Eighth Edition

Basic Reading Inventory

Pre-Primer Through Grade Twelve and Early Literacy Assessments

Jerry L. Johns

Distinguished Teaching Professor Emeritus
Northern Illinois University

KENDALL/HUNT PUBLISHING COMPANY
4050 Westmark Drive · Dubuque, Iowa 52002

Project Team

President & Chief Executive Officer: Mark C. Falb
Vice President, Director of National Book Program:
  Alfred C. Grisanti
Editorial Development Supervisor: Georgia Botsford
Vice President, Production Editorial:
  Ruth A. Burlage
Production Manager: Jo Wiegand
Production Editor: Angela Williams
Design Manager: Jodi Splinter
Cover Designer: Deb Howes

Author Information for Correspondence and Workshops

Jerry L. Johns, Ph.D.
Consultant in Reading
2105 Eastgate Drive
Sycamore, IL 60178
E-mail: *jjohns@niu.edu*
815-895-3022

Books by Jerry L. Johns

Spanish Reading Inventory (two editions)
Balanced Reading Instruction: Teachers' Visions and Voices (edited with Laurie Elish-Piper)
Secondary & College Reading Inventory (two editions)
Literacy for Diverse Learners (edited)
Handbook for Remediation of Reading Difficulties
Informal Reading Inventories: An Annotated Reference Guide (compiled)
Literacy: Celebration and Challenge (edited)

Books by Jerry L. Johns and Susan Davis Lenski

Improving Reading (three editions)
Improving Writing: Resources, Strategies, and Assessments
Early Literacy Assessments & Teaching Strategies (with Laurie Elish-Piper)
Reading & Learning Strategies for Middle & High School Students (with Mary Ann Wham)
Celebrating Literacy: The Joy of Reading and Writing (with June E. Barnhart, James H. Moss, and Thomas E. Wheat)
Language Arts for Gifted Middle School Students

Ordering Information

Address: Kendall/Hunt Publishing Company
         4050 Westmark Drive, P.O. Box 1840
         Dubuque, IA 52004-1840

Telephone: 800-247-3458, Ext. 5

Web site: www.kendallhunt.com

Photos by Susan Johns and JM IMAGES

ISBN 0-7872-5832-6

Printed in the United States of America
10 9 8 7 6 5 4 3

Dedicated to My Family

Annette

Beth & Dominique

My Mom and My Brothers and Sisters

Yours Truly, Nancy, Tom, Mary (Mom), Dan, Susan, & Becky

And My Niece and Nephew

Coté Anne & Jesse

Brief Contents

 Part One

Basic Reading Inventory Manual 1

 Part Two

Basic Reading Inventory Forms 119

 Part Three

Appendices, References, and Index 385

Contents

 Part One

Basic Reading Inventory Manual

Section 1   Overview 3

Section 2   Administration and Scoring Procedures 19

Section 3   Determining the Student's Three Reading Levels 49

Section 4   Instructional Uses of Inventory Results 57

Section 5   Timesaving Administration Procedures 79

Part Two

Basic Reading Inventory Forms

Form A   Oral Reading   121

Form B   Oral Reading   171

Form C   Optional   221

Form D   Silent Reading   271

Form LN   Narrative   309

Form LE   Expository   347

Part Three

Appendices, References, and Index

Appendix A: Early Literacy Assessments   387

Appendix B: Procedures for Eliciting and Evaluating Passage Retellings   437

Appendix C: Form E: Extra Passages   443

Appendix D: Summary Sheets 451

References 459

Index 469

How to Use the Basic Reading Inventory CD-ROM 473

Basic Reading Inventory Administration and Scoring Procedures 476

About the Author

JERRY L. JOHNS

Jerry Johns has been recognized as a distinguished professor, writer, and outstanding teacher educator. He completed his B.A. at Oakland University with special honors. He taught in the public schools in Pontiac, Michigan, while working on his M.A. at Michigan State University. After receiving his M.A., Dr. Johns was awarded a fellowship to pursue doctoral studies at MSU. He served as an instructor at Michigan State, teaching various reading courses. Then he accepted the position of special reading teacher for the Waterford, Michigan Public Schools where he taught students with severe reading problems. Dr. Johns has had a long, distinguished career at Northern Illinois University. He was also Visiting Professor at Western Washington University and the University of Victoria in British Columbia.

In addition to his major teaching responsibilities, Dr. Johns has been elected to leadership positions at the local, state, national, and international levels. He has been president of the Northern Illinois Reading Council, the Illinois Reading Council, and the College Reading Association. He also served on the Board of Directors of the International Reading Association and will be the Association's president in 2002–2003. In addition, Dr. Johns has served on numerous committees of the International Reading Association and other professional organizations. His more than 400 presentations and workshops for professional organizations and school systems involved travel throughout the world.

Dr. Johns has numerous publications, including his well-known *Basic Reading Inventory* (now in its 8th edition) and the third edition of *Improving Reading: Strategies and Resources.* He has recently co-authored *Early Literacy Assessments & Teaching Strategies, Reading & Learning Strategies for Middle & High School Students,* and *Improving Writing: Resources, Strategies, and Assessments.* He also co-edited *Balanced Reading Instruction: Teachers' Visions and Voices* and developed a *Spanish Reading Inventory.* All his books are published by Kendall/Hunt (1-800-247-3458, ext. 5). He has authored nearly 300 articles, monographs, pamphlets, books, and research studies. Dr. Johns also serves on the editorial advisory boards for *Reading Psychology* and *Reading Research and Instruction.*

Dr. Johns has been the recipient of numerous awards for his contributions to various professional organizations. He received the Outstanding Service Award from the College Reading Association and was honored by the Illinois Reading Council with induction into the Reading Hall of Fame. Other recognitions include the Alpha Delta Literacy Award for Scholarship, Leadership, and Service to Adult Learners and the A.B. Herr Award for outstanding contributions to the field of reading. His most recent recognition is the Outstanding Teacher Educator in Reading Award presented by the International Reading Association.

Dr. Johns now serves as a consultant and speaker to schools and professional organizations. He is also an officer in the International Reading Association. Dr. Johns enjoys travel and driving his sports car—an Ontario orange 1971 Corvette convertible.

List of Figures and Tables

Figures

Tables

Preface

The Basic Reading Inventory provides a complete assessment package—consisting of this book, complete with CD-ROM, a video that demonstrates an administration of an inventory with a teacher and student, and a separate CD-ROM that contains tracking software.

The Basic Reading Inventory is used by classroom teachers, students in preservice education, teachers taking introductory and advanced reading courses, reading specialists, Title I teachers, learning disability teachers, tutors, teacher aides, school psychologists, and school systems that offer inservice work in reading assessment.

The book explains how to administer, score, and interpret the Basic Reading Inventory. Included are graded word lists and graded passages that can be used to help teachers place students in appropriate reading materials, assess comprehension, and determine the student's strategies for word identification and comprehension. Four methods are explained to help assess comprehension. Because this text includes numerous examples, strategy lessons, and summary aids, it will enable professionals of diverse training to enhance reading instruction in classrooms, resource rooms, diagnostic centers, and clinics.

NEW TO THIS EDITION

In preparing the eighth edition of the Basic Reading Inventory, I have devoted my efforts to refining those components that warranted revision, clarification, expansion, and updating. The guiding question for any revision is: Will the change improve the inventory? Many of the revisions are in response to suggestions from users of the inventory.

CD-ROM (INCLUDED WITH EACH BOOK)

Each book contains a dual platform CD-ROM that contains video clips demonstrating the Basic Reading Inventory with a teacher and student. The Performance Booklets and the Record Booklet are also provided on this CD-ROM and can be reproduced for noncommercial educational purposes by teachers for use in their classrooms. These copies may not be sold, and further distribution is expressly prohibited. An icon is keyed to the text alerting the reader to refer to the CD-ROM when a demonstration of the inventory is appropriate.

A sample of the Basic Reading Inventory Tracking Software (BRITS) is now included on the CD-ROM included with this book. Please install this software to see how much easier it is to record and track performance of a student or a class of students after the Basic Reading Inventory has been administered.

Forms for Pre-Primer Through Grade Eight (Forms A, B, C, D)

New graded passages are given in Form B, ranging from the beginning stages of reading (pre-primer) through grade eight. Forms A, C, and D cover these grade levels as well.

New to this edition is an informal miscue tally for each passage in Forms A, B, C, and D. Completing the miscue tally assists the teacher in making informed decisions about a student's reading so that instruction can be responsive to the student's needs. Ideas presented in Section 6 may be useful for instructional interventions.

Form A is comprised of narrative passages designed for oral reading and may be used as a pretest. If desired, the passages in Form A may be used for silent reading.

Form B, the new form, consists of narrative passages. It is also designed for oral reading and can serve as a posttest. Form B passages may also be used for silent reading.

Form C consists of both narrative and expository passages. It is an extra form that can be used for additional assessment or to supplement selected passages in the other forms. The passages may be read orally or silently.

Form D is designed for silent reading. It contains expository passages at the higher grade levels because students often encounter such materials when reading content area texts. There is also a provision for orally reading a portion from the passages in Form D. If desired, the passage in Form D may be used for oral reading.

Forms for Grade Three Through Grade Twelve (Forms LN and LE)

Forms LN and LE are particularly useful for silent reading and to gather additional insights about a student's reading. Form LN (narrative passages) and LE (expository passages) each contain ten longer passages (250 words) that range in difficulty from grade three through grade twelve.

BASIC READING INVENTORY VIDEO

The new edition continues the tradition of providing a complete assessment package, including a professional, full-color videotape designed to train teachers, prospective teachers, aides, diagnosticians, and other professionals involved in teaching students to read. It demonstrates a sample administration of the Basic Reading Inventory to a student.

Packaged with the videotape are master copies of how the reading was scored for the student being assessed. Transparencies may be made from these masters to assist with training. This videotape can be used individually or with others to gain experience and competence in administering the Basic Reading Inventory. I welcome the opportunity to consult with schools and districts to help carry out effective training programs.

BASIC READING INVENTORY TRACKING SOFTWARE
(See demonstration included on the CD-ROM packaged in this book.)

The power of contemporary technology is now available with the Basic Reading Inventory Tracking Software CD-ROM (BRITS) for tracking a student's performance after the Basic Reading Inventory has been administered.

The software is designed to allow a school or district to record each individual student's scores. These scores can be recorded for up to four years, including a pretest and a posttest for each year. By using this software, professionals can view each student's progress, individual strengths, and weaknesses. The total class can also be viewed as to the average scores on all numerical data and the total number of each reading level for the group. Once entered, the data can be sorted and averaged for various demographics—boys, girls, Title I, and students in special education.

The software will automatically compile miscue summaries and graphs for all data entered. Similar summaries can be printed for each student's comprehension performance.

For further information about this valuable resource, please contact Kendall/Hunt Publishing Company, using the information on the copyright page. I am indebted to my friends at Kendall/Hunt for their wonderful support and vision. They are always open to new ideas, and they work hard to bring these ideas to fruition.

Note to Readers

Users of the eighth edition will find a number of refinements and clarifications in the text. I have sought to strengthen the Basic Reading Inventory by listening to professionals throughout the United States and Canada. I am indebted to all those colleagues, students, teachers, and reading specialists who have offered help, constructive criticism, and encouragement.

The Basic Reading Inventory has existed in one form or another for over thirty years. It has helped thousands of teachers make their instruction more responsive to students—many of whom struggle in reading. I want to thank all of you for your generous sharing. You are indeed partners in this edition of the Basic Reading Inventory.

Jerry L. Johns

Acknowledgments

Special appreciation is extended to the following professionals who assisted with the eighth edition by fieldtesting, suggesting ideas, raising questions, or providing support.

Violet Adams, Colorado Christian University
Pat Adamson, Fort Garry SD #5
Dawn Andermann, Steward, IL
Rebecca Anderson, The University of Memphis
Tanya Anderson, University of Manitoba
Marce Armstrong, Smith Elementary
Deborah Augsburger, Northern Illinois University
Phyllis Augsburger, Plantation, FL
Sandie Baade, Valley Park Elementary School
June E. Barnhart, Northern Illinois University
Diane S. Barr, Lincoln Elementary School
Liz Beardmore, Reading Clinic Assistant
Vicki Beatty, Temecula Valley Unified School District
Deborah Begoray, The University of Winnipeg
Cathy Belben, Nooksack Valley Junior/Senior High School
Kathy Bell, Caesar Rodney School District
Linda Bell, Lexington High School
Roberta L. Berglund, Reading Consultant
Linda Bingham, New Braunfels, TX
Lois Blanks, Mt. Auburn Elementary School
Carole L. Bond, The University of Memphis
Karen Brauer, Fulton Elementary Schools
Susan Brenner, Clarion University
Estelle J. Brown, Glassboro State College
Maria Brown, Durant Elementary School
Marti Brueggeman, Ashland University
Diane E. Bushner, Salem State College
Mary Cahill, Winnipeg Child Guidance Clinic
Ronda Campbell, The University of Memphis
Doreen B. Cannon, Steward, IL
Kay Carson, Kaneville Community Unit School District
Louise Carson, Partners for Learning
Martha Carter, Milwaukee Public Schools
Susan Casey, Lane School

Marietta Castle, Consultant
Lois Catrambone, Concordia University/ District 97
Joseph Chojnacki, Cheektowaga Central High School
James G. Christmann, Cheektowaga Central High School
Leann Clark, UW-Milwaukee
Cheryl Coseglia, Arlington Heights School District
Elizabeth Cox, Sparta High School
Karen Crabtree, University of Northern Colorado
Ken Crawford, Nooksack Valley Junior/Senior High School
Elise Crowell, Maplebrook Elementary School
Kathy Crum, Stuart Elementary
Joyce Cullen, Aurora, CO
James W. Cunningham, The University of North Carolina at Chapel Hill
Barbara Debevec, Vacaville School District
Tanya Delaney, Sydney, Australia
Peggy DeLapp, Minneapolis Public Schools
JoAnn Desmond, Frankfort Public Schools
Carla Ann Diehl, Clarion University
Lynn Dieter, Maine Township High School East
Clark Duncan, Maine Township High School East
Susan Dunlap, Lexington High School
Melinda Eckhardt, Maine Township High School East
Richard Egel, Littlejohn School
Carolyn Eichenberger, St. Louis University
Laurie Elish-Piper, Northern Illinois University
Laurie Erdman, Kaneville Community Unit School District
Francine Falk-Ross, Northern Illinois University
Phyllis Fantauzzo, Rider College
Jim Farrell, Maine Township High School East
Frederick J. Fedorko, East Stroudsburg University

Lou Ferroli, Rockford College

Peter Fisher, National Louis University

Linda Fligg, Highlands Ranch, CO

Celia Flores, San Antonio, TX

Judi Francis, Coquitam School District

Kim Frank, San Antonio, TX

M. K. Gillis, Southwest Texas State University

Susan Mandel Glazer, Rider College

Steve Granzyk, Maine Township High School East

Sandy Gray, Hill Elementary School

Thomas Gunning, Southern Connecticut State University

Deborah Hackbarth, Seattle, WA

Sue Hanson, Hinckley Elementary School

James Harris, West Aurora School District 129

Renee Harris, Jefferson Middle School

Julie Hatcher, Hill Elementary School

Donna Hathaway, Rowan College of New Jersey

Shonah J. Hayden, Lancaster Central School District

Jean Higdon, Jefferson School

Glenda Hildreth, Rockford Public Schools

Margaret H. Hill, University of Houston–Clear Lake

Daniel R. Hittleman, Queens College

Debra Housel, Churchville-Chili Central School District

Kay Howard, Nicholson Elementary

Megan Hunniford, Tasmania, Australia

Betty Hurst, Bower School

Elliott Hurtig, Maine Township High School East

Heidi Hutson, Maine Township High School East

Sandra Imdieke, Northern Michigan University

Elizabeth Ingles, Centennial Elementary School

Ellen Jampole, SUNY-Courtland

Sharon Jennings, Indian Prairie School District No. 204

Nancy Johns, Lincoln Middle Elementary School

Rick Johnson, Naperville School District 204

Billie Jones, Beaver Valley Elementary School

Roseanne Joyner, Missouri Southern State College

Jerald Kantrovich, Maine Township High School East

Marian Kasprzak, Cheektowaga Central High School

Gloria H. Kenyon, Denver, CO

Charles Kessler, Maine Township High School East

Nancy Kiger, University of Central Florida

Caryn King, Grand Valley State University

Patti Kinsman, Biloxi, MS

Pam Knudsen, Lexington High School

Lisa Koeller, Moline High School

Christie Koester, South-Western City Schools

Barbara Koffman, Partners for Learning

Maureen Korczykowski, Cheektowaga Central High School

Sandra Krickeberg, Waubonsie Valley High School

Sharon Kulhanek, Medaille College

Leona Laouras, Maine Township High School East

Deborah Layne, Brook Forest Elementary School

Steven Layne, Butler Junior High School

Richard Lefort, Maine Township High School East

Susan Davis Lenski, Illinois State University

Heather Lind, Lindenhurst, IL

Joni Lindgren, Greenman Elementary

Sally Lipa, SUNY Geneseo

Jim Lonergan, Maine Township High School East

Richard Luckritz, Maine Township High School East

Mary Ludeman, Oxford, MI

Karen Mack, Chesbro School

Eileen Madden, Maine Township High School East

Anne Marie Magliari, Yorkville Grade School

Kathy Malpede, Pioneer Elementary School

Jane Mantazo, Florida Atlantic University

Peggy Marciniec, Lester School

Harold Martin, Maine Township High School East

Sandra McCormick, The Ohio State University

Jennifer Mesko, Graduate Student

Louise Milasauskis, Auburn Public Schools

Sophie Miller, Vaughn Elementary

David W. Moore, Arizona State University-West

Chierie Moriarty, Graduate Student

Barbara Moss, University of Akron Emeritus

Lynn Kremsner Mullenbruck, Ridgeland School District 122

Ester Muñoz, Sam Houston Elementary

Susan B. Neuman, University of Michigan

Susan Nikkee, Fort Garry School District #5

Vikie Norris, Winnipeg Child Guidance Clinic

Sheree Novotny, May Elementary School

Ruth E. Olle, Genoa Middle School

Lloyd O. Ollila, Victoria, B.C.

Mary W. Olson, University of North Carolina at Greensboro

Robert Olson, Maine Township High School East

Michael F. Opitz, University of Southern Colorado

Elizabeth Osborne, Pismo Beach, CA

Nancy Padak, Kent State University

Ramona Pearson-Amos, Graduate Student
Alicia R. Pérez, Donna, TX
Roberta Price, Cheektowaga Central High School
Karen Pritchard, Schneider Elementary School
Leona Prock, Simon Fraser University
Pam Prusow, Lee School
Carolyn Pumphrey, Lexington High School
Velma Rangel, Moye Elementary
Timothy V. Rasinski, Kent State University
Ronald S. Reigner, State University of West Georgia
Kathy Resener, Lexington High School
Marilyn Rinehart, Maine Township High School East
Marilyn Roark, Palatine, IL
Sue Robinson, Nooksack Valley Junior/Senior High School
Kay Rollings, Lexington High School
Lori Russell, McCleery Elementary
Joan Ryerkerk, Upper Iowa University
Mary Dayton Sakari, University of Victoria
Olga de Santa Anna-O'Brien, Santa Cruz City Schools
Peggy Sauser, Lincoln Elementary School
Anna Schaber, Student Worker
Marjorie Schallmo, Cheektowaga Central High School
Mary Lorae Schcopner, Treasure Hills Elementary
Marcia Scheppele, Waterloo Community School District
Joelle Schlesinger, Reading Recovery Teacher Leader
Patricia Schmidt, LeMoyne College
Paula Schoenfelder, Indiana Prairie School District No. 204
Judithe Schreiner, Concordia University
Jennifer Schuaneueldt, Southern Utah University
Gary L. Shaffer, State University of West Georgia
Pat Shannon, Nooksack Valley Junior/Senior High School
Brenda Sharts, Cleveland County Schools
Cherie Durfee Smith, Chesbro Elementary School
Kate Smith, Weimar, TX
Lana Smith, The University of Memphis
Gary Smithey, Henderson State University
Norman Stahl, Northern Illinois University

Susan A. Stan, Elgin High School
Dixie Stebbins, Winnipeg Child Guidance Clinic
Karen Stinson, Upper Iowa University
Nancy Stone, University of Wisconsin-Oshkosh
Melody Studer, Chouteau Elementary School
Donna Stupple, Maine Township High School East
Louise Sullivan, Mullica Hill, NJ
Kathleen Sweeney, Grant Elementary School
Cheryl Troyer, St. Charles Public Schools
JoAnne Vacca, Kent State University
Rich Vacca, Kent State University
Stephanie Vickers, Portland, OR
Kerryn Vincent, Sydney, Australia
Kristine Voreis, Jefferson Middle School
Cheryl Wacholz, Winnipeg Child Guidance Clinic
Barbara Walker, Oklahoma State University
Carol Warren, West Aurora School District #129
Deborah P. Watson, Hartford Public Schools
Patty Welker, Kaneville Community Unit School District
Mary Ann Wham, University of Wisconsin-Whitewater
Diane Williams, Mountain View Elementary School
Martin Woerter, Maine Township High School East
Leslie M. Woldt, Chula Vista Elementary School
John T. Wolinski, Salisbury State University
Dan Wood, Nooksack Valley Junior/Senior High School
Ralph Wurster, Maine Township High School East
Dennis Wyatt, Maine Township High School East
Barbara Wynes, University of Manitoba
Therese Yonikus, Naperville School District 203
Hazel Zahradnik, Winnipeg Child Guidance Clinic
Beverly Zakaluk, University of Manitoba

Special thanks to:

Teachers in Derby, KS
Teachers in Cleveland County Schools
Teachers in a Northwest Regional Educational Service Alliance Workshop
Graduate students at Northern Illinois University
Teachers in DeKalb, IL

PART ONE

Basic Reading Inventory Manual

SECTION ONE

Overview

HELPING TEACHERS MAKE INSTRUCTION DIFFERENT

Teachers can help students make significant progress in reading. While methods come and go, teachers remain the staple in providing quality reading instruction that is responsive to their students. Responsive instruction has many qualities, and a fundamental principle is attention to individual differences.

A recent position statement of the International Reading Association (2000) titled *Making a Difference Means Making It Different*, notes that students "have a right to reading assessment that identifies their strengths as well as their needs . . ." (p. 7). The Basic Reading Inventory is one resource to help gather information for instructional decision making in reading. It can be used to estimate the student's instructional level—the level at which the student is challenged but not overwhelmed. It is the level where the student can profit from reading instruction (Spiegel, 1995). Unfortunately, many students are placed in materials that are too difficult for them (Johnston and Allington, 1995). If students are placed in instructional materials where they are able to pronounce approximately 95 percent of the words, they tend to be successful readers who are on task (Adams, 1990).

Responsive instruction is more likely to be provided if teachers know the student's reading needs (Kibby, 1995). According to Manning (1995), valuable information can be obtained by noting the behaviors of students as they read orally in instructional materials. The Basic Reading Inventory provides one means through which teachers can systematically gain insights into the student's reading. Teachers can study and analyze the student's abilities in word identification and comprehension. These can then be used as an important basis for responsive instruction and high-quality instructional decisions the teacher needs to make (Farr, 1992). "Assessment practices should enrich teaching and learning" (Tierney, 1998, p. 388). The Basic Reading Inventory can help teachers "to become better informed and make better decisions" (Tierney, 1998, p. 388). Such decisions can be used to help develop individual literacy plans for students (Felknor, 2000). The end result should help students become more efficient and effective readers.

COMPONENTS OF THE BASIC READING INVENTORY

The Basic Reading Inventory is an individually administered informal reading test. Composed of a series of graded word lists and graded passages, the inventory helps teachers gain insights into students' reading behavior. Inventory results will help support the daily instructional decisions teachers need to make (Farr, 1992; Gillet and Temple, 2000; Johns, 1996). Five types of comprehension questions follow each passage: topic, fact, inference, evaluation, and vocabulary. This section explains the purposes of the Basic Reading Inventory, gives directions for administering and scoring the inventory, and provides concrete assistance for interpreting the findings of the inventory so that the results can be used to improve students' reading. The development of the Basic Reading Inventory is described in Section 8.

There are six forms (A, B, C, D, LN, LE) of the Basic Reading Inventory, each denoted by one or more capital letters.

- ▶ Forms A, B, and C contain word lists ranging from pre-primer (beginning reading) through grade twelve and passages ranging from the pre-primer level through the eighth grade.

- ▶ Form D contains passages ranging from the pre-primer level through the eighth grade and is designed specifically for silent reading.

- ▶ Forms LN and LE each contain ten passages of 250 words ranging in difficulty from third grade to twelfth grade.

Four numerals are used to code the grade level of the word lists and/or passages in the Basic Reading Inventory. Table 1.1 contains the code.

Table 1.1   Code of Grade Levels for the Six Forms of the Basic Reading Inventory

Grade Level	Form of the Basic Reading Inventory					
	A	B	C	D	LN	LE
Pre-Primer	AA	BB	CC	DD	—	—
Primer	A	B	C	D	—	—
1	A 7141	B 7141	C 7141	D 7141	—	—
2	A 8224	B 8224	C 8224	D 8224	—	—
3	A 3183	B 3183	C 3183	D 3183	LN 3183	LE 3183
4	A 5414	B 5414	C 5414	D 5414	LN 5414	LE 5414
5	A 8595	B 8595	C 8595	D 8595	LN 8595	LE 8595
6	A 6867	B 6867	C 6867	D 6867	LN 6867	LE 6867
7	A 3717	B 3717	C 3717	D 3717	LN 3717	LE 3717
8	A 8183	B 8183	C 8183	D 8183	LN 8183	LE 8183
9	A 4959	B 4959	C 4959	—	LN 4959	LE 4959
10	A 1047	B 1047	C 1047	—	LN 1047	LE 1047
11	A 1187	B 1187	C 1187	—	LN 1187	LE 1187
12	A 1296	B 1296	C 1296	—	LN 1296	LE 1296

PRE-PRIMER AND PRIMER LEVELS

For the pre-primer and primer levels, capital letters designate the level.

▶ The pre-primer level is designated by two capital letters.

▶ The primer level is designated by one capital letter.

GRADE LEVELS 1–9

For the remaining levels through grade nine, the teacher can determine the grade level of the word list or passage by determining which two numerals are identical.

In Table 1.1, for example, A 7141 indicates that the word list or passage in form A is at the first-grade level because there are two 1's. The code B 8183 indicates the word list or passage in Form B is at the eighth-grade level because there are two 8's. A similar procedure is followed for the remaining word lists and passages when two numerals are the same within each grade level.

GRADE LEVELS 10–12

For the word lists and passages at grades ten, eleven, and twelve, the first two numerals indicate the grade level.

BRI Forms

Six forms of the Basic Reading Inventory are included so that a variety of goals can be achieved.

▶ Forms A and B assess the student's oral reading. Teachers often use Form A as a pretest. Form B may be used as a posttest. It is especially important that students above the primary grades engage in silent reading.

► Form C can be used either to estimate the student's listening level or as a post-test to help assess growth in reading. The passages in Form C can also be used for additional oral or silent reading opportunities to better estimate the student's reading levels or to further study the student's reading behavior.

► Form D is specifically designed for assessing silent reading.

► Forms LN and LE, because of their length (250 words), permit a more in-depth appraisal of the student's ability to read narrative and expository materials. The passages in these two forms may be read orally and/or silently.

Table 1.2 shows how the various forms of the Basic Reading Inventory may be used.

Table 1.2   Uses of Basic Reading Inventory Forms

Form	Primary Use	Other Uses
A	Oral Reading Pretest	Silent Reading Listening Level
B	Oral Reading Posttest	Silent Reading Listening Level
C	Oral Reading Listening Level	Silent Reading Pretest Posttest
D	Silent Reading	Oral Reading Pretest Posttest
LN	Silent Reading	Oral Reading Listening Level
LE	Silent Reading	Oral Reading Listening Level

Early Literacy Assessments

A series of early literacy assessments are included in Appendix A. These assessments are especially useful for students who find the easiest word lists and passages difficult and who could be called emergent readers. A separate Record Booklet, directions, and ten assessments are found in Appendix A:

1. Alphabet Knowledge
2. Writing
3. Literacy Knowledge
4. Wordless Picture Reading
5. Caption Reading
6. Auditory Discrimination
7. Phoneme Awareness
8. Phoneme Segmentation
9. Basic Word Knowledge
10. Pre-Primer Passages

Johns, Lenski, and Elish-Piper (1999) have also developed a series of fifteen early literacy assessments accompanied by complementary teaching strategies. Consult this resource for helpful assessments and suggestions for instruction.

PURPOSES OF THE BASIC READING INVENTORY

On the basis of the student's performance on the word lists and graded passages, the teacher can gain insights into the student's:

▶ **independent reading level**—the level at which the student reads fluently with excellent comprehension.

▶ **instructional reading level**—the level at which the student can make maximum progress in reading with teacher guidance.

▶ **frustration level**—the level at which the student is unable to pronounce many of the words and/or is unable to comprehend the material satisfactorily.

▶ **strategies for word identification**—the teacher can evaluate the student's ability to use sight vocabulary, phonic analysis, context cues, and structural analysis to pronounce words.

▶ **fluency**—the teacher can determine the student's rate of reading (in words per minute).

▶ **strengths and weaknesses in comprehension**—the teacher can evaluate the student's ability to answer various types of comprehension questions.

▶ **listening level**—the highest level of material that the student can comprehend when it is read to him or her.

Observations can also be made regarding the student's interests, attitudes, self-monitoring strategies, general approach to various tasks, and reading behavior (such as engagement, persistence, and predictions).

BACKGROUND INFORMATION ON READING LEVELS AND THE LISTENING LEVEL

A major function of the Basic Reading Inventory is to identify a student's three reading levels: independent, instructional, and frustration. Numerous questions have been raised about standards for evaluating a student's performance on reading inventories (Johns, 1976; 1990a). Although some research (Anderson and Joels, 1986; Johns and Magliari, 1989; Powell, 1971) indicates that the original criteria suggested by Betts (1946) are too high for determining the instructional level for students in the primary grades, other studies (Hays, 1975; Homan and Klesius, 1985; Morris, 1990; and Pikulski, 1974) report contradictory findings. In addition, Ekwall (1974, 1976) has presented evidence that supports retaining the traditional Betts criteria. Teachers should remember that the numerical criteria for reading levels are not *absolute standards*; they are *guidelines* to help teachers evaluate a student's reading. Each of the three reading levels presented here will be considered from two viewpoints: the teacher's and the student's. The listening level will also be discussed.

What Is the Independent Reading Level?

Level	Characteristics	Types of Reading
Independent (Easy)	Excellent comprehension (90%+) Excellent word recognition (99%+) Few or no repetitions Very fluent	All schoolwork and reading expected to be done alone Pleasure reading Informational reading

Teacher's Viewpoint

The independent reading level is that level at which the student can read fluently without teacher assistance. In other words, the student can read the materials independently with excellent comprehension. This is the level of supplementary and recreational reading. The material should not cause the student any difficulty. If the student reads orally, the reading should be expressive with accurate attention to punctuation. At this level, the student's reading should be free from finger pointing, vocalizing, lip movement, poor phrasing, and other indications of general tension or problems with the reading material.

In order to be considered at the student's independent level, materials should be read with near-perfect accuracy in terms of word recognition. Even in a situation of oral reading at sight, the student should generally not make more than one significant miscue in each 100 running words. With respect to comprehension, the student's score, when 10 comprehension questions of various types are asked, should be no lower than 90 percent. In short, the student should be able to fully understand the material.

If a retelling strategy is used, a student "will be able to reflect most of the content of a selection and will reflect it in an organized fashion." In a narrative passage, the student will recount events in the proper order. In expository passages, the student's retelling will reflect the text structure or organization of that material. For example, a passage with the main idea followed by supporting details will usually be retold in the same manner (Johnson, Kress, and Pikulski, 1987, p. 14).

It is important that the above criteria for determining a student's independent reading level be applied with careful teacher judgment. The criteria, especially the near-perfect accuracy for word recognition, may have to be modified somewhat in evaluating a student's performance. The younger reader, for example, may frequently substitute *a* for *the* and vice versa while reading. An older student may omit or substitute a number of words that do not seriously interfere with fluency and/or a good understanding of the passage. Miscues of this nature should be regarded as acceptable; they are not significant. If the teacher has correctly determined the student's independent reading level, the student will experience little difficulty with materials that are written at or below that particular level.

Student's Viewpoint

Because most students have never heard of the various reading levels, they would not refer to the percentages and related behavioral characteristics just described. A student might, however, describe the independent reading level in these terms: "I can read this book by myself, and I understand what I read. I like reading books like this; they're easy."

What Is the Instructional Reading Level?

Level	Characteristics	Types of Reading
Instructional (Just right; comfortable)	Good comprehension (75–85%) Good word recognition (95%+) Fluent A few unknown words Some repetitions	Guided reading Basal instruction Texts used or instruction

Teacher's Viewpoint

The instructional reading level is that level at which the student can, theoretically, make maximum growth in reading. It is the level at which the student is challenged but not frustrated. Many teachers are interested in finding the student's instructional level so they can provide classroom reading materials at that level (Felknor, Winterscheidt, and Benson, 1999; McTague, 1997). At the instructional level, the student should be free from externally observable symptoms of difficulty, such as finger pointing, produced by the reading materials. Although the student might experience some difficulties when reading classroom materials at sight, most of these difficulties should be overcome after the student has had an opportunity to read the same material silently. In other words, oral rereading should be definitely improved over oral reading at sight. If the student is to make maximum progress from instruction, he or she should encounter no more difficulty in reading materials than can be adequately dealt with through good teaching.

In order to be considered at the student's instructional level, materials should be read with not more than 5 miscues in each 100 words in terms of word recognition. According to Adams (1990, p. 113), "there is evidence that achievement in reading is improved by placement in materials that a student can read orally with a low error rate (2 percent to 5 percent), and that students placed in materials that they read with greater than 5 percent errors tend to be off-task during instruction." Although some difficulties will probably arise in word recognition, the student should be able to use contextual cues, phonics, and other strategies to decode most unknown words. In terms of comprehension, the student should miss fewer than 3 of 10 comprehension questions.

If a retelling strategy is used, a student responding to instructional level materials will "reflect less content than at an independent level. The organization of the passage will be less complete and some minor misinterpretations and inaccuracies may begin to appear." In essence, the student is able to share the overall sense and content of the passage (Johnson, Kress, and Pikulski, 1987, p. 17).

It is at the instructional level that the student will have the best opportunity to build new reading strategies. This is the level at which guided reading instruction is likely to be most successful (Lenski, 1998). Teachers need to be sure that books used for reading instruction are at students' instructional levels.

Student's Viewpoint

A student might describe the instructional level in these terms: "I can understand what I am taught from this reading book. Some of the words are hard, but after the teacher gives me some help, the story is easy to read."

What Is the Frustration Level?

Level	Characteristics	Types of Reading
Frustration (Too hard)	Poor comprehension (≤50%) Poor word recognition (≤90%) Word-by-word reading Many unknown words Rate is slow Lack of expression Fidgeting	Materials for diagnostic purposes Avoid instructional materials at this level Occasional self-selected material when interested and background knowledge are high

 ### Teacher's Viewpoint

The frustration level is that level at which the student should not be given materials to read. A serious problem in many classrooms is that a large number of students are asked to read books at their frustration levels. Students at their frustration levels are unable to deal with the reading material. Numerous behavioral characteristics may be observed if students are attempting to read materials that are too difficult for them. Some students may actually refuse to continue reading their books. Other students may exhibit lack of expression in oral reading, lip movement during silent reading, difficulty in pronouncing words, word-by-word reading, and/or finger pointing. A study by Jorgenson (1977) found that as reading material became more difficult, teachers judged their students as becoming more impatient, disturbing to the classroom, and reliant for directions on persons other than themselves.

The criteria for the frustration level, in addition to the behavioral characteristics just noted, are 10 or more miscues in every 100 words (90 percent or less) and comprehension scores of 50 percent or less. For example, a student who could not correctly pronounce 90 or more words in a 100-word selection and who could not answer at least half of the questions asked by the teacher is likely reading material that is too difficult.

If a retelling strategy is used, "materials at a frustration level are recalled incompletely or in a rather haphazard fashion. Bits of information may be recalled, but they are not related in any logical or sequential order." Questions asked by the teacher tend to go unanswered. In addition, behaviors such as finger pointing and tenseness may appear (Johnson, Kress, and Pikulski, 1987, p. 20).

Student's Viewpoint

Because reading materials at this level are too difficult for the student, it is likely that the frustration level would be described in these terms: "This book is too hard. I hate to read when books are this hard. I hardly know any of the words." Other students will say nothing when books are too difficult for them to read, but the perceptive teacher will note when books are at a student's frustration level. The teacher can then provide or suggest other materials that are at the student's independent or instructional levels.

What Is the Listening Level?

The listening level is the *highest* level at which the student can understand material that is read *to* him or her. Determining this level can help the teacher ascertain whether a student has the potential to improve as a reader. When a substantial difference exists between the student's instructional level and listening level (generally a year or more), it usually indicates that the student should be able to make significant growth in reading achievement with appropriate instruction. The larger the difference, the more reason for the teacher to believe that the student can profit from instruction that is responsive to the student's needs in reading. Many students who struggle with reading can improve if they are given quality instruction and placed in reading materials at their instructional levels.

The criteria for the listening level are a minimum comprehension score of at least 70 percent. In other words, the student should miss no more than 3 of 10 comprehension questions. It is also important for the teacher to informally assess whether the student's vocabulary and language structure in conversations are as complex as that used in the reading passage.

Schell (1982), after reviewing several studies relating to the listening level, cautioned teachers not to use the procedure with students in grades one through three. He argued that reading comprehension and listening comprehension are not approximately equal for students in the primary grades; moreover, neither grow at approximately equal rates until about sixth grade. For these reasons, teachers should not use the listening level procedure with students in the primary grades.

PREPARATION FOR ASSESSMENT

Understand the Procedures

To prepare for assessment, the teacher first needs to be familiar with the procedures for administering and scoring the Basic Reading Inventory. These procedures are discussed in Section 2. What is needed for assessment? There are four basic items:

1. This manual.

2. A piece of heavy paper to cover the passage when necessary.

3. A performance booklet in which the teacher will record the student's responses.

4. A desk or table and two chairs. It is recommended that right-handed teachers seat the student on their left. Left-handed teachers should do the opposite.

PHYSICAL ENVIRONMENT

When using the reading inventory with a student, the teacher needs a desk or table and two chairs located in an area reasonably free from excessive noise and distractions.

SELECTING WORD LISTS AND PASSAGES

The student will read from selected pages in this manual. To aid in locating word lists and passages, consult the quick reference guide printed on the inside front cover. Some teachers purchase tabs and place them at the beginning of the word lists and passages so they can easily locate the different forms. Other teachers remove the students' reading materials and arrange them in a binder or notebook for easy reference.

While the student reads, the teacher records the student's performance and makes notes on the graded word lists and the graded passages in a performance booklet.

Permission is granted to users of the Basic Reading Inventory to reproduce all, or any part, of the six performance booklets that follow the student copies of the reading inventory. **Note:** The student copies of the word lists and passages may not be reproduced.

The validity of a student's performance on the Basic Reading Inventory is related to how completely and accurately the teacher is able to record the student's reading performance and answers to the comprehension questions. A tape recorder, therefore, is recommended as a method of self-checking until the teacher's recording of the student's performance becomes automatic and swift. These tape recordings can also be placed in portfolios or other record-keeping devices.

OVERVIEW OF ADMINISTRATION AND SCORING PROCEDURES

To evaluate the student's reading, it is recommended that the teacher administer the reading tests included in the Basic Reading Inventory in the following manner.

Word Recognition in Isolation

Select a graded word list at a reading level that will be easy for the student. Ask the student to pronounce the words rapidly. Record the student's responses in the sight column beside the corresponding word in the performance booklet.

Return to mispronounced or unknown words for a second attempt and note the student's responses in the analysis column. Administer successive word lists until the student is no longer able to achieve a total of at least 14 words correct or until the student becomes frustrated. Examples of student and teacher copies of word lists are shown in Figure 1-1. To view the student and teacher copies of the word lists, consult the Quick Reference Guide printed on the inside front cover.

SCORING WORD RECOGNITION IN ISOLATION

Total the correct responses in the sight and analysis columns. Consult the criteria in the scoring guide at the bottom of the teacher's word lists to determine a rough estimate of the reading level achieved on each graded word list. Record the number-correct scores and the reading levels in the Word Recognition, Isolation column on the summary sheet of the performance booklet.

List A-A		List A	
1.	me	1.	show
2.	get	2.	play
3.	home	3.	be
4.	not	4.	eat
5.	he	5.	did
6.	tree	6.	brown
7.	girl	7.	is
8.	take	8.	boat
9.	book	9.	call
10.	milk	10.	run
11.	dog	11.	what
12.	all	12.	him
13.	apple	13.	wagon
14.	like	14.	over
15.	go	15.	but
16.	farm	16.	on
17.	went	17.	had
18.	friend	18.	this
19.	about	19.	around
20.	some	20.	sleep

List A-A		Sight	Analysis	List A		Sight	Analysis
1.	me*	___	___	1.	show	___	___
2.	get*	___	___	2.	play*	___	___
3.	home	___	___	3.	be*	___	___
4.	not*	___	___	4.	eat*	___	___
17.	went*	___	___	17.	had*	___	___
18.	friend	___	___	18.	this*	___	___
19.	about	___	___	19.	around*	___	___
20.	some*	___	___	20.	sleep	___	___

Number Correct ___ ___   Number Correct ___ ___
Total ___   Total ___
*denotes basic sight word from   *denotes basic sight word from
  Revised Dolch List   Revised Dolch List

Scoring Guide for Graded Word Lists

Independent	Instructional	Frustration
20 19	18 17 16 15 14	13 or less

Figure 1-1 *(Left)* Sample Student Copy of Graded Word Lists; *(Right)* Sample Teacher Copy of Word Lists from Performance Booklet

Word Recognition in Context (Passages)

Ask the student to read aloud the graded passage **one level below** the highest independent level achieved on the graded word lists. As the student reads the passage, record miscues on the corresponding copy of the passage found in the performance booklet. A miscue occurs when the student's oral reading of a passage differs from the printed passage. **For example**, a miscue results if the student says *wood* when the word in the passage is *good*. Substituting *wood* for *good* is called a miscue. Other major types of miscues are omissions, insertions, and mispronunciations. A suggested method for recording a student's miscues can be found in Figure 2-3 on page 26. Examples of student and teacher passages are shown in Figure 1-2. To view the student and teacher copies of the passages, consult the Quick Reference Guide printed on the inside front cover.

SCORING WORD RECOGNITION IN CONTEXT (PASSAGES)

To find the word recognition in context score, count the number of miscues (total or significant) in each graded passage and record the numeral in the appropriate box (total or significant). To determine reading levels, consult the appropriate set of criteria in the scoring guide at the bottom of the teacher's passage. Then

Bill at Camp

It was the first time Bill went to camp. He was very happy to be there. Soon he went for a walk in the woods to look for many kinds of leaves. He found leaves from some maple and oak trees. As Bill walked in the woods, he saw some animal tracks. At that moment, a mouse ran into a small hole by a tree. Bill wondered if the tracks were made by the mouse. He looked around for other animals. He did not see any. The last thing Bill saw was an old bird nest in a pine tree.

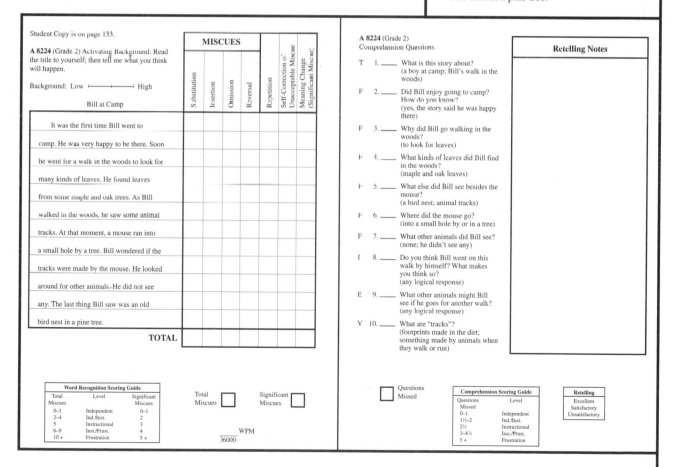

Figure 1-2 *(Top)* Sample Student Copy of Graded Passage; *(Bottom)* Sample Teacher Copies of Graded Passage and Comprehension Questions from Performance Booklet

record the number of miscues and the corresponding reading levels in the Word Recognition, Context column on the summary sheet of the performance booklet.

Comprehension Questions

Ask the comprehension questions that accompany the passage in the performance booklet and record the student's responses. Continue administering graded passages until the student is unable to answer half of the comprehension questions or makes so many miscues that frustration is apparent. Also, watch for behaviors associated with frustration: lack of expression, word-by-word reading, excessive fidgeting, and so on. **Discontinue assessment when frustration is evident.**

SCORING THE COMPREHENSION QUESTIONS

To find the student's comprehension score for each passage, count the number of comprehension questions answered incorrectly. Then record the numeral in the box provided.

To convert the comprehension scores into reading levels, consult the criteria on the scoring guide at the bottom of the teacher's copy. Then record the number of questions missed and the corresponding reading levels for oral and silent reading in the appropriate Comprehension columns on the summary sheet of the performance booklet.

Teacher judgment must be exercised at the pre-primer level because the limited number of questions may not permit precise measurement of achievement. At this level, a retelling of the passage by the student instead of the comprehension questions may be a better indicator of the student's reading ability.

HOW TO USE THIS MANUAL

Teachers or prospective teachers who have limited knowledge of reading inventories will profit by reading the entire manual carefully. It is written to permit self-study.

Teachers or specialists who are already familiar with reading inventories can read sections of interest and use the remainder of the manual as needed. Because reading inventories differ in their orientation, Sections 3 and 4 may be especially helpful.

Once familiarity with the Basic Reading Inventory is achieved, there is a shortened administration procedure that may be used by teachers and specialists who are interested primarily in placing students at their instructional levels or assessing their reading. The alternate timesaving administration procedure explained in Section 5 is intended to provide greater flexibility for teachers and specialists as they seek to estimate reading levels and assess reading strategies.

GUIDE TO UNDERSTANDING BASIC READING INVENTORY*

Comprehension can often be enhanced by posing questions about the reading *before* you actually begin the reading. With this in mind, I suggest the following:

1. Read the questions for each section.

2. Read the section looking for the answers to the questions.

3. Somehow make a notation when you discover an answer for one of the questions (write notes in the margin).

Keep in mind that the answers to *all* of these questions are explicitly stated in the text. That is, answers are "right there." Nonetheless, for some of them you might have to "think and search" because the answers may be in separate sentences or paragraphs.

QUESTIONS TO AID UNDERSTANDING OF THE BASIC READING INVENTORY

Section 2

GRADED WORD LISTS

1. What can be gained by establishing rapport?

2. What are four purposes for administering the graded word lists?

3. Why do you need to use the graded word lists with caution?

4. What do you need to administer the graded word lists?

5. What are the two scores that can be derived from the graded word lists?

6. How many word lists do you have the student read?

GRADED PASSAGES (ORAL READING)

1. What is a miscue?

2. How are miscues recorded?

3. Why might a warm-up passage be helpful?

4. With which passage should you begin?

5. Johns states that you should have the student read the title and predict what the passage might be about. What can you learn by doing so?

6. What should you do after the student has predicted?

7. What is your major task while the student reads?

8. What do you do after the student finishes reading a passage?

9. How accurate do responses to comprehension questions need to be?

10. When should you have the student stop reading the passages?

---

*Shared by Michael F. Opitz and adapted with permission. From Jerry L. Johns, *Basic Reading Inventory* (8th ed.). Copyright © 2001 by Kendall/Hunt Publishing Company (1-800-247-3458, ext. 5). May be reproduced for noncommercial educational purposes.

DETERMINING READING LEVELS FROM THE WORD RECOGNITION IN CONTEXT SCORES

1. What do you need to consider as you go about determining a student's three reading levels?

2. How is a student's word recognition score found?

3. What are *significant miscues*?

4. How should you count significant miscues on the pre-primer selections?

5. How is the percentage found?

DETERMINING READING LEVELS FROM THE COMPREHENSION QUESTIONS

1. What is the comprehension score?

2. How is the comprehension score derived?

3. How is the comprehension score determined for the pre-primer level?

DETERMINING READING LEVELS FROM SILENT READING

1. Which passage should be used to begin silent reading?

2. What do you do as the student reads silently?

3. What do you do after the passage has been read?

4. What is the student asked to reread orally?

5. What does the oral rereading enable you to assess?

6. How many passages does the student read?

DETERMINING RATE OF READING

1. Where would you find the formula for determining a student's rate of reading?

2. How many words per minute (WPM) would the average third grader read orally in the fall of the year?

3. What would be an estimate of a third grader's silent reading rate?

DETERMINING LISTENING LEVEL

1. What does a student's listening level convey?

2. What procedure do you use to determine listening level?

3. What are some limitations for using the listening level as an indicator of reading potential?

Section 3

1. Is it possible for some students to have a range of several grades within the instructional level?

2. What should you use when attempting to make decisions about students' reading levels?

3. Are the reading levels determined by using this inventory entirely accurate?

Section 4

DETERMINING STRENGTHS AND WEAKNESSES IN WORD IDENTIFICATION

1. What are some questions that can be used to guide your analysis?

2. Study Strategy 2: Advanced Qualitative Analysis.

DETERMINING STRENGTHS AND WEAKNESSES IN COMPREHENSION

1. What are some questions you can use to assess the student's comprehension?

2. What are five types of comprehension questions used in the BRI?

3. Study Strategy 1: Analysis by Question Type.

SECTION TWO

Administration and Scoring Procedures*

*See Section Five for Timesaving Procedures

Because the Basic Reading Inventory is an informal test, there is no set of procedures that must be followed rigidly. The teacher, nevertheless, must be thoroughly familiar with the recommended procedures for administration prior to asking a student to read the graded word lists and passages. The Basic Reading Inventory will take some time to administer initially until greater familiarity with the procedures is achieved. After a teacher is familiar with the procedures, the inventory flows smoothly and will take less time to administer.

Before giving the Basic Reading Inventory, the teacher needs to have a general idea of the student's reading ability. The teacher can gather this information by—

▶ consulting the student's cumulative record from the previous year to note the level at which the student was reading

▶ noting the student's reading performance in the classroom

Regardless of the method used to decide where to begin administration of the inventory, it is important that the student experience success with the initial graded word lists and passages. Therefore, the teacher needs to begin the inventory at a level where the student is likely to find the material easy.

The recommended procedure for administering and scoring the reading inventory is given in this section, with teacher's frequently asked questions provided at the end of the section.

ESTABLISHING RAPPORT AND GAINING INSIGHTS

If the reading inventory is to yield valid, reliable, and useful results, it is necessary to obtain the student's cooperation. In an effort to establish rapport, the teacher may wish to give the student some idea about how his or her reading will be evaluated. The teacher may also want to explore the student's interests and answer questions about the assessment procedure. This brief discussion may help to reduce the anxiety that often accompanies an assessment. Teachers should note that rapport is not always fully established before the administration of a reading inventory actually begins. In some cases, rapport is steadily increased throughout the assessment. In other cases, interaction between the teacher and the student may become strained during the assessment. If this occurs, the teacher should attempt to reestablish rapport.

CD View Laurie (teacher) establishing rapport with Ben (student).

During the early stages of establishing rapport, as well as throughout the administration of the reading inventory, the teacher has the opportunity to gain valuable diagnostic information in several areas. The teacher can appraise the student's oral language facility and background knowledge through informal conversation and observe how well the student responds to specific comprehension questions that are asked after the graded passages are read. The teacher may also gain insight into how the student attempts to decode unknown words by asking, "What do you do when you come to unknown words?" or "What did you do to finally figure out that word?" The teacher may also ask specific questions such as, "What is reading?" and "What do you do when you read?" to gain insights into how the student views the reading process. When the teacher feels that adequate rapport has been established, it is generally advisable to begin the reading inventory with the graded word lists.

Some students, especially young ones or readers who struggle, may become tired during the administration of the inventory. In such instances, "refresher" breaks can be used or the assessment can be spread over two periods. For example, the graded word lists can be given during one sitting and the graded passages can be given at another sitting. Because the graded word lists and passages increase in difficulty, it is permissible to explain this fact to the student before assessment begins. Some teachers encourage students to say "pass," "skip it," "not yet," or "I don't know" when difficult words or questions are encountered.

GRADED WORD LISTS

There are at least four reasons for giving the graded word lists.

▶ First, the word lists will provide the approximate level at which the student should begin reading the graded paragraphs.

▶ Second, the teacher will be able to study some of the student's word identification strategies (such as structural analysis and phonics) and assess "how well the student recognizes words automatically" (Gillet and Temple, 2000, p. 107).

▶ Third, the word lists can be used to classify the student's word recognition ability as above, at, or below grade level.

▶ Fourth, the teacher can assess the extent of the student's sight vocabulary and basic sight vocabulary.

Basic sight words on the graded word lists are indicated with an asterisk (*). These words are found on the Revised Dolch List (Johns and Lenski, 2001; Johns, Lenski, and Elish-Piper, 1999) and comprise over 50 percent of the running words found in all types of printed materials.

Because the word lists are not a natural reading situation, extreme caution should guide the teacher. The teacher cannot examine all word identification strategies through the student's performance on the graded word lists. Phonics, structural analysis, and sight vocabulary are the three most common areas that can be observed. It is not possible to explore the student's overall word identification strategies and the balance between phonics and context, because the words are presented in isolation. All aspects of a student's word identification repertoire deserve careful attention, because they can provide potential instructional insights. The best judgments about the student's word identification strategies result from a careful analysis of the student's oral reading of the graded passages coupled with insights from the graded word lists.

The graded word lists do not assess the student's ability to comprehend and are, therefore, an inappropriate measure of overall reading ability. Goodman (1965) has demonstrated that students decode much more readily when words appear in context than when they appear in lists. Also, Marzano and others (1978) have cautioned teachers about basing assessment solely on a word recognition test.

☑ Administering Graded Word Lists

To administer the graded word lists, the teacher will need the word lists for the student and the performance booklet in which the student's responses will be recorded. The recommended procedure for administering the graded word lists is to present the student with the graded list of words and ask him or her to pronounce them rapidly. If a student reads a word correctly within one second, it is defined as a sight word (Leslie and Caldwell, 1995). As the student reads down each list of words, the teacher records the student's responses in a performance booklet. The word list the teacher initially selects should, if at all possible, be very easy for the student.

It is important for the teacher to record the student's responses promptly because any delays are likely to result in incorrect reporting. The use of a tape recorder may prove quite helpful for the teacher. The graded word lists are continued until the student is no longer able to achieve a total score of at least 14 correct words or when the

View Laurie (teacher) administering a third-grade word list to Ben (student).

teacher observes that the task has become frustrating for the student. Teacher judgment plays an important role in the administration of the entire inventory.

☑ Scoring Graded Word Lists

The teacher derives three scores for each graded word list administered to the student (see Figure 2-1). One score represents the student's immediate responses to the words and is called the *sight* score. The second score represents the student's correction of the words missed during the sight presentation. The opportunity for the student to study each word missed in an attempt to pronounce it is called the *analysis* score. If the student does not know or mispronounces any words on the first attempt (that is, at sight), the teacher returns to each of these words after the student has finished the list and provides the student with an opportunity to analyze the word in an attempt to arrive at its correct pronunciation. The student's *immediate* responses are recorded by the teacher in the sight column. The responses the student makes when given an opportunity to study the words missed are recorded in the analysis column. The third score is the total of the sight and analysis scores. The total score can be used as a rough indicator of reading levels.

✍ SCORING JEFF'S GRADED WORD LISTS

To show how the graded word lists are scored, Figure 2-1 contains Jeff's performance on the pre-primer and primer word lists. An empty space next to a word means that Jeff pronounced it correctly. (Some teachers put a check mark for each correct word, because it lessens students' perceptions of when they get a word wrong.) Miscues in word recognition are noted as follows: "DK" indicates that he said "I don't know." Single letters or phonetic symbols represent Jeff's attempt to pronounce the word. The plus (+) indicates that he corrected a miscalled word. When Jeff said a word which was different from the stimulus word, it is noted in the appropriate column. Other pertinent comments that might have diagnostic significance (for example, skips unknown words; uses phonic knowledge; knows basic sight words; quite persistent; gives up easily) can also be noted by the teacher.

Jeff's scores are shown at the bottom of each column of words. For the pre-primer (A-A) word list, the score of 16 indicates that he correctly pronounced 16 of the 20 words on the sight presentation. These 16 words were known automatically. The 4 words not correctly pronounced during the sight presentation were numbers 2, 3, 6, and 20. From his score on the *analysis* column, the teacher can note that Jeff corrected 3 of his initial miscues (numbers 2, 3, and 6), thereby achieving a total score of 19 correct words. At the primer level Jeff achieved a score of 15 on the sight presentation and a total score of 18 because he corrected 3 (numbers 1, 10, and 18) of his initial miscues.

The teacher can use the total number of words Jeff correctly pronounced on each graded word list for a very general idea of his reading levels. To convert total scores to a rough estimate of the various reading levels, the teacher should compare the total number of correct words for each list of words to the scoring guide at the bottom of the word lists in the performance booklet. This scoring guide is also reproduced in Table 2.1.

Table 2.1 Scoring Guide for Graded Word Lists		
Independent	**Instructional**	**Frustration**
20 19	18 17 16 15 14	13 or less

List A-A (Pre-Primer)	Sight	Analysis	List A (Primer)	Sight	Analysis
1. me*			1. show	she	+
2. get*	got	+	2. play*		
3. home	house	+	3. be*		
4. not*			4. eat*		
5. he*			5. did*		
6. tree	tr-	+	6. brown	D.K.	br-
7. girl			7. is*		
8. take*			8. boat		
9. book			9. call*		
10. milk			10. run*	ran	+
11. dog			11. what*		
12. all*			12. him*	his	his
13. apple			13. wagon		
14. like*			14. over*		
15. go*			15. but*		
16. farm			16. on*		
17. went*			17. had*		
18. friend			18. this*	that	+
19. about*			19. around*		
20. some*	same	same	20. sleep		

*denotes basic sight word from Revised Dolch List

Number Correct   _16_   _3_

Total   _19_

*denotes basic sight word from Revised Dolch List

Number Correct   _15_   _3_

Total   _18_

Scoring Guide for Graded Word Lists

Independent	Instructional	Frustration
20 19	18 17 16 15 14	13 or less

Figure 2-1   Jeff's Performance on Two Graded Word Lists

☑ Determining Reading Levels—Graded Word Lists

From Jeff's responses in Figure 2-1, the teacher can note that he achieved a total score of 19 correct words on the pre-primer list. According to the scoring guide below the word lists, a score of 19 would indicate an independent level. The total score of 18 for the primer word list indicates an instructional level. From the results reported thus far, it is not possible to estimate Jeff's frustration level. The teacher would need to continue with additional word lists until Jeff mispronounced 7 words or appeared to be having considerable difficulty. When this point is reached, the teacher would proceed to the graded passages. Keep in mind that reading levels estimated with word lists represent only rough indications of reading ability. The inadequacies of graded word lists are recognized by teachers who know that some students can identify words in isolation that cause difficulty in reading materials. Other students who have difficulty with words in isolation can identify words in reading materials. It is important, therefore, for teachers to recognize the limitations of graded word lists and to use this knowledge when scoring and interpreting inventory results.

✍ RECORDING JEFF'S WORD RECOGNITION SCORES FOR GRADED WORD LISTS

Figure 2-1 shows that Jeff achieved a total score of 19 on the pre-primer list and 18 on the primer list. These scores should then be entered on the summary sheet similar to that shown in Figure 2-2 and reproduced at the beginning of the performance booklets for Forms A, B, C, and D. To determine the reading levels corresponding to these two scores, consult Table 2.1 or the scoring guide at the bottom of the word lists. Using the criteria, Jeff achieved an independent level on the pre-primer word list and an instructional level on the primer word list. Note that the abbreviations *Ind.* and *Inst.* are written on the summary sheet to indicate the levels achieved.

The teacher should check his or her understanding of this procedure by finding the reading levels that correspond to Jeff's performance on the first- through third-grade word lists as noted in Figure 2-2. This task can be accomplished by taking the total score given in Figure 2-2 for the first-grade word list (20) and finding the corresponding reading level from the scoring guide (Table 2.1). The reading level should then be entered next to the number of words correct. This procedure can be repeated for the scores on the second-grade and third-grade word lists.

GRADED PASSAGES

Prior to actually administering the graded passages, the teacher must develop some system for recording the student's responses. There are numerous systems and techniques for coding reading miscues (Barr, Blachowicz, and Wogman-Sadow, 1995; Collins and Cheek, 1993; Gillet and Temple, 2000; Goodman, Watson, and Burke, 1987; Johnson, Kress, and Pikulski, 1987; Manzo and Manzo, 1993; McCormick, 1999). A miscue is "an oral reading response that differs from the expected response to the written text" (Harris and Hodges, 1981, p. 199). Miscues "provide a rich source of information for analyzing language and reading development" (Harris and Hodges, 1995, p. 155). Figure 2-3 contains examples of miscues and a suggested method for recording them during oral reading. The teacher should carefully study and learn or adapt the suggested procedure so that it can be used and referred to later when actual examples of a student's oral reading are considered.

Because there is a transition from the word lists to the reading passages, some teachers find a "practice" passage helpful. Warm-up passages are found in Appendix C. These passages and questions may be used at the teacher's discretion. **It is generally**

| Grade | Word Recognition | | | | | | Comprehension | |
| | Isolation (Word Lists) | | | | Context (Passages) | | Oral Reading Form A | |
	Sight	Analysis	Total	Level	Miscues*	Level	Questions Missed	Level
PP	16	3	19	*Ind.*	0	*Ind.*	0	
P	15	3	18	*Inst.*	1		½	
1	16	4	20		2		0	
2	14	2	16		5		1½	
3	9	2	11		10		5	

*Refers to *total* miscues in this example

Figure 2-2   Summary Sheet for Jeff's Performance on the Basic Reading Inventory

recommended to begin administering the graded passages at least one level below the student's highest independent level on the graded word lists. If a student, for example, achieved independent levels on the word lists for the pre-primer, primer, first-, and second-grade levels, it is recommended that the teacher begin the graded passages at the first-grade level. If the student is unable to read that passage at the independent level, the teacher should go to the next lower level and continue to move down until an independent level is found or the pre-primer passage is reached. Then, the teacher should return to the starting point and proceed until the student reaches a frustration level. In the event that the pre-primer passage is too difficult for the student to read, carefully selected Early Literacy Assessments in Appendix A may be used.

☑ Administering Graded Passages

Before actual reading begins, cover the passage with a heavy sheet of paper. Have the student read the title of the passage silently and predict or share what it might be about. The student's sharing can yield several valuable pieces of information: (1) the background experiences/knowledge the student associates with the title; (2) the student's ability to make predictions; and (3) the student's vocabulary and ability to express himself or herself. During this prereading sharing, the teacher may note the student's ideas and informally evaluate the student's background on a scale of low to high.

 View Laurie (teacher) administering a second-grade passage to Ben (student).

Background: Low |————|————| High

This scale accompanies each graded passage in the performance booklet and can be found near the top of the page on the left. The teacher should not describe what the passage is about, explain key concepts, or use vocabulary from the passage because the student's comprehension may be artificially enhanced. Once the student has shared or predicted, the teacher should uncover the passage. The student should then be given a

SUBSTITUTIONS

Jim saw the boy.

OMISSIONS

Poor little ~~Baby~~ Bear could not move from the tall tree.

INSERTIONS

He strolled along the path and soon was deep in the forest.

REVERSALS

Are they twins?

REPETITIONS

   A. Correcting a miscue

      Baby Bear did not know where he was.

   B. Abandoning a correct form

      He stayed alone in the pine tree all night.

   C. Unsuccessfully attempting to correct an initial miscue

      He had slept hard all night.

   D. Plain repetition

      Jim saw a bear.

ADDITIONAL MARKINGS

   A. Partial words

      The hunters rescued the boys.

   B. Nonword substitutions

      People on the frontier had shooting contests.

   C. Punctuation ignored

      . . . from some maple and oak trees/As Bill

   D. Intonation

      He played a record that was his favorite.

   E. Word pronounced by examiner

      Men on the frontier often had shooting contests.

   F. Dialect

      He went home.

   G. Lip movement

      place LM in margin

   H. Finger pointing

      place FP above word

   I. Vocalization

      place V in text

Figure 2-3   A Suggested Method for Recording a Student's Oral Reading Miscues

reason to read the passage; for example, to find out more about the title, to check predictions made about the passage, or the like. The student should also be told that comprehension questions will be asked after the passage has been read. The teacher might say something like the following: "Read the passage aloud and think about what you're reading. I'll ask you some questions when you're done reading."

✍ Recording Miscues During Oral Reading

While the student is reading from the graded passage, the teacher uses a performance booklet to keep a careful record of the exact way in which the student reads the passage. Some students may need to be told a word if they pause for ten or fifteen seconds; however, the recommended procedure is to encourage students to read the graded passages using their strategies for word identification without any teacher assistance. The suggested method for recording a student's oral reading, presented in Figure 2-3, should be a valuable aid to the teacher or prospective teacher who has not yet developed a system for recording. The teacher's major task is to record the manner in which the student reads the passage by noting omissions, insertions, substitutions, and other miscues. In addition, the teacher should note hesitations, word-by-word reading, finger pointing, monitoring strategies, and so on. If desired, the teacher may time the student's reading using a stopwatch or a watch with a second hand. There is a place in the performance booklet to note the number of seconds it takes the student to read the passage. Performing division will result in the student's rate of reading in words per minute (WPM). Any timing should be done in an inconspicuous manner because some students, if they see they are being timed, do not read in their usual way. In addition, some students may focus more on pronouncing words quickly than trying to understand the passage. Further discussion of how to determine rate of reading is found under Determining Rate of Reading later in this section.

Four Ways to Assess Comprehension

After the student finishes reading the passage, the teacher may assess comprehension by asking the comprehension questions, integrating the concept of engagement with the questions, using retelling, or combining retelling with the questions. Many teachers prefer to ask the comprehension questions.

Ask Comprehension Questions. Each reading passage above the pre-primer level contains 10 comprehension questions. The general procedure is for the teacher to remove or cover the passage and ask the student the comprehension questions. Write the student's verbatim responses to the comprehension questions or underline the "answers" given in the performance booklets. Noting the student's responses will make scoring the questions much easier. The teacher will also be able to analyze the reasoning used by the student. The student's answers to the comprehension questions need not conform exactly to the answers in the performance booklets; responses similar in meaning to the printed answer should be scored as correct. In addition, some students may need to be told that the answers to some questions (vocabulary, evaluation, and inference) are not stated directly in the passage. For these questions, always give credit for responses that demonstrate understanding and/or logical thinking.

CD View Laurie (teacher) asking Ben (student) comprehension questions after he read a second-grade passage.

The teacher should not help the student arrive at the correct answers to the questions (use a + for questions answered correctly). If a comprehension question is answered incorrectly (use a –), note the student's response, and go on to the next question. The teacher may, however, ask for clarification if the answer for a particular question is not clear. Neutral probes such as "Tell me more," "What else?" or "Explain that further" often help students elaborate on partial answers. Half credit may be given for partial answers. Continue with subsequent passages until the student is unable to answer satisfactorily at least half of the comprehension questions or makes many miscues.

Integrate the Concept of Engagement with the Questions. Manzo and Manzo (1993) have suggested the "engagement" concept to enhance comprehension assessment. Basically, the teacher determines whether the student's responses to comprehension questions are congruent or incongruent. All correct responses are congruent. Incorrect responses "may be congruent (related but incorrect) or incongruent (unrelated as well as incorrect). An increase of congruent responses is a sound sign that the student is engaged" (Manzo and Manzo, 1993, p. 92). Unfortunately, so-called remedial students answer 55 to 80 percent of teachers' questions with totally incongruent responses (Manzo and Manzo, 1995).

Teachers who wish to integrate the engagement concept while asking the comprehension questions should follow these guidelines:

▶ All comprehension questions scored as correct (+) are a sign of engagement. For correct responses that are "especially full, fresh, or elaborated in some meaningful and appropriate way," circle the numeral beside the comprehension question (Manzo and Manzo, 1993, p. 467).

▶ For comprehension questions scored as incorrect (–), a decision needs to be made: Is the incorrect response congruent (related to the passage in some meaningful way) or incongruent (not related to the passage in some meaningful, logical way)? For incorrect responses that are incongruent, place an X on the numeral beside the comprehension question.

General guidelines for evaluating engagement can be found in Section 4 of this manual. More extensive information can be found in an inventory developed by Manzo, Manzo, and McKenna (1995).

Use Retelling. McCormick (1995, p. 174) notes several advantages to using retellings. They can assist the teacher in "determining whether students have noted important information, whether they can reproduce it in a manner that makes sense, and whether their background knowledge has an effect on the way they interpret the substance of the text." The teacher can also informally assess the student's short-term retention. In retelling, the student is asked to orally recall a passage after it has been read. The teacher could say, "After you have read the passage, you will be asked to retell it in your own words."

Other ways to initiate the retelling include the following probes:

▶ Tell me what the passage (story or text) is about.

▶ Tell me as much as you can about what you have just read.

▶ What is the passage (story or text) about?

Goodman, Watson, and Burke (1987) have offered suggestions to teachers who are interested in gaining proficiency in using a retelling strategy to assess the student's comprehension. A few of their suggestions for teachers who want to use retelling procedures include:

1. familiarity with the passage

2. not giving the student information from the passage

3. asking open-ended questions

4. retaining any nonwords or name changes given by the student

Once a teacher becomes familiar with the graded passages, it is possible to use a retelling strategy to assess comprehension. In a retelling strategy, the teacher invites the student to tell everything about the passage that has just been read. The teacher may ask specific questions without giving the student information that has not already been mentioned. Using Jeff's reading of the second-grade passage in Figure 2-4 for illustration, the teacher would first ask him to tell about what he read. Suppose Jeff said that the passage is about a boy who went to camp for the first time. The teacher could encourage Jeff to relate further events and also ask him the boy's name. Through experience, the teacher will gain confidence in extracting the main ideas and important details in the passages without asking the comprehension questions.

There are some probes that teachers have found useful. Consider adapting and using the following probes (Lipson and Wixson, 1991, p. 198):

▶ Tell me more about what you have read.

▶ Tell me more about what happened.

▶ Tell me more about the people who you just read about.

▶ Tell me more about where this happened.

To judge student retelling, the categories *excellent* (independent level), *satisfactory* (instructional level), and *unsatisfactory* (frustration level) may be used. At the independent level, the student recalls central or key events, remembers important facts, retains the sequence of events, and relates most of the content in an organized manner. At the instructional level, the student recalls most central or key events, remembers *some* important facts, retains the *general* sequence of events, and relates an overall sense of the content. At the frustration level, the student typically recalls bits of information in a rather haphazard manner with little apparent organization. There is space for retelling notes beside the comprehension questions in the performance booklet. Teachers who choose to use retelling may circle excellent, satisfactory, or unsatisfactory in the retelling box at the bottom of the space for retelling notes in the performance booklet.

While retelling is a viable option, it "is not an easy procedure for students, no matter what their ages" (Morrow, 1988, p. 128). In addition, retelling requires considerable teacher judgment, and there is no widely used, generally accepted criteria for judging student retellings of passages. Harris and Sipay (1990) also note that retellings place a heavy demand on the student's ability to retrieve and organize information in the passage. Johnson, Kress, and Pikulski (1987) believe that it is somewhat premature to recommend retelling for widespread practical use. Teachers interested in pursuing this strategy in greater depth may find the work of professionals such as Glazer and Brown (1993), Kalmbach (1986), McCormick (1999), Morrow (1985, 1988), and Wilde (2000) worthy of consideration. In addition, Appendix B contains several procedures and suggestions for using retelling.

Combine Retelling with the Questions. In actual practice, many teachers feel more comfortable in combining the retelling strategy with some of the comprehension questions. This procedure permits the teacher to maintain the necessary flexibility to gather the information needed to make an accurate assessment of the student's understanding of the passage. The recommended procedure is to invite retelling, during which time the teacher uses an asterisk or R (for retelling) to note the comprehension questions answered. The remaining questions are asked after the retelling. This technique capitalizes on the strengths of both assessment procedures while minimizing their weaknesses.

☑ Scoring Jeff's Graded Passage

Figure 2-4 contains Jeff's oral reading performance on a second-grade passage. The notations indicate that he substituted *Bob* for *Bill*, *so* for *soon*, *was* for *saw*, and *minute* for *moment*. These four substitutions were not corrected. He also inserted *trees*. Based on a total (quantitative) count, Jeff made 5 miscues. The numeral 5 is recorded in the "Total Miscues" box at the bottom of the page. The miscue tallies in the chart should not be done until after the assessment has been completed.

On the 10 comprehension questions shown in Figure 2-5 Jeff responded freely and demonstrated the ability to answer various types of questions (+ indicates correct responses; – indicates incorrect responses; underlining indicates student's responses). Jeff didn't know why Bill went walking (so he earned no credit) and apparently forgot the name of one kind of leaf Bill found in the woods (hence he received half credit); nevertheless, his understanding of the passage was quite good. From the general criteria for the three reading levels at the bottom of Figure 2-4, it would appear that this passage is at Jeff's instructional level, because he made 5 *total* miscues and had comprehension in the *Ind./Inst.* range.

DETERMINING READING LEVELS—GRADED PASSAGES

The teacher can determine whether the passage is at the student's independent, instructional, or frustration level by considering: (1) the accuracy with which the student reads; and (2) the student's behavior while reading. In order to determine the accuracy with which the student reads the passage, the teacher must determine the student's word recognition score. The word recognition score is found by determining the number of either *total* or *significant* miscues the student makes during the oral reading of the graded passages. Teachers, depending on their philosophies, can count miscues in one of two ways: total miscues or significant miscues.

Word Recognition

COUNTING TOTAL MISCUES

Determining the word recognition in context score by counting the student's total miscues is a *quantitative* analysis of oral reading behavior. The teacher counts all miscues, regardless of type, and uses this total to help determine the student's reading level. In this procedure, all miscues are given equal weight in scoring the student's oral reading. The teacher may find it easier to count total miscues during the actual administration of the reading passages. After the Basic Reading Inventory has been administered, further analysis, if desired, may be undertaken to determine significant miscues and to complete the miscue tally to the right of the passage.

Various guidelines have been offered for counting total miscues. After a review of five studies, Morris (1990) found that investigators counted miscues differently; nevertheless, there was consensus on certain types of miscues. Based on this information, and a careful review of the literature, it is recommended that the teacher count the following for total miscues:

▶ substitutions

▶ omissions (words and punctuation)

▶ insertions

▶ self-corrections (see comments in the following paragraph)

▶ examiner aid (however, giving aid is not recommended)

Student Copy is on page 133.

A 8224 (Grade 2) Activating Background: Read the title to yourself; then tell me what you think will happen.

Background: Low ├────────┼────────┤ High

Bill at Camp

	Substitution	Insertion	Omission	Reversal	Repetition	Self-Correction of Unacceptable Miscue	Meaning Change (Significant Miscue)
	MISCUES						
It was the first time Bill *Bob* went to							
camp. He was very happy to be there. Soon *So*							
he went for a walk in the woods to look for							
many kinds of leaves. He found leaves							
from some maple *trees* ∨ and oak trees. As Bill							
walked *was* in the woods, he saw some animal							
tracks. At that moment, a mouse *minute* ran into							
a small hole by a tree. Bill wondered if the							
tracks were made by the mouse. He looked							
around for other animals. He did not see							
any. The last thing Bill saw was an old							
bird nest in a pine tree.							
good phrasing and intonation **TOTAL**							

Word Recognition Scoring Guide		
Total Miscues	Level	Significant Miscues
0–1	Independent	0–1
2–4	Ind./Inst.	2
5	Instructional	3
6–9	Inst./Frust.	4
10 +	Frustration	5 +

Total Miscues ☐   Significant Miscues ☐

WPM
$\overline{)6000}$

Figure 2-4   Jeff's Performance on a Graded Passage

A 8224 (Grade 2)
Comprehension Questions

Retelling Notes

T 1. **+** What is this story about?
(a boy at camp; Bill's walk in the woods) *Bill at camp*

F 2. **+** Did Bill enjoy going to camp? How do you know?
(<u>yes</u>, the story said <u>he was happy there</u>)

F 3. **−** Why did Bill go walking in the woods?
(to look for leaves)
to find animals

F 4. **1/2** What kinds of leaves did Bill find in the woods?
(<u>maple</u> and <u>oak</u> leaves)
What else? I don't know

F 5. **+** What else did Bill see besides the mouse?
(<u>a bird nest</u>; animal tracks)

F 6. **+** Where did the mouse go?
(<u>into a small hole</u> by or in a tree)

F 7. **+** What other animals did Bill see?
(none; <u>he didn't see any</u>)

I 8. **+** Do you think Bill went on this walk by himself? What makes you think so?
(any logical response) *Yes, he didn't talk to anyone*

E 9. **+** What other animals might Bill see if he goes for another walk?
(any logical response)
deer and squirrels

V 10. **+** What are "tracks"?
(<u>footprints</u> made in the dirt; something made by animals when they walk or run)

1½ Questions Missed

Comprehension Scoring Guide	
Questions Missed	Level
0–1	Independent
1½–2	Ind./Inst.
2½	Instructional
3–4½	Inst./Frust.
5 +	Frustration

Retelling
Excellent
Satisfactory
Unsatisfactory

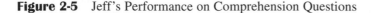

Figure 2-5   Jeff's Performance on Comprehension Questions

In counting total miscues, a number of special considerations are warranted. First, dialect variations (such as *goed* for *went*), hesitations, and repetitions should not be included in the count of total miscues although they may be recorded for later study and analysis. Second, the *consistent* mispronunciation of a word more than once in a passage should only be counted once. For example, if a student reads *Bob* for *Bill* repeatedly in the passage, it should be counted as only one miscue. This same guideline also applies to situations where a nonsense name is used for a proper name or any other word. Third, if a student omits an entire line, it should be counted as one miscue. Finally, self-corrections provide evidence that the student is monitoring his or her reading, and some teachers prefer not to count such miscues. Numerous self-corrections, however, impact fluency and rate of reading. If such miscues are not counted, they should still be considered as a source of information in the overall determination the student's reading levels. It is important that all the above information be considered carefully when the teacher is analyzing the student's word identification and comprehension strategies.

COUNTING SIGNIFICANT MISCUES

Determining the word recognition in context score by counting only significant miscues is a *qualitative* analysis of oral reading behavior. Some evidence (for example, Goodman, 1972; Goodman and Marek, 1996; Lipton, 1972; Recht, 1976) seems to suggest that certain substitutions, insertions, omissions, and the like do not seriously damage the student's understanding of the passage; hence, such miscues should not be counted as significant.

It must be remembered that accurate recognition is not the major objective in reading. *The goal is always meaning.* Because even proficient readers make errors on unfamiliar material, teachers must resist the temptation to meticulously correct all inconsequential mistakes. They must always ask whether a particular miscue really makes a difference (Goodman, 1971, p. 14).

It would appear that the best advice to give teachers and prospective teachers for counting significant miscues is to include those omissions, insertions, substitutions, and other miscues that appear to affect comprehension. In short, significant miscues alter the meaning of the passage. The following method is suggested:

1. Count the total number of miscues in the passage.

2. Find the total of all dialect miscues, all corrected miscues, and all miscues that do not change the meaning.

3. Subtract this total from the remaining miscues. The result is the number of significant miscues.

A comprehensive, chronological annotated bibliography of miscue analysis has been compiled by Brown, Goodman, and Marek (1996). In addition, Wilde (2000) has provided numerous helpful and practical suggestions for conducting a miscue analysis so the results can be used for instruction.

☑ Scoring Jeff's Oral Reading

From Jeff's oral reading of a second-grade passage, as recorded in Figure 2-4, it is apparent that he made five total miscues. If a teacher decided to count *total* miscues to determine Jeff's score in word recognition, he or she would record the numeral 5 in the "Total Miscues" box and circle the corresponding level (Instructional) in the Word Recognition Scoring Guide (see Table 2.2). Then, the numeral and the level would be written on the summary sheet of the performance booklet. The same procedure would be used to determine the word recognition score for the other graded passages.

If a teacher decided to count *significant* miscues, each of the five miscues would be evaluated within the context of the passage to determine whether the meaning of the passage was affected. After such an analysis, three of the miscues Jeff made (*Bob*, *so*, and *was*) appear to be significant. The teacher would record the numeral 3 in the "Significant Miscues" box and circle the corresponding level (Instructional) in the Word Recognition Scoring Guide. Then the numeral and the level would be recorded on the summary sheet of the performance booklet.

Figure 2-2 contains various scores when the teacher decided to count *total* miscues. By consulting Table 2.2 or the appropriate section of the Word Recognition Scoring Guide at the bottom of each passage, the teacher should determine the reading levels that correspond to the various scores and place the appropriate levels in Figure 2-2. For example, at the pre-primer level, Jeff's *total* miscue count was 0. This score corresponds to a reading level of "Independent" which is written as *Ind.* in the appropriate column of Figure 2-2. For practice, write in the appropriate levels for primer, first, second, and third grade. Remember to use "Total Miscues" from the Word Recognition Scoring Guide.

Table 2.2   Scoring Guide for Words in Context for Forms A, B, C, and D

Word Recognition Scoring Guide		
Total Miscues	Level	Significant Miscues
0–1	Independent	0–1
2–4	Ind./Inst.	2
5	Instructional	3
6–9	Inst./Frust.	4
10+	Frustration	5+

Observation of Reading Behaviors and Other Evidence

In addition to counting miscues, the teacher should also note other evidence that may be helpful in determining the appropriateness of the passage:

► finger pointing

► phrasing (fluent, adequate, poor)

► flushed face or anxiety

► frustration

► refusals

► attitude

► persistence

► monitoring strategies

► background knowledge

► overall engagement

Teachers who use the Basic Reading Inventory report that such behaviors and observations are often as helpful as actual miscue counts in helping to determine whether a particular passage is easy, about right, or too difficult for the student. At the very least, these observations can provide additional information as tentative judgments are made regarding a student's oral reading and reading levels.

Determining Reading Levels from Comprehension Questions or Retelling

The comprehension score is determined by counting the number of questions missed. To convert this score into one of the three reading levels, the teacher would consult Table 2.3 or the scoring guide at the bottom of each passage. For example, if Jeff missed five comprehension questions, that passage would be at his frustration level.

Table 2.3 Scoring Guide for Comprehension	
Questions Missed	Level
0–1	Independent
1$\frac{1}{2}$–2	Ind./Inst.
2$\frac{1}{2}$	Instructional
3–4$\frac{1}{2}$	Inst./Frust.
5+	Frustration

The above procedure, however, is not directly applicable to the pre-primer passages, because they contain only five questions. Teacher judgment must be exercised in determining the student's comprehension score. If the teacher decided that the score from the pre-primer level did not accurately reflect the student's achievement, it would be permissible for the teacher to place more emphasis on the score at the primer level when summarizing the results of all passages administered.

Teachers who choose to use the retelling strategy to assess comprehension may (1) determine a percent score from the student's retelling or (2) identify the passage as one of the three reading levels without noting a specific percent of comprehension. Teachers who choose to use retelling may also circle *excellent* (independent), *satisfactory*, (instructional), or *unsatisfactory* (frustration) in the retelling box at the bottom of each graded passage in the performance booklet. The main issue to be kept in mind is whether the student's comprehension of the passage is judged to be at the independent, instructional, or frustration level.

✍ RECORDING JEFF'S COMPREHENSION SCORES FOR THE GRADED PASSAGES

Figure 2-2 contains Jeff's scores for the comprehension questions in the pre-primer through third-grade levels. The teacher, by consulting Table 2.3 or the scoring guide below each passage, should determine the reading level that corresponds to each comprehension score and place these levels in Figure 2-2. When a student's scores fall between the reading levels, teacher judgment must be used. The recommended procedure is to record *Ind./Inst.* or *Inst./Frust.* on the summary sheet. The scoring guide indicates areas that require teacher judgment. The determination of reading levels requiring teacher judgment is discussed in Section 3.

Determining Reading Levels from Silent Reading

Select a form of the Basic Reading Inventory that the student did not read orally. Form D is specifically designed for silent reading. **It is recommended that the teacher begin the silent reading at the highest passage where the student achieved an independent level during oral reading.** If this procedure does not result in an independent level for silent reading, proceed to easier passages until an independent level is determined or the pre-primer passage is read. Then, return to the original starting point and continue until the student reaches a frustration level.

As the student reads the passage silently, the teacher times the student's reading and notes behavioral characteristics such as lip movement and finger pointing. Following silent reading, the passage is removed and the student's comprehension is assessed with comprehension questions, a retelling strategy, or a combination of the two.

Then the student is given the passage and asked to locate and orally reread a sentence in the passage that answers the question posed by the teacher. The question is located below the passage in Form D of the performance booklet. The correct sentence in the passage is printed in bold type. According to Johnson, Kress, and Pikulski (1987), the oral rereading enables the teacher to assess the student's ability to (1) skim for specific information, (2) read for specific information and stop when that purpose has been achieved, and (3) demonstrate oral reading ability after the material has been read silently. Generally, oral rereading following silent reading should be better than the oral reading at sight from another passage at the same level of difficulty. For example, if a student reads one third-grade passage orally and a different third-grade passage silently, the sentence orally reread from the silent passage should generally be read more accurately and fluently than the passage read at sight.

When the student finds and rereads the sentence orally, the teacher should record the reading in the same manner as was done on the passages read orally at sight. The teacher can also note how the student located the sentence that was read (for example, skimmed to locate the information; reread the passage from the beginning; seemed confused).

The student continues to read increasingly difficult passages until a frustration level is determined. The various scores and corresponding reading levels should be entered at the appropriate place on the summary sheet. These silent reading levels can be used in conjunction with the student's oral reading performance to arrive at estimations of the three reading levels.

RATE OF READING

A formula for determining a student's rate of reading is provided on each graded-passage page in the performance booklet. The 6,000 for each graded passage above the pre-primer level for Forms A, B, C, and D was determined by multiplying the number of words per selection (100) by sixty. For Forms LN and LE, a similar procedure was used. The teacher who wants to determine a student's rate of reading can do so by using the formula provided. The teacher should record as the divisor of the formula the time (in seconds) the student takes to read the passage. Perform the necessary division, and the resulting numeral will be a rough estimate of the student's rate in words per minute (WPM). For example, suppose a middle-grade student took 70 seconds to read the fourth-grade selection on Form A. The teacher would divide 6,000 by 70. The result is a reading rate of approximately 86 words per minute (WPM).

$$
\begin{array}{r}
85.7 \text{ WPM} \\
70{\overline{\smash{\big)}\,6000}} \\
\underline{560} \\
400 \\
\underline{350} \\
500 \\
\underline{490}
\end{array}
$$

Teachers are enouraged to make general notes about a student's rate (for example, read very quickly; read slowly but accurately; seems to think that fast is best). A slow rate beyond second grade is usually a symptom that the student lacks a large sight vocabulary and effective word identification strategies.

Another estimate of a student's reading rate can be determined by averaging the rates for those passages where the student misses three or fewer comprehension questions. This procedure has the advantage of using a larger sample of behavior and taking comprehension into account. It should also be remembered that reading rate can vary according to the material being read, the student's interest and familiarity with the material, the purpose for which it is being read, and whether reading is done orally or silently. The teacher who chooses to determine reading rate should average oral and silent reading rates separately.

COMBINING READING RATES FOR SHORTER AND LONGER PASSAGES

The passages in Forms A, B, C, and D each contain 100 words (except for the pre-primer level) and differ in length from the 250-word passages in Forms LN and LE. If the teacher wishes to combine the results from passages in both forms (for example, Form A and Form LN), the following procedure should be used:

1. Select passages where the student missed three or fewer comprehension questions. Keep oral and silent reading separate in the calculations.

2. Add the total number of words read for all the passages where the student missed three or fewer questions and multiply by 60. The resulting numeral becomes the dividend.

3. Add the times it took the student to read each passage. This numeral is used as the divisor.

4. Complete the necessary division to determine the approximate reading rate.

For example, the data in Table 2.4 is from Terell who read seven passages orally. His resulting reading rate is approximately 80 words per minute (WPM).

Table 2.4   Data for Terell's Reading Rate

Level of Passage	Number of Words	Time (in Seconds)	
4 (A 5414)	100	70	
5 (A 8595)	100	80	80.4 WPM
6 (A 6867)	100	90	970)78000
4 (LN 5414)	250	160	7760
5 (LN 8595)	250	190	4000
6 (LN 6867)	250	180	3880
7 (LN 3717)	250	200	
	1300	970	
	× 60		
	78000		

NORMS FOR ORAL AND SILENT READING RATES

Large-scale norms for *oral* reading fluency have been reported by Hasbrouck and Tindal (1992). These norms were developed by having students in grades two through five read passages at sight for one minute from their grade level text, regardless of their instructional level. The resulting norms, shown in Table 2.5, are based on over 7,000 students and provide "words correct per minute" at the 75th, 50th, and 25th percentiles for students in grades two through five during three periods (fall, winter, spring) of the school year. Because the norms are reported in words correct per minute (WCPM), comparing the WPM as determined by the Basic Reading Inventory procedures to the WCPM norms in Figure 2.5 should be done informally, realizing that different procedures have been used to determine the numerals. These differences mean that the WPM procedures outlined in this manual result in figures that are less conservative than the WCPM procedures. Comparisons can still be made and used to make informal decisions about the student's rate of reading. The percentiles within each grade should be especially useful to help teachers track and monitor progress of students within a particular grade and compare growth to established standards.

Table 2.5   Median Oral Reading Rates for Students in Grades Two Through Five

Grade	Percentile	Fall WPM*	Winter WPM	Spring WPM
	75	82	106	124
2	50	53	78	94
	25	23	46	65
	75	107	123	142
3	50	79	93	114
	25	65	70	87
	75	125	133	143
4	50	99	112	118
	25	72	89	92
	75	126	143	151
5	50	105	118	128
	25	77	93	100

* Reported in words correct per minute

Forman and Sanders (1998) established norms for the reading rates of first-grade students over a five-year period. Their procedure involved randomly selecting students in each of the school district's fourteen schools who were judged by their teachers as making average grade-level progress in reading. The goal was to identify average students. Any students recommended for special reading services, special education, or believed to be reading above grade level were not included in the study. Over a five-year period, they had first graders read stories while recording miscues and seconds for reading. Increasingly difficult stories were read throughout the school year. Mean accuracy (in percentage of words pronounced correctly) and reading rate (in mean words per minute) were determined for over 1,100 students for each of the three time periods shown in Table 2.6. These norms may be useful to teachers who wish to have some empirical standards for the reading rates of first-grade students.

Teachers should keep in mind that the rates, based on over 3,000 students, are restricted to a single large school district whose students generally score above average in state and national reading assessments. The standard deviations give some indication of the wide range of rates among first-grade students. Adding and subtracting one standard deviation (22) to the mean rate of 54 means that approximately two-thirds of the students will have rates between 32 and 76 words per minute in December and January of first grade.

Table 2.6   Mean Oral Reading Rates for "On-Grade Level" First Graders

Months	Number of Students	Mean Accuracy	Mean Rate* (WPM)	Standard Deviation
Dec.–Jan.	1,173	95%	54	22
Feb.–March	1,192	96%	66	24
April–May	1,166	96%	79	26

*Reported in words per minute

Carver (1989, p. 165) has provided information on *silent* reading rates that "may be helpful to teachers who administer informal reading inventories." The figures he presents are the average rates of students in that *particular* grade who can *understand* material at *that* grade level. Although Carver's figures are in standard word lengths, they may be useful as a rough indication of the average rates at which average students in a particular grade read with understanding. Users of the Basic Reading Inventory, then, can use the figures presented in Table 2.7 when evaluating a student's silent reading ability.

Table 2.7   Silent Reading Rates for Students in Various Grades Who Understand the Material

Grade	1	2	3	4	5	6	7	8
WPM	<81	82–108	109–130	131–147	148–161	162–174	175–185	186–197

	9		10		11		12	
	198–209		210–224		225–240		241–255	

THE LISTENING LEVEL

In addition to the three reading levels, the teacher may wish to get a rough estimate of the student's listening level or potential for substantial growth in reading. Intelligence tests are sometimes used to estimate potential for reading; however, their limitations have led some teachers to read graded passages to a student and determine the highest level of material that the student can understand. Undertaking such a procedure is known as determining the student's listening level. This procedure should **not** be used with students in the primary grades (Schell, 1982).

Determining the Listening Level

The teacher should select a form of the Basic Reading Inventory that was not used for either oral or silent reading. The listening level is determined after the *teacher* reads increasingly difficult passages to the student. The teacher should first read the title and develop a purpose for listening to the passage. Procedures similar to those used for oral and silent reading may be used: Invite the student to predict what the passage will be about and then have the student *listen* to the content in the passage as the teacher reads a passage *to* the student. After the passage has been read, the teacher assesses the student's comprehension with the questions, a retelling strategy, or a combination of the two. The criteria for estimating the student's listening level is a comprehension score of three or fewer questions missed. The teacher should also informally note the student's ability to use vocabulary and language structures as complex as those used in the passage read.

It is recommended that the teacher begin reading a passage that is not higher than the student's instructional level. The teacher should then continue reading more difficult passages until the student misses more than three comprehension questions. The *highest* passage at which the student misses three or fewer questions is his or her listening level.

Scoring Tom's Listening Level

Suppose, for example, that Tom is a fifth-grade student who has a fourth-grade instructional level for oral and silent reading. The teacher wishes to determine his listening level or potential. The teacher should choose a passage at the fourth-grade level from a form of the Basic Reading Inventory that Tom has not read orally or silently. After the teacher reads the passage aloud, Tom responds to the comprehension questions. If Tom misses three or fewer questions, the teacher continues reading increasingly difficult passages until Tom misses more than three questions. The highest level at which Tom meets this criterion is identified as his listening level. To illustrate this procedure, consider the data in Table 2.8.

Table 2.8   Data for Tom's Listening Level

Level of Passage	Comprehension Questions Missed
4 (C 5414)	0
5 (C 8595)	2
6 (C 6867)	3
7 (C 3717)	4

Based on these data, Tom's listening level would be sixth grade, because that was the highest level at which he missed three or fewer questions. Because his listening level (sixth grade) is higher than his instructional level (fourth grade), the teacher has reason to believe that Tom has the potential to increase his reading ability. Harris and Sipay (1990) suggest a two-year discrepancy between the listening level and the instructional level as a rough criterion for practical significance. In this instance, Tom's listening comprehension can be viewed as a favorable prognostic sign; namely, Tom should be able to understand material at the sixth-grade level once he acquires the necessary reading competence.

There are, of course, some limitations for using the listening level as an indicator of reading potential. Limitations within the assessment process as well as a student's auditory handicaps and/or unfamiliarity with standard English reduce the importance that the teacher should attach to a listening level. In addition, bright students in the middle and upper grades may have reading abilities that exceed their listening abilities.

For these reasons, teachers should consider the listening level as a rough estimate of reading potential that needs to be supported from observation and the results of measures of intellectual capacity.

Figure 2-6 on page 48 provides a summary of procedures for administering and scoring the Basic Reading Inventory.

Frequently Asked Questions

1. Must every student be given the Basic Reading Inventory?

No. Use the inventory with those students who you believe need further assessment in reading: students who score very high or very low on standardized reading survey tests or students who need assessment of their word identification or comprehension skills. The Basic Reading Inventory is also useful with students who have transferred into your school system. Remember that the basic assessment strategy described in this manual can be used with instructional materials in your classroom (such as trade books, literature-based readers, and language experience stories) to help make your instruction more responsive to students' needs.

2. Are informal reading inventory (IRI) results appropriate additions to my students' portfolios?

Certainly. One of the guiding principles for literacy portfolios is that assessment should be a multifaceted process (Valencia, 1990). Results and insights (both yours and the student's) from an IRI can help chronicle reading development. Some teachers audio tape the student's reading and responses to the IRI and include the tape in the portfolio. Teachers have used multiple indications of performance for many years. Continue using observations, your judgments, running records, daily work, and other informal and formal assessments. McCormick (1999) has provided an excellent discussion for beginning, maintaining, and evaluating portfolios. She has also included ideas for portfolio conferences.

3. What should I do if a student finds a particular passage extremely easy or difficult?

The diversity of students' experiences and backgrounds may make a particular passage much easier or more difficult than its assigned readability level. You can generally note this problem when the student's reading of a particular passage is much better or worse than would be predicted from the student's performance on previous passages. When you believe that a passage is inappropriate, the recommended procedure is to substitute a passage at the same level from a different form of the reading inventory. Then use the total results from the student's reading to make your judgments.

4. Do some comprehension questions tap the student's background and experience?

For most of the questions in the Basic Reading Inventory, the student must recall or use information from the passage to answer the question. These types of questions are called passage dependent. Some questions, however, are not totally passage dependent. The most notable ones are the vocabulary questions. Two other types of questions (inference and evaluation) encourage students to use their knowledge, background, and experience in conjunction with the information presented in the passage to engage in what some reading authorities identify as higher-level thinking. Raphael (1986) refers to such questions as author and you. Such questions invite students to make explicit connections between the ideas in the passage and their own background knowledge and experience. Teachers are generally pleased with the variety of questions contained in the Basic Reading Inventory.

Frequently Asked Questions

5. May I omit some comprehension questions?

Yes, you may omit questions to shorten the administration time, because it takes about ten seconds for each question to be asked and answered. Some teachers omit the vocabulary questions because they are least dependent on the passage. In other words, students are often able to use their backgrounds and experiences to give correct responses to the vocabulary questions. The evaluation and inference questions encourage students to integrate information in the passage with their background knowledge in order to give a satisfactory response. Because such responses are not based entirely on the text, some teachers prefer to omit these questions. You can probably omit one question without changing the scoring guide at the bottom of each passage in the performance booklet.

Another alternative is replacing some of the questions with others that you believe are more important in assessing the student's comprehension. How you conceptualize the nature of comprehension will likely influence the types of questions you ask. The author's view is that if comprehension is assessed with questions, an effort should be made to tap the student's ability to recall the literal information *and* to reason beyond the information given in the passages. That is why evaluation and inference questions are also included.

6. Are the answers provided with the comprehension questions the only acceptable answers?

No. You may decide that some students' responses are both logical and reasonable even though they differ from the "answer" in the parentheses under the question. In such cases, give the student credit. The age and grade of the student should also be taken into consideration when you are scoring responses. In essence, use your knowledge of students when scoring the comprehension questions.

7. What should I do if a student uses experience (not information in the passage) to correctly answer a factual question even though it is not the answer in parentheses?

After you acknowledge the student's response, ask what the passage said. In essence, the student's answers to factual questions should be tied to information presented in the passage. If the student is unable to remember and the initial response (based on experience) was correct, you may want to give half credit.

8. What should I do when students fail to see that they should use their experience along with information in the passage to answer an inference or evaluative question?

Gently remind students that, based on what they read, you want to know what they think. When the student says, "It didn't say," you might respond, "That's right, but I want to know what you think." Feel free to encourage students to use their experience.

9. Is it acceptable to reword questions that the student doesn't seem to understand?

Yes. You should not, however, provide information that will help the student answer the question. In addition, if you find that many students experience difficulty with a particular question, you may want to develop a replacement question of your own.

Frequently Asked Questions

10. Why do first graders sometimes have difficulty with the pre-primer and primer passages?

Generally, students at the early stages of reading, especially those taught with literature-based readers or trade books, are most familiar with the vocabulary used in such books. Because the Basic Reading Inventory is not designed for use with specific reading materials, differences in vocabulary may exist, particularly at the pre-primer and first-grade passages. You should take this information into consideration when you assess reading and determine the student's three levels. You may also find the Early Literacy Assessments in Appendix A to be especially helpful with emergent readers.

11. How should I assess the reading of students who are unable to read the easiest word lists and passages?

Remember that emergent readers and older students experiencing difficulty in reading may find the easiest word lists and passages difficult. When this situation occurs, the language experience approach (LEA) is recommended. A concrete object, photograph, or experience is used to engage the student in discussion. Then the teacher writes down the student's dictation and has the student read the LEA story. This strategy can be used to probe what students have learned about how the reading process works. Walker (2000, pp. 247–48), Gillet and Temple (2000, pp. 283–84) and Lipson and Wixson (1991, pp. 479–82) offer some concise assistance for launching, maintaining, and using dictated stories. Appendix A contains a variety of Early Literacy Assessments. Included are informal ways to assess literacy knowledge, phoneme segmentation awareness, auditory discrimination, alphabet knowledge, picture reading, and so on. The informal assessment devices will be especially useful for students who are unable to read the easiest word lists and passages. Additional assessments for the early stages of reading can be found in Johns, Lenski, and Elish-Piper (1999).

12. Why are some passages narrative and others expository?

Narrative passages generally tell a story. Expository passages inform by presenting information. Both types of literature are commonly found in schools, and students need to be able to read both types of texts.

Forms A, B, and LN of the Basic Reading Inventory contains narrative passages. Form C contains mostly narrative passages. Form D, starting in grade two, contains expository passages. Form A is designed for oral reading, and you can assess the student's ability to deal with narrative discourse. Form LN contains longer narrative passages (250 words) than Form A (100 words). You can use Form LN for oral or silent reading.

In the upper grades, the content areas become more important, so Forms D and LE contains expository passages at and above the second-grade level. Because students often read their content area texts silently, Form D assesses silent reading with expository materials. Form LE contains longer expository passages and may be used for oral or silent reading. With these various forms, you have the resources to help you gain a more complete picture of the student's reading. Both teachers and research have found that expository passages can cause students greater difficulty. McCormick (1999) notes that expository text structures are commonly more difficult to comprehend than the story structures of narrative materials. One reason such a situation exists may be a student's lack of experience with expository materials. Another reason may be the differences in structure between the two types of literature. If, for example, a student has difficulty with the expository passages, you may have gained valuable knowledge to use in your instructional program.

Frequently Asked Questions

13. Why do illustrations accompany only the pre-primer passages of the reading inventory?

Illustrations can make reading material attractive. They can also capture the interest of a student. Pictures, however, sometimes provide clues to help the student understand the passage. Because the Basic Reading Inventory is designed to assess how a student uses language cues to construct meaning from print, illustrations are restricted to the pre-primer passages.

14. What are miscues and what's the difference between total miscues and significant miscues?

Miscues occur when a student's oral reading of the passage results in a version that differs from the printed passage. Common miscues include substitutions, omissions, and insertions. A miscue can be as minor as substituting *a* for *the* in the following sentence: I saw the squirrel run up *the* tree. Other miscues can be significant: substituting *horse* for *house* in the sentence, Dad parked the car in the garage and walked into the *house*. It is important to remember that miscues are a natural part of the reading process.

The number of miscues a student makes can merely be counted; this procedure is called quantitative analysis or total miscues. Such analysis does not take into account the quality of the student's miscues; therefore, all miscues are given equal weight.

A qualitative analysis counts significant miscues. It is a search to gain insights into a student's reading by making judgments about the student's miscues. In a qualitative analysis, some miscues are rated of higher quality than others. To determine significant miscues, evaluate each miscue in the passage in which it occurs and judge the extent to which the meaning of the sentence or passage is altered. Generally, significant miscues change the meaning of the passage. Whether you choose to count total miscues or significant miscues is up to you. The scoring guide contains both options.

Below are some examples of miscues that teachers considered significant because of the change in meaning involved.

Student:	Here comes a *cat*.
Text:	Here comes a *car*.
Student:	While gathered *above* the council fire . . .
Text:	While gathered *about* the council fire . . .
Student:	The summer had been a dry one, *usual* . . .
Text:	The summer had been a dry one, *unusual* . . .
Student:	The flower got its name from its *stage* habit . . .
Text:	The flower got its name from its *strange* habit . . .
Student:	They threw leaves into the *yard*.
Text:	They threw leaves into the *air*.
Student:	He unlocked the *bank* door.
Text:	He unlocked the *back* door.
Student:	He *sniffled* slowly down the street.
Text:	He *shuffled* slowly down the street.
Student:	Jim put the *bird* on the snow.
Text:	Jim put the *bread* on the snow.
Student:	Only he would know the amount in each dose.
Text:	Only he would know the *correct* amount in each dose.

Frequently Asked Questions

Here are some examples of miscues that were not considered significant because only a minimal change of meaning was involved.

Student: . . . sailing over the *middle* line . . .
Text: . . . sailing over the *midline* . . .

Student: . . . and scored. *The* game ended.
Text: . . . and scored *as* the game ended.

Student: *Ooh!* What fun!
Text: *Wow!* What fun!

Student: She went with her parents to the pet *store*.
Text: She went with her parents to the pet *shop*.

Student: . . . trees fell *on* the ground.
Text: . . . trees fell *to* the ground.

Student: Dale *was* the strongest player on the team *and* was up first.
Text: Dale, the strongest player on the team, was up first.

Student: The Tigers and *the* Jets were playing . . .
Text: The Tigers and Jets were playing . . .

Finally, here are some "gray area" examples for which greater teacher judgment is needed to determine whether the miscues are significant.

Student: The *kick* went sailing . . .
Text: The *ball* went sailing . . .

Student: The children helped by *carrying* bits of wood.
Text: The children helped by *carting* bits of wood.

Student: This is *funny*.
Text: This is *fun*.

Student: . . . some would take *the* wood and start . . .
Text: . . . some would take *this* wood and start . . .

15. What should I do when the student mispronounces proper nouns?

First, do not include multiple mispronunciations of the same word in counting miscues. Count only one miscue. Second, encourage the student to use strategies to pronounce the word by saying, "Just do the best you can." Third, use the student's pronunciation if the word appears in a question. Finally, in some instances you may pronounce the word for the student because of the frustration that is evident. Be sure you make a note about the student's behavior (for example, unable to go on until I pronounced the word; tried several pronunciations; is aware that the word is mispronounced but seems to have the basic meaning).

16. What guidelines should be used if I decide to count only significant miscues?

Miscues are generally significant when:

1. the meaning of the sentence or passage is significantly changed or altered and the student does not correct the miscue.
2. a nonword is used in place of the word in the passage.
3. only a partial word is substituted for the word or phrase in the passage.
4. a word is pronounced for the student.

Frequently Asked Questions

Miscues are generally *not* significant when:

1. the meaning of the sentence or passage undergoes no change or only minimal change.
2. they are self-corrected by the student.
3. they are acceptable in the student's dialect (*goed home* for *went home, idear* for *idea*).
4. they are later read correctly in the same passage.

17. Should I help students with words they don't know?

Every time a student is told an unknown word is one less opportunity to gain insights into the student's reading. There will probably be some rare instances where you tell a student a word; nevertheless, the recommended procedure is to remain silent or to say, "Do the best you can." Then you can note the strategies (or lack of them) that the student uses frequently, occasionally, or not at all. There is some evidence (McNaughton, 1981) that students were less accurate and self-corrected a smaller proportion of their miscues when they received immediate as compared with delayed correction. You may, therefore, want to be selective about telling students unknown words.

18. How do passages in the Basic Reading Inventory and the Early Literacy Assessments relate to levels for Guided Reading and Reading Recovery?

Using criteria summarized by Reutzel and Cooter (2000) and the work of Gunning (1998), the chart below contains approximations of the passages in the Basic Reading Inventory and Early Literacy Assessments. These approximations should be used along with your experience and professional judgment.

Grade Level	Early Literacy Assessments	Basic Reading Inventory Passage Code	Guided Reading Level	Reading Recovery Level
Caption Reading	Caption Reading	—	A	1–3
Easy Sight Word	EE-1		A	4–6
Pre-primer	EE-2	A-A, B-B, C-C, D-D (4 Passages)	B	7–8
Primer	—	A, B, C, D (4 Passages)	C–E	9–11
1	—	7141 (4 Passages)	F–I	12–17
2	—	8224 (4 Passages)	J–M	18–28
3	—	3183 (6 Passages)	N–P	30–38
4	—	5414 (6 Passages)	Q–R	39–40
5	—	8595 (6 Passages)	—	41–44

Note: In addition to the above questions, Felknor, Winterscheidt, and Benson (1999) provide thoughtful answers to nearly thirty questions related to selecting, administering, scoring, and using IRIs.

Basic Reading Inventory Administration and Scoring Procedures

To determine a student's independent, instructional, and frustration levels, administer the graded word lists and graded passages included in the Basic Reading Inventory as follows:

WORD RECOGNITION IN ISOLATION: Select a graded word list at a reading level that will be easy for the student. Ask the student to pronounce the words rapidly. Record the student's responses in the sight column beside the corresponding word list in the performance booklet.

Return to mispronounced or unknown words for an attempt at analysis and note the student's responses in the analysis column. Administer successive word lists until the student is no longer able to achieve a **total** score of at least 14 correct words or until the student becomes frustrated.

Scoring: Total the correct responses in the sight and analysis columns. Consult the criteria on the scoring guide at the bottom of the word lists to determine a rough estimate of the reading level achieved on each graded word list. Record the number-correct scores and the reading levels on the summary sheet of the performance booklet.

WORD RECOGNITION IN CONTEXT: Ask the student to read aloud the passage graded one level *below* the highest independent level achieved on the graded word lists. As the student reads the passage, record all miscues such as omissions, repetitions, substitutions, and the like on the corresponding copy of the passage found in the performance booklet.

Scoring: Count the number of *total* miscues or *significant* miscues (those that affect meaning) in each graded passage.

To determine reading levels from the word recognition in context scores, consult the criteria on the scoring guide at the bottom of the passage. Record the score and the reading levels on the summary sheet of the performance booklet.

COMPREHENSION: Ask the comprehension questions that accompany the passage in the performance booklet and record the student's responses. Continue administering graded passages until the student has many word recognition miscues or is unable to answer half the comprehension questions. Also, watch for behavior associated with frustration: lack of expression, word-by-word reading, excessive anxiety, and so on.

Scoring: Count the number of comprehension questions missed.

To convert these scores into reading levels, consult the criteria on the scoring guide at the bottom of the questions. (Teacher judgment must be exercised at the pre-primer level because the limited number of questions may not permit precise measurement of achievement.) Record the scores and the reading levels on the summary sheet of the performance booklet.

Figure 2-6   Basic Reading Inventory Administration and Scoring Procedures

Determining the Student's Three Reading Levels

ASSIMILATING JEFF'S RESULTS

Once the teacher has summarized the results for graded word lists, words in context, and passage comprehension, estimates of the student's independent level, instructional level, and frustration level can be determined. Figure 3-1 contains a summary of Jeff's performance on Form A of the Basic Reading Inventory. The various scores and levels should correspond to the teacher's efforts to complete the examples that were presented in Figure 2-2 (page 25). The teacher should check his or her results from Figure 2-2 with Figure 3-1 and resolve any discrepancies.

From the data presented in Figures 2-2 and 3-1, it would appear that Jeff's independent levels are pre-primer, primer, and first grade. Because the independent level is the *highest* level at which Jeff can read books by himself, first grade would be his independent level. Materials at the second-grade level of difficulty should provide the basis for instruction. At this level Jeff should make maximum progress under teacher guidance. The third-grade level, according to the criteria, appears to be his frustration level. In summary, Jeff's three reading levels are: independent—first grade, instructional—second grade, and frustration—third grade.

EXAMPLES—BOB'S AND PABLO'S READING LEVELS

It should be noted that most summary sheets, unlike Figure 3-1, will not provide the teacher with such clear distinctions among the three reading levels. When discrepancies arise, the teacher must use judgment in determining the student's three levels. Frequently, it is wise to consider the student's performance *preceding and following* the level in question, as well as the student's performance *within* a particular passage.

Generally, the recommended procedure is to place a bit more emphasis on comprehension if word identification on the graded word lists and in context is clearly instructional level or better. **Remember that the goal of reading is constructing meaning from print.** The ability to pronounce words automatically *is* important; nevertheless, word identification must always be judged with regard to the student's ability to under-

Grade	Word Recognition						Comprehension	
	Isolation (Word Lists)				Context (Passages)		Oral Reading Form A	
	Sight	Analysis	Total	Level	Miscues*	Level	Questions Missed	Level
PP	16	3	19	Ind.	0	Ind.	0	Ind.
P	15	3	18	Inst.	1	Ind.	½	Ind.
1	16	4	20	Ind.	2	Ind./Inst.	0	Ind.
2	14	2	16	Inst.	5	Inst.	1½	Ind./Inst.
3	9	2	11	Frust.	10	Frust.	5	Frust.

*Refers to *total* miscues in this example

Figure 3-1   Summary of Jeff's Performance on Form A of the
Basic Reading Inventory

stand the passage. In addition, give greater emphasis to silent reading comprehension in the upper grades.

It is also important to take the behavioral characteristics of the student at each reading level into consideration to aid in proper placement. A student, for example, may have percentages high enough to read independently at a certain level of difficulty; however, the student may appear to be quite nervous and exhibit behavioral characteristics that lead the teacher to conclude that such a level is too difficult for independent reading. It is prudent for teachers to exercise extreme care in determining a student's three reading levels. It is always best to give a student easier material than to give or recommend a book to the student that might be difficult and frustrating.

In most cases the three reading levels serve as a starting point for effective reading instruction. Because the reading levels are determined in a relatively short period of time, they may not be entirely accurate. The teacher should not, therefore, consider a student's three reading levels to be rigid and static. If, in working with the student, the teacher finds that the student's various reading levels are not accurate, the necessary adjustments should be made. Keep in mind that the passages in the Basic Reading Inventory provide a limited sample of student reading behavior. Adjustments, based on classroom performance, should be made when necessary.

Estimating Bob's Reading Levels

Interpreting the summary of Bob's reading, presented in Figure 3-2, requires some teacher judgment. Note that *total* miscues are recorded for word recognition in context.

All the scores for the first- and third-grade levels present no problems, because the numerals correspond to those given in Tables 2.1, 2.2, and 2.3. At the second-grade level, however, word recognition in context is below the criteria in Table 2.2 for a clear independent level. Because Bob's other two scores at the second-grade level are marked independent, the teacher may hypothesize that second grade is his independent level. For the fourth-grade level, Bob achieved the instructional/frustration level for word recognition in context; in addition, his scores for word recognition in isolation and comprehension are at the frustration level. Bob is unable to comprehend the material satis-

| Grade | Word Recognition | | | | | | Comprehension | |
| | Isolation (Word Lists) | | | | Context (Passages) | | Oral Reading Form A | |
	Sight	Analysis	Total	Level	Miscues*	Level	Questions Missed	Level
1	20	0	20	Ind.	1	Ind.	1	Ind.
2	19	1	20	Ind.	4	Ind./Inst.	1	Ind.
3	13	2	15	Inst.	5	Inst.	2½	Inst.
4	8	3	11	Frust.	8	Inst./Frust	6	Frust.

*Refers to *total* miscues in this example

Figure 3-2 Summary of Bob's Performance on Form A of the Basic Reading Inventory

factorily, so the teacher hypothesizes that fourth grade is Bob's frustration level. Now, by analyzing Bob's performance *within* a given graded passage and *between* the four graded passages, the teacher may verify earlier hypotheses and make a judgment that his three reading levels are: independent—second grade, instructional—third grade, and frustration—fourth grade.

Teachers should also note that it is possible for some students to have a range of several grades within the instructional level. If, for example, Bob's scores in Figure 3-2 were changed so that the comprehension score at the second-grade level was two questions missed, his three reading levels would probably be: independent—first grade, instructional—second grade and third grade, and frustration—fourth grade. Given a range of instructional levels, where should Bob be placed for instruction? The recommended procedure is to place him in second-grade reading materials and carefully monitor his progress. If he does well at this level, the teacher should consider a temporary placement in third-grade reading materials. Generally, it is easier to move a student to a higher level than to a lower level.

Estimating Pablo's Reading Levels

Another summary sheet that requires teacher judgment is shown in Figure 3-3. Study the percentages and make a judgment with regard to Pablo's independent, instructional, and frustration levels before continuing. Note that **significant** miscues are recorded for word recognition in context.

At the fourth-grade level, the teacher must resolve Pablo's word recognition score in context. Two significant miscues could be either independent or instructional; however, by examining the other scores *within* that level, the teacher should judge fourth grade as his independent level because of his near-perfect scores in these areas. The fifth-grade level requires judgment in oral reading comprehension. Because the score in comprehension is near the independent level (one or fewer questions missed) and the other three scores within this level are independent, the teacher should conclude that the fifth-grade level is also independent. At the sixth-grade level, the two significant miscues for word recognition in context is probably best identified as instructional because Pablo's other three scores are instructional.

| Grade | Word Recognition | | | | | | Comprehension | | | |
| | Isolation (Word Lists) | | | | Context (Passages) | | Oral Reading Form A | | Silent Reading Form D | |
	Sight	Analysis	Total	Level	Miscues*	Level	Questions Missed	Level	Questions Missed	Level
4	20	0	20	Ind.	2	Ind./Inst.	0	Ind.	1	Ind.
5	19	1	20	Ind.	1	Ind.	1½	Ind./Inst	1	Ind.
6	16	2	18	Inst.	2	Ind./Inst.	2½	Inst.	2½	Inst.
7	16	1	17	Inst.	4	Inst./Frust	4½	Inst./Frust	5	Frust.
8	10	4	14	Inst.	5	Frust.	5	Frust.	6	Frust.

*Refers to *significant* miscues in this example

Figure 3–3 Summary of Pablo's Performance on Form A and Form D of the Basic Reading Inventory

The seventh-grade level requires teacher judgment in two areas: word recognition in context and oral reading comprehension. Both of these scores, according to the scoring guide, appear to be nearer the frustration level, so a tentative judgment for the seventh-grade level is frustration. Judgment is required at the eighth-grade level because the words in isolation score is instructional. The other three scores are clearly frustration. In addition, because the seventh-grade was judged to be frustration, the eighth-grade level, by definition, would also be frustration.

The teacher must now decide on Pablo's reading levels. From the earlier judgments, his three reading levels would probably be independent—fifth grade, instructional—sixth grade, and frustration—seventh grade. Although Pablo is quite good at pronouncing words at the seventh-grade level, the teacher placed considerable emphasis on comprehension and decided that this level was too difficult.

CONTRASTING EXAMPLES— AARON'S AND HEM'S READING LEVELS

Teachers who have given reading inventories have noticed that some students make many miscues but are still able to answer the comprehension questions. Other students are able to recognize most of the words but have difficulty answering the comprehension questions. How are the reading levels of such students best estimated?

Estimating Aaron's Reading Levels

Aaron's reading performance is presented in Figure 3-4. Look at Aaron's performance in word recognition. It is clear that by fifth grade he is having difficulty pronouncing words in the word lists and graded passages. His comprehension, however, is

Grade	Word Recognition						Comprehension	
	Isolation (Word Lists)				Context (Passages)		Oral Reading Form A	
	Sight	Analysis	Total	Level	Miscues*	Level	Questions Missed	Level
PP								
P								
1								
2								
3	18	2	20	Ind.	1	Ind.	0	Ind.
4	15	3	18	Inst.	5	Inst.	2½	Inst.
5	11	2	13	Frust.	10	Frust.	3	Inst./Frust.
6	9	1	10	Frust.	11	Frust.	2	Ind./Inst.

*Refers to *total* miscues in this example

Figure 3-4   Summary of Aaron's Performance on Form A of the Basic Reading Inventory

not clearly frustration at grades five or six. Aaron appears to have great difficulty in word recognition, but his comprehension could be characterized as near instructional level at grade five and clearly instructional at grade six. Because the goal of reading is comprehension, some teachers may tend to emphasize Aaron's ability to comprehend in spite of many miscues. There is a problem with this sort of emphasis—it fails to acknowledge that both word recognition and comprehension must be taken into account when determining reading levels. An over-emphasis on comprehension may lead to placement in materials where Aaron would make many miscues and likely regard reading as a frustrating experience. He would have to work so hard to construct meaning that the joys of reading would be lost.

The reflective teacher will recognize the need to help Aaron strengthen his sight vocabulary and skills in word identification. Based on the data in Figure 3-4, Aaron's independent reading level is third grade. His instructional level is best characterized as grade four because his scores for words in isolation, words in context, and comprehension are all instructional level. Grade five would be Aaron's frustration level because of his great difficulty with word recognition. The teacher should realize that Aaron has the ability to comprehend at higher levels—possibly because his background knowledge allows him to compensate for his limited abilities in word recognition. A systematic analysis of Aaron's miscues should provide the basis for specific instruction that is responsive to Aaron's needs. Responsive instruction, coupled with plenty of reading materials at Aaron's instructional level, will likely result in strengthening his sight vocabulary, fluency, and overall confidence in reading.

Estimating Hem's Reading Levels

In contrast to Aaron, Hem has the ability to recognize words (see Figure 3-5). His scores for words in isolation and words in context never reach the frustration level. Comprehension, however, is an entirely different matter. He has no clear independent level in comprehension. Even at second grade, Hem is experiencing difficulties with comprehension. Those difficulties persist with each of the subsequent passages Hem reads. The ability to pronounce words without adequate comprehension is often characterized as word calling or barking at print. Situations of this type do not occur frequently, but they suggest that a student may have limited background experiences, poor vocabulary knowledge, lowered mental abilities, or limited oral language skills in English.

The teacher should explore possible explanations for Hem's reading behavior. It is possible that his background experiences are limited. Based on the data available, Hem does not have a clear independent level. The teacher might still consider second grade to be his independent level as long he has the necessary background for the selection being read. Third grade could be Hem's instructional level, but the teacher must be sure that needed concepts and ample background are built before reading. Materials at grades four and five should not be used for instruction unless adequate attention is devoted to ensure that Hem has the necessary background experiences. The teacher will probably need to help Hem expand his meaning vocabulary, to teach him that the goal of reading is comprehension, and to develop strategies he can use for comprehension monitoring. Plenty of easy reading in materials where Hem possesses the necessary background knowledge coupled with retellings and discussions about the material should help Hem strengthen his reading.

| Grade | Word Recognition | | | | | | Comprehension | |
| | Isolation (Word Lists) | | | | Context (Passages) | | Oral Reading Form A | |
	Sight	Analysis	Total	Level	Miscues*	Level	Questions Missed	Level
PP								
P								
1								
2	20	0	20	Ind.	0	Ind.	3	Inst./Frust.
3	19	1	20	Ind.	1	Ind.	4	Inst./Frust.
4	17	2	19	Ind.	2	Ind./Inst.	5	Frust.
5	16	1	17	Inst.	3	Ind./Inst.	5	Frust.

*Refers to *total* miscues in this example

Figure 3-5 Summary of Hem's Performance on Form A of the Basic Reading Inventory

Instructional Uses of Inventory Results

In addition to using the Basic Reading Inventory to estimate a student's three reading levels, the results can also be used to study the student's reading behavior. Kibby (1995) notes that a key question in a diagnostic decision-making model is determining which reading strategies and skills are strengths and limitations for the student. Carefully evaluating a student's performance on reading inventories cannot be surpassed for the wealth of useful diagnostic data that they provide. Three strategies for evaluating inventory results are suggested for word identification. Two strategies are provided for analyzing the student's comprehension.

DETERMINING WORD IDENTIFICATION STRATEGIES

Any system of analyzing the student's word identification strategies should be guided by a careful and thoughtful analysis of oral reading performance. Conrad and Shankin (1999) suggest helpful ways to use miscues to understand the student's reading. In addition, Johnson, Kress, and Pikulski (1987) provide several questions that may help guide the overall analysis:

▶ Does the student's oral reading reflect a balanced use of sight vocabulary, context clues, phonics, structural analysis, and syntactic clues? Do weaknesses appear to exist in any of these areas?

▶ Is the student's oral reading fluent or is the student's reading hesitant or word by word?

▶ To what extent do the student's miscues alter or interfere with the meaning of the passages read?

▶ When miscues occur, does the student appear to be monitoring his or her reading by rereading, correcting unacceptable miscues (those that adversely affect meaning), and/or noting that the passage is difficult? Are the miscues influenced by the student's dialect?

▶ Does the student's limited vocabulary, background, or concept development appear to be affecting oral reading?

▶ Are any patterns suggested by analyzing the student's miscues and oral reading behavior?

STRATEGY 1: SIMPLE ERROR ANALYSIS

3 Strategies for Evaluating Inventory Results

1—Simple Error Analysis

2—Miscue Analysis Tally

3—Advanced Qualitative Analysis

Simple error analysis is one method for analyzing the miscues made during oral reading in an effort to find patterns. These patterns may indicate certain tendencies in word identification or general reading behavior. By recording a student's miscues from the reading inventory on a sheet similar to that in Figure 4-1, the teacher may make hypotheses about a student's needs in reading. The recommended procedure is to **use miscues from passages that are at the student's independent, instructional, and instructional/frustration levels**. Suppose, for example, that Sam's errors from the oral reading passages revealed the information contained in Figure 4-1. Based on these data, it would appear that Sam is able to apply the initial sounds in those words he has difficulty pronouncing. He has difficulty, however, with the middle of words. After further analysis of his medial errors, it would seem that a lack of vowel knowledge may be contributing to his difficulties in word recognition. It is also evident that many of these miscues are substitutions that distort the meaning of the reading selection. Sam may be helped with the strategy lessons from Scenario 5 in Section 6. Sam has also made several other substitutions; however, these substitutions (*a* for *the*; *road* for

SUBSTITUTIONS			
Different Beginnings	**Different Middles**	**Different Endings**	**Different in Several Parts**
	ran for rain *naw – now* *well – will* *walk – work* *barn – burn*	*fly – flew* *had – have* *big – bigger* *in – into*	*a for the* *road – street* *big – huge*
Insertions	**Omissions**	**Repetitions**	**Miscellaneous**
big *always*	*she* *spiders* *many*	///	

Figure 4-1   Summary of Sam's Oral Reading Performance

street, and so on) do not result in significant changes in the meaning of the passage and do not require any instruction. The repetitions Sam made may indicate a problem that requires the attention of the teacher or the implementation of an effective reading strategy. Teachers should evaluate such repetitions within the context of Scenario 1 in Section 6.

A different student may show weaknesses in other areas. Pete, for example, may have many words under the section "Omissions." Perhaps he does not attempt to pronounce many of the words he does not recognize immediately. Pete may, therefore, need instruction in developing more effective strategies for anticipating words through the use of contextual and syntactic cues (see Scenarios 2 and 3 in Section 6).

Still another student may fail to recognize many word endings. Such miscues may be indicative of a possible problem in structural analysis (*s, es, ed, ing,* and so on). Teachers should remember, however, that some speakers of a particular dialect may omit word endings. Miscues of this type, as long as they make sense in the reader's dialect, should not be regarded as significant; furthermore, they do not require instructional intervention.

When analyzing word recognition by charting miscues, the teacher must be careful to base conclusions on patterns of miscues, not just a few miscues in any given category. Remember that only miscues at the student's independent and instructional levels should be charted for analysis, because the frustration level indicates that the reading process has broken down. Miscues noted at the student's frustration level may be used to verify tendencies noted at the student's independent and instructional levels. The graded word lists, if used in this type of analysis, should be kept separate because research (Allington and McGill-Franzen, 1980) has revealed that students made different miscues when reading the same words in a random order instead of in context.

The teacher's hypotheses regarding a student's tendencies in word identification should be considered tentative and verified or discounted through classroom instruction. The teacher should also remember that word identification is not an end in itself; it is a means for constructing meaning of the material. It is often possible for a student to construct meaning from reading material even when the student makes several miscues. Instruction in word identification, therefore, should be based on strategies that will help the student comprehend text and develop greater automaticity in word recognition.

STRATEGY 2: MISCUE ANALYSIS TALLY

The teacher's passages for Forms A, B, C, and D have provisions to tally miscues and other reading behaviors as shown in Figure 4-2. The tallies should be completed after the assessment session with the student has been completed.

The example in Figure 4-2 is based on Jeff's oral reading noted in Figure 2-4. Each miscue should be considered and tallied accordingly. Jeff substituted *Bob* for *Bill* so a tally mark is placed in the substitution column. Because this miscue resulted in a meaning change, a tally mark is also placed under the meaning change column. The same columns were also marked for the miscue *so* because it was a miscue that also changed the meaning. The miscue *trees* is an insertion, so a tally mark is placed in the insertion column on the appropriate line of the text. The teacher judged that this miscue did not change the meaning, so no other column is marked. The miscue *was* is a reversal, and a tally mark is placed in the reversal column. This miscue resulted in a meaning change, and a tally mark was placed in the meaning change column corresponding to the appropriate line of text. The miscue *minute* for *moment* was a substitution that the teacher felt did not result in a significant meaning change; therefore, a tally mark was only placed in the substitution column corresponding to the line of text where the miscue was made.

Once the tallies for miscues and other reading behaviors are completed for **all** the passages read by the student, they can be summarized on the two sample charts shown in Figure 4-3. These charts are also contained in Appendix D for teacher reproduction and use.

After completing the miscue tally and reading behavior summary charts, the teacher can look for patterns in order to hypothesize areas where the student might profit from strategy lessons. In the sample charts shown in Figure 4-3, the student appears to have a pattern of omissions. The teacher might offer responsive instruction for omissions by considering some of the ideas in Scenario 3 in Section 6. The student in this example also corrected a number of miscues that changed the meaning. Behavior of this sort should be seen as a reading strength, and the student should be praised for monitoring reading and using correction strategies.

STRATEGY 3: ADVANCED QUALITATIVE ANALYSIS

A more advanced system for analyzing miscues has been developed by Christie (1979) and is presented in Figure 4-4. This system draws upon the work of Goodman, Watson, and Burke (1987) and the suggestions of Williamson and Young (1974). The following qualitative analysis has been adapted, with permission, from Christie. For convenience, the procedure is presented in a five-step outline form.

Student Copy is on page 133.

A 8224 (Grade 2) Activating Background: Read the title to yourself; then tell me what you think will happen.

Background: Low ⊢————+————⊣ High

Bill at Camp

Passage	Substitution	Insertion	Omission	Reversal	Repetition	Self-Correction of Unacceptable Miscue	Meaning Change (Significant Miscue)
	MISCUES						
Bob It was the first time Bill went to	/						/
camp. He was very happy to be there. *So* Soon	/						/
he went for a walk in the woods to look for							
many kinds of leaves. He found leaves							
trees from some maple ⌄ and oak trees. As Bill		/					
was walked in the woods, he saw some animal				/			/
minute tracks. At that moment, a mouse ran into	/						
a small hole by a tree. Bill wondered if the							
tracks were made by the mouse. He looked							
around for other animals. He did not see							
any. The last thing Bill saw was an old							
bird nest in a pine tree.							
good phrasing and intonation **TOTAL**	3	/	0	/	0	0	3

Word Recognition Scoring Guide		
Total Miscues	Level	Significant Miscues
0–1	Independent	0–1
2–4	Ind./Inst.	2
5	Instructional	3
6–9	Inst./Frust.	4
10 +	Frustration	5 +

Total Miscues [5]

Significant Miscues [ ]

WPM
)6000

Figure 4-2 Jeff's Miscue Tally and Reading Behavior on a Graded Passage

Total Miscues Across Passages Read	Type of Miscue			
	Substitution	**Insertion**	**Omission**	**Reversal**
	3	2	8	0

Other Reading Behaviors (Totals)	**Repetition**	**Self-Correction of Unacceptable Miscues**	**Meaning Change**
	2	6	2

Figure 4-3   Sample Miscue Tally and Reading Behavior Summary Charts

Teachers who decide to use this type of analysis may be interested in purchasing Basic Reading Inventory Tracking Software that automatically completes the prediction and correction strategies when the data are entered. For further information about this software, contact Kendall/Hunt Publishing Company at 1-800-247-3458, ext. 5.

STEP 1—SELECT MISCUES FOR ANALYSIS

A. Select miscues from oral passages at the student's **independent** and **instructional** levels only. Record the following types of miscues on the Analysis Sheet:
  1. substitutions
  2. omissions
  3. insertions
  4. word-order reversals
  5. nonwords

B. Do *not* use the following types of miscues:
  1. repetitions
  2. hestitations
  3. prompts
  4. disregard for punctuation
  5. omissions of entire lines of text
  6. variations in pronunciation involving dialect
  7. partial words

STEP 2—RECORD MISCUES ON THE ANALYSIS SHEET

A. Record each type of miscue as follows:
  1. substitutions

	MISCUE	**TEXT**

        glad
    The girl was very sad.

glad	sad

  2. omissions

    He went to ~~the~~ church.

——	the

  3. insertions

        very
    The road was narrow.
              ^

very	——

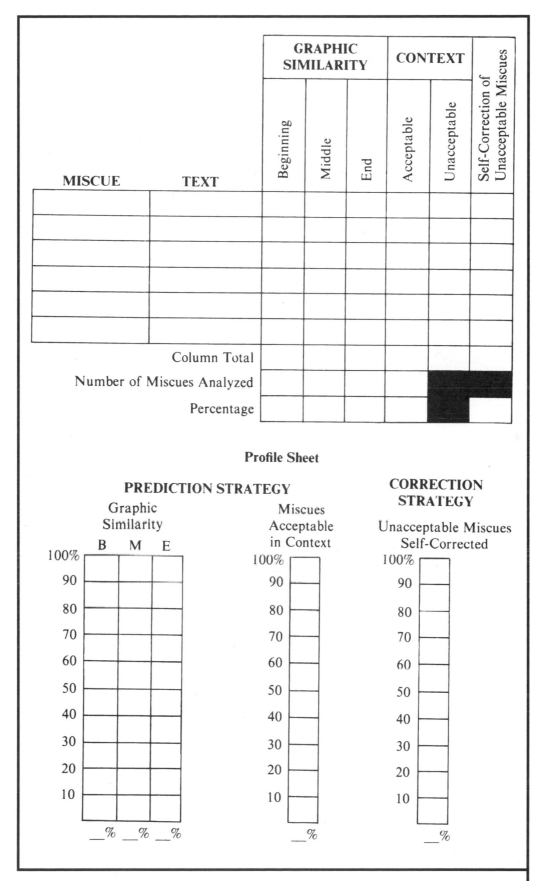

Figure 4-4   System for the Qualitative Analysis of Miscues

4. word order reversals

at her desk quietly
Jill sat quietly at her desk.

at her desk quietly	quietly at her desk

5. nonwords

redon
The region was large.

redon	region

B. Special Rules
1. Record identical substitutions only once.
2. If the reader makes several attempts at a word, record the first complete word or nonword substitution.

2. stars
1. st–
Example: He went up the stairs.

MISCUE	**TEXT**
stars	stairs

3. If a miscue causes the reader to immediately make another miscue in one apparent thought, record as one complex miscue.

have danced
Example: He could^dance all night.

have danced	dance

STEP 3—ANALYZE MISCUES

A. Graphic Similarity
1. Miscues to Analyze
a. Only substitutions of a single word or nonword for a single text item should be analyzed for graphic similarity.
b. Do *not* analyze omissions, insertions, reversals, or substitutions that involve more than one word. In these cases, draw *Xs* through the three boxes under GRAPHIC SIMILARITY.
c. Example:

went
He walked to ~~the~~ school.

MISCUE	TEXT	GRAPHIC SIMILARITY Beginning	Middle	End
went	walked	✓		
——	the	X	X	X

2. Judging Graphic Similarity
a. Compare the sequence and shape of the letters in the miscue with those in the text item. Place a check in the appropriate box if the beginning, middle, and/or end of the miscue is graphically similar to the corresponding part of the text item.
b. Guidelines for judging graphic similarity
(1) divide the miscue and text item into corresponding thirds.
(2) Use the following criteria for judging the different thirds as being graphically similar:

      (a) *Beginning*—the first letter of the miscue and the first letter of the text item must be identical.

      (b) *Middle* and *End*—the letters in the miscue and text item need only be similar in sequence and configuration.

   (3) Special cases

      (a) Two-letter text items—place an *X* in the "Middle" box and judge only for beginning and ending similarity.

      (b) One-letter text items—place an *X* in the "Middle" and "End" boxes and judge only for beginning similarity.

  c. Examples:

MISCUE	TEXT	GRAPHIC SIMILARITY Beginning	Middle	End
men	man	✓	✓	✓
here	said		✓	
his	this		✓	✓
walk	walked	✓	✓	
cub	carry	✓		
meal	material	✓		✓
be	by	✓	✗	
if	it	✓	✗	
the	a		✗	✗
an	on		✗	✓

B. Acceptability in Context

  1. Judge all miscues recorded on the Analysis Sheet for acceptability in context. Refer to the graded passages that were coded to make these judgments.

  2. To judge the acceptability of a miscue, take the following two factors into consideration:

    a. *Syntax*—Is the miscue grammatically acceptable in the manner in which the sentence was read?

    b. *Semantics*—Does the miscue make sense in the context of the sentence and the preceding portion of the passage?

3. Marking the Analysis Sheet
   a. If the miscue meets **both** criteria, check the box in the "Acceptable" column.
   b. If either criterion is not met, check the box in the "Unacceptable" column.
   c. If the unacceptable miscue is successfully self-corrected by the reader, place a check in the "Self-Correction of Unacceptable Miscues" column.

	CONTEXT		Self-Correction of Unacceptable Miscues
	Acceptable	Unacceptable	
Acceptable in context; no self-correction	✓		
Unacceptable in context; no self-correction		✓	
Unacceptable in context; self-correction		✓	✓

STEP 4—DETERMINE TOTALS AND PERCENTAGES

(This step is completed automatically if the Basic Reading Inventory Tracking Software is used.)

A. Graphic Similarity
   1. Count the number of checks in each column (Beginning, Middle, and End) and place the totals in the boxes marked Column Total.
   2. For each column, count the number of boxes that do not have Xs in them. Place each total in the box marked Number of Miscues Analyzed.
   3. Determine the percentage for each column by dividing each Column Total by the Number of Miscues Analyzed and then multiplying by 100.

B. Acceptability in Context
   1. Count the number of checks in the "Acceptable" column and enter the total in the appropriate Column Total box.
   2. "Acceptable" column *only*
      a. Enter the total number of miscues analyzed for acceptability in context in the box marked Number of Miscues Analyzed. (This should equal the total number of miscues recorded on the Analysis Sheet.)
      b. Determine the percentage of miscues acceptable in context by dividing the Column Total by the Number of Miscues Analyzed and then multiplying by 100.

C. Percentage of Unacceptable Miscues That Were Self-Corrected
   1. Count the number of checks in the "Unacceptable" column and enter the total in the appropriate Column Total box.

2. Count the number of miscues in the "Unacceptable" Column that were self-corrected. Be sure to count only self-corrections for **Unacceptable** miscues. Place this total in the Column Total box in the "Self-Correction of Unacceptable Miscues" column.
3. Determine the percentage of unacceptable miscues that were self-corrected by dividing the Column Total of "Self-Correction of Unacceptable Miscues" by the Column Total of "Unacceptable" miscues and then multiplying by 100. Place this percentage in the Percentage Column under "Self-Correction of Unacceptable Miscues."

| MISCUE | TEXT | GRAPHIC SIMILARITY | | | CONTEXT | | Self-Correction of Unacceptable Miscues |
		Beginning	Middle	End	Acceptable	Unacceptable	
men	man	✓	✓	✓		✓	✓
here	said		✓			✓	✓
his	this		✓	✓		✓	
walk	walked	✓	✓		✓		
cub	carry	✓				✓	✓
meal	material	✓		✓		✓	
be	by	✓	✗			✓	✓
if	it	✓	✗			✓	
the	a		✗	✗	✓		
an	on		✗	✓		✓	✓
Column Total		6	4	4	2	8	5
Number of Miscues Analyzed		10	6	9	10	■	■
Percentage		60	67	44	20	■	63

STEP 5—COMPLETE PROFILE SHEET

(This step is completed automatically if the Basic Reading Inventory Tracking Software is used.)

A. Transfer the percentages from the Analysis Sheet to the blanks below the appropriate bar graphs as shown here.
B. Darken in the bar graphs.

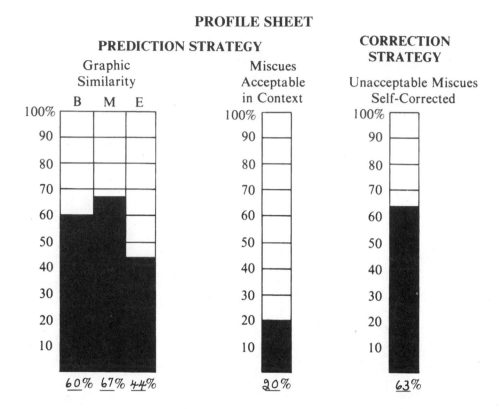

PROFILE SHEET

PREDICTION STRATEGY

CORRECTION STRATEGY

Graphic Similarity

Miscues Acceptable in Context

Unacceptable Miscues Self-Corrected

60% 67% 44%   20%   63%

Once the teacher completes the three parts of the Profile Sheet, he or she can develop reading strategy lessons. The two Prediction Strategy graphs help to determine whether the student is relying on graphic cues, context cues, or both in predicting upcoming text and decoding unknown words. When both graphs are similar, the student has a balanced prediction strategy. If, on the other hand, the two graphs show a marked difference, the student may be depending excessively on one type of cue.

If the Graphic Similarity graph is high and the Context graph is low, the student may be relying excessively on graphic cues. If this is the case, reading strategy lessons that emphasize the use of context cues may be warranted. See Scenarios 3 and 6 in Section 6.

When the Graphic Similarity graph is low and the Context graph is high, the student may be relying heavily on context cues. Strategy lessons could include asking the student a question like, "What word do you know that begins like _____ that would make sense?"

The Correction Strategy graph shows the percentage of unacceptable miscues that were self-corrected by the student. When a large percentage of unacceptable miscues are not corrected (when the Correction Strategy graph is low), the student may need to be taught strategies for monitoring his or her reading. Strategy lessons to help the reader develop a sensitivity to correcting miscues that disrupt meaning may also be needed. Scenario 5 in Section 6 contains some useful suggestions. Several additional resources for instructional techniques can be found in the work of Crawley and Merritt (1996),

Davis and Lass (1996), Irwin and Baker (1989), Johns and Lenski (2001), Manzo and Manzo (1993), McCormick (1999), and Walker (2000).

ANALYZING COMPREHENSION

To guide the overall assessment of the student's comprehension, the following questions should be considered in the teacher's appraisal:

▶ Does the student appear to know that comprehension is the goal of reading?

▶ Does the student appear to possess the background (concepts and vocabulary) necessary for understanding the passage?

▶ Are there significant differences between the student's oral and silent comprehension?

▶ Do significant comprehension differences exist between narrative and expository passages?

▶ Are there significant differences in comprehension between the shorter passages and the longer passages?

▶ Does the student appear to have difficulties with specific types of comprehension questions?

▶ What does the student do when comprehension becomes difficult?

▶ Does the student monitor his or her reading and use appropriate fix-up strategies?

2 Strategies for Analyzing Comprehension

1—Analysis of comprehension by question type

2—Analysis by level of comprehension

The Basic Reading Inventory contains five different types of comprehension questions coded as follows: (F) fact, (T) topic, (E) evaluation, (I) inference, and (V) vocabulary. Two strategies are suggested for analyzing comprehension performance. For each strategy, **only comprehension questions at the student's independent, instructional, and instructional/frustration levels should be analyzed**. Comprehension questions at the student's frustration level may be used to verify tendencies at the student's independent and instructional levels.

Lest teachers glibly use the classification scheme suggested, it must be emphasized that these categories of comprehension questions, although widely used, have little or no empirical support (Schell and Hanna, 1981). In other words, many reading tests claim to measure comprehension skills that authorities cannot show to exist. Although such analysis lacks empirical support, Johnson, Kress, and Pikulski (1987) believe such a procedure is useful to help identify general tendencies in comprehension. Spache (1976) notes that comprehension is composed of three essential elements: (1) a word meaning factor, (2) a relationships-among-ideas factor, and (3) a reasoning factor. He goes on to say that "when the reading teacher has determined by repeated observations that the student apparently does not use a certain type of essential thinking, the remedial course is quite obvious. She may repeatedly ask the student to attempt to answer questions that appear to sample the missing cognitive process" (p. 269). It is believed that the following strategies described for determining strengths and weaknesses in comprehension offer two systematic ways to gather preliminary evidence indicating that some aspect of a student's comprehension may need attention. The teacher can then support or refute this tentative need through the student's performance in classroom activities. If a need exists, the teacher can develop appropriate strategy lessons. Teachers need to remember that the scheme for analyzing comprehension performance is intended to be used informally. It should aid the teacher's judgment, not replace it.

Grade	Fact (F-6)* Oral	Topic (T-1) Oral	Evaluation (E-1) Oral	Inference (I-1) Oral	Vocabulary (V-1) Oral
P	2/6	0/1	0/1	0/1	0/1
1	1/6	0/1	0/1	0/1	0/1
2	3/6	0/1	0/1	1/1	0/1
3	2/6	0/1	1/1	1/1	0/1
Ratio Missed	8/24	0/4	1/4	2/4	0/4
Percent Missed	33%	0%	25%	50%	0%

*Indicates the type of question and the number of questions in each graded paragraph. For example, F indicates a fact question and 6 signifies that each graded passage contains six F questions.

Figure 4-5 Summary of Dan's Comprehension Performance in Oral Reading

STRATEGY 1: ANALYSIS OF COMPREHENSION BY QUESTION TYPE

The teacher can analyze comprehension after recording the number and types of questions the student misses on each passage read at the independent, instructional, and instructional/frustration levels. An example of this procedure, using Dan's comprehension scores, is shown in Figure 4-5. Using such a procedure may enable the teacher to discern patterns of possible difficulty in comprehension. If the teacher uses the Basic Reading Inventory Tracking Software, all ratios and percentages are automatically calculated when the data are entered. Dan's performance on the comprehension questions marked in Figure 4-5 indicates possible strengths in answering topic and vocabulary questions. Areas of possible weakness include answering fact, evaluation, and inference questions. Because of the limited data on which these hypotheses are based, Dan's silent reading should also be considered. These hypotheses should then be verified or discounted through observation and instruction.

Now, consider Tony's errors on the comprehension questions. To determine Tony's tendencies in comprehension, the teacher should complete Figure 4-6 by determining the ratios of comprehension questions missed and the corresponding percentages. First, record the number of questions answered and the number of questions missed for each question type. Second, determine the percent of errors by dividing the number of errors by the total number of that question type and multiplying by 100. For example, Tony responded to 30 fact questions and missed 4 of them. His error rate for the fact questions was 13 percent (4 ÷ 30 = .13; .13 × 100 = 13%). What are Tony's possible strengths and weaknesses in comprehension?

During oral reading, Tony missed 4 of 30 fact questions (13%), 3 of 5 topic questions (60%), 2 of 5 evaluation questions (40%), 1 of 5 inference questions (20%),´and 2 of 5 vocabulary questions (40%). Based on these percentages, answering topic ques-

Grade	Fact (F-6) Oral	Topic (T-1) Oral	Evaluation (E-1) Oral	Inference (I-1) Oral	Vocabulary (V-1) Oral
4	_1_/6	_0_/1	_0_/1	_0_/1	_0_/1
5	_0_/6	_0_/1	_1_/1	_1_/1	_0_/1
6	_1_/6	_1_/1	_0_/1	_0_/1	_0_/1
7	_0_/6	_1_/1	_0_/1	_0_/1	_1_/1
8	_2_/6	_1_/1	_1_/1	_0_/1	_1_/1
Ratio Missed	_4_/_30_	__/__	__/__	__/__	__/__
Percent Missed	_13_%	__%	__%	__%	__%

Figure 4-6   Tony's Comprehension Performance in Oral Reading

tions may be hypothesized as an area of weakness. A possible strength is in the area of recalling facts. It seems most appropriate from this analysis to identify errors in topic questions as a possible weakness and responses to fact questions as a possible strength. Whether the areas of evaluation, inference, and vocabulary warrant instructional intervention should be based on additional information gained from classroom observations and relevant performance on reading tasks.

When a student reads orally and silently, it is recommended that the results be combined for both sets of graded passages. This procedure enables the teacher to get a larger sample of behavior on which to make hypotheses. The teacher should remember that the student may not always read the same number or level of oral and silent passages. Figure 4-7 contains Tony's comprehension performance from the graded passages that were analyzed previously, as well as his silent reading performance on a different set of graded passages from the Basic Reading Inventory. The teacher should complete Figure 4-7 by determining the ratio of questions answered incorrectly and the corresponding percentages. First, total the ratio of questions missed for oral reading and silent reading separately. For the fact questions, Tony missed 4 of 30 questions in oral reading and 6 of 30 questions in silent reading. Second, add these numerals to complete the "Total Ratio Missed" column. Tony missed 10 of the 60 fact questions. Third, determine the percent of fact questions missed. ($10 \div 60 = .16; .16 \times 100 = 16\%$). After determining Tony's comprehension performance for topic, evaluation, inference, and vocabulary questions, compare the results to Table 4.1. Remember that the ratios and percentages are calculated automatically when the Basic Reading Inventory Tracking Software is used for data entry.

A comparison of Tony's oral and silent reading comprehension is shown in Table 4.1. The teacher should check his or her work and resolve any discrepancies. Because the number of questions upon which the total percentages are calculated has increased,

Grade	Fact (F-6) Oral	Silent	Topic (T-1) Oral	Silent	Evaluation (E-1) Oral	Silent	Inference (I-1) Oral	Silent	Vocabulary (V-1) Oral	Silent
4	1/6	0/6	0/1	0/1	0/1	0/1	0/1	1/1	0/1	0/1
5	0/6	0/6	0/1	0/1	1/1	0/1	1/1	0/1	0/1	0/1
6	1/6	1/6	1/1	1/1	0/1	0/1	0/1	0/1	0/1	1/1
7	0/6	3/6	1/1	0/1	0/1	0/1	0/1	0/1	1/1	0/1
8	2/6	2/6	1/1	1/1	0/1	0/1	0/1	0/1	1/1	1/1
Ratio Missed	4/30	6/30	3/5	_/_	1/5	_/_	1/5	_/_	2/5	_/_
Percent Missed	13%	20%	60%	_%	20%	_%	20%	_%	40%	_%
Total Ratio Missed	10/60		_/_		_/_		_/_		_/_	
Total Percent Missed	16%		_%		_%		_%		_%	

Figure 4-7   Tony's Comprehension Performance in Oral and Silent Reading

Table 4.1 Summary of Tony's Comprehension Performance in Oral and Silent Reading										
	Fact Oral	Silent	Topic Oral	Silent	Evaluation Oral	Silent	Inference Oral	Silent	Vocabulary Oral	Silent
Ratio Missed	4/30	6/30	3/5	2/5	1/5	0/5	1/5	1/5	2/5	2/5
Percent Missed	13%	20%	60%	40%	20%	0%	20%	20%	40%	40%
Total Ratio Missed	10/60		5/10		1/10		2/10		4/10	
Total Percent Missed	16%		50%		10%		20%		40%	

the hypotheses about Tony's strengths and weaknesses should have greater validity. His answers to fact, evaluation, and inference questions appear to be areas of strength. Errors on topic and vocabulary questions may be hypothesized as areas of weakness. Because these findings are generally consistent with those based on Tony's oral reading, the combined analysis should give the teacher greater confidence in the hypotheses made.

STRATEGY 2: ANALYSIS BY LEVEL OF COMPREHENSION

A second way to analyze comprehension performance is by classifying the various types of comprehension questions into logical categories. Numerous classification schemes have been developed (Raphael, 1986; Tatham, 1978). It is recommended that teachers use two levels of comprehension. Category one, lower-level comprehension, is composed of the six fact questions. Category two, higher-level comprehension, is composed of topic, evaluation, inference, and vocabulary questions. The logic behind the two categories is that the first is based on literal or explicit comprehension, whereas the second is based on thinking beyond the ideas stated in the graded passages. The student's ability to reason and use experiences is assessed in the latter category. Although the evaluation, inference, and vocabulary questions may not be completely passage dependent, they can help teachers evaluate a student's vocabulary and ability to reason beyond the printed text. Even some of the factual questions may not be totally passage dependent, depending on student's prior knowledge. Viewed from this perspective, comprehension is only partially contextual. Johnston (1983, p. 34) argues strongly that "since no two individuals will have identical prior knowledge, the construction of tests which are free of bias at the individual level is impossible. Furthermore, it can be argued that it would be undesirable in any case since a reading comprehension test uninfluenced by prior knowledge would certainly not be measuring comprehension as it is understood theoretically."

Other classification schemes are also possible; the teacher is encouraged to modify the scheme suggested to conform to his or her own conception of comprehension. The two categories of comprehension suggested make it possible for teachers to view comprehension more holistically when planning instruction for students. Table 4.2 contains the results of such an analysis for Tony's scores that were reported earlier.

The results of the global analysis reveal that Tony's major difficulties are in the higher-level comprehension area. If a more detailed analysis of this area is desired, the comprehension questions may be arranged by type and analyzed.

Table 4.2   Summary of Tony's Two-Level Comprehension Performance

	Lower-Level Comprehension (Fact Questions Only)		Higher-Level Comprehension (All Other Questions)	
	Oral	Silent	Oral	Silent
Ratio Missed	4/30	6/30	7/20	5/20
Total Ratio	10/60		12/40	
Total Percent Missed	16%		30%	

INTEGRATING THE CONCEPT OF ENGAGEMENT

Another way to enhance comprehension assessment is to use the "engagement" concept (Manzo and Manzo, 1993). In short, the teacher determines whether the student's responses to comprehension questions are congruent or incongruent. All correct responses are congruent. Incorrect responses "may be congruent (related but incorrect) or incongruent (unrelated as well as incorrect). An increase of congruent responses is a sound sign that the student is engaged" (Manzo and Manzo, 1993, p. 92).

In Section 3, it was noted that teachers who wish to integrate the engagement concept while asking the comprehension questions should follow two guidelines to record relevant data:

▶ All comprehension questions scored as correct (+) are a sign of engagement. For correct responses that are "especially full, fresh, or elaborated in some meaningful and appropriate way," circle the numeral beside the comprehension question (Manzo and Manzo, 1993, p. 467).

▶ For comprehension questions scored as incorrect (−), a decision needs to be made: Is the incorrect response congruent (related to the passage in some meaningful way) or incongruent (not related to the passage in some meaningful, logical way)? For incorrect responses that are incongruent, place an X on the numeral beside the comprehension question.

If these two pieces of data have been recorded on appropriate pages of the performance booklet, they can be used to informally assess engagement. An example of this procedure, using Kendrick's responses to comprehension questions, is shown in Table 4.3. Kendrick had one response to the questions at the fourth-grade level that was elaborated in some meaningful and appropriate way. None of the questions on the fifth-grade passage was elaborated; however, one response was rated as incongruent. For the sixth-grade passage, two questions were elaborated. Kendrick had four incongruent responses for the seventh-grade passage.

Table 4.3 Summary of Kendrick's Comprehension Engagement				
	Grade Level of Passage			
	4	5	6	7
Correct responses especially full, fresh, or elaborated (numerals circled)*	1	0	2	0
Incongruent incorrect responses **unrelated** to the passage in some meaningful, logical way (numerals with Xs)*	0	1	0	4

*Refers to numerals beside the comprehension questions in the performance booklet.

To evaluate a student's responses, the following guidelines should be used. First, more than one elaboration per passage may be "taken as evidence of an alert mind that is engaged and being driven by meaning" (Manzo and Manzo, 1993, p. 467). Second, more than three incongruent responses (illogical, far out) to questions "is an indication that engagement was weak and nonproductive" (Manzo and Manzo, 1993, p. 467).

Based on these guidelines, Kendrick was quite engaged for the sixth-grade passage. For the seventh-grade passage, Kendrick's engagement was weak. The teacher can use this information along with other qualitative criteria and observations to better understand a student's overall comprehension.

Now, consider Juan's engagement based on the data presented in Table 4.4. Using the guidelines just presented, what tentative conclusions regarding Juan's engagement are appropriate? For the second- and third-grade passages, Juan was engaged; however, on the fourth-grade passage, Juan's engagement was weak. No specific conclusions regarding engagement are appropriate for the fifth-grade passage.

According to Manzo and Manzo (1993, p. 467), "it is too soon to say if any significant meanings can be attached to the absence of elaborations." While future research is being conducted on the concept of engagement, teachers are encouraged to use the simple recording system in order to possibly add a richer interpretation of factors that may influence comprehension.

Table 4.4   Summary of Juan's Comprehension Engagement

	Grade Level of Passage				
	1	2	3	4	5
Correct responses especially full, fresh, or elaborated (numerals circled)*	0	2	3	0	1
Incongruent incorrect responses **unrelated** to the passage in some meaningful, logical way (numerals with Xs)*	0	0	0	4	2

*Refers to numerals beside the comprehension questions in the performance booklet.

INSTRUCTIONAL INTERVENTIONS GRID

To help teachers make instruction more responsive to the student's needs based on the results of the Basic Reading Inventory, classroom observations, and the student's daily work, there are numerous sources for ideas. The author and his colleagues have prepared several easy-to-use strategy books to help teachers in their quest to enhance student achievement in reading.

Early Literacy Assessments & Teaching Strategies (Johns, Lenski, and Elish-Piper, 1999) contains fifteen different assessments (two forms) to help assess emergent readers through third grade. In addition to the brief, useful assessments, over 225 teaching strategies, ideas, and activities are presented. A few of these strategies are referenced on the instructional interventions grid on the next two pages. If, for example, the teacher wishes to help a student become more flexible in the use of word-identification strategies, the teacher would consult the general area of Identifying Words. The last entry in that area refers the teacher to Section 3.13 in *Early Literacy Assessments*.

Improving Reading: Strategies and Resources (Johns and Lenski, 2001) contains a wealth of teaching strategies, practice activities, games, and reproducible materials to use with students—over 600 pages. The ideas in this resource book support a wide range of learners. Teachers from kindergarten through high school have used the strategies in earlier editions to energize their instruction with average students as well as with students who struggle in reading. The third edition of *Improving Reading* contains

Instructional Interventions Grid for Responsive Instruction

General Area Specific Interventions	Resource Books		
	Early Literacy Assessments & Teaching Strategies	Improving Reading: Strategies and Resources	Reading & Learning Strategies for Middle & High School Students
Emergent Literacy			
Oral Language		2.1	
Concepts About the Nature and Purpose of Reading	3.3, 3.5	2.2	
Knowledge of the Alphabet	3.7	2.3	
Auditory Discrimination		2.4	
Concept of a Word		2.5	
Rhyming	3.6, p. 123	2.6	
Syllabic Awareness		2.7	
Alphabetic Principle		2.8	
Onsets and Rimes	p. 123	2.9	
Phonemic Awareness	3.6, p. 124–125, 3.9	2.10	
Visual Discrimination		2.11	
Letter and Word Reversals		2.12	
Sense of Story	3.4	2.13	
Identifying Words			
Phonics: Consonants	3.10–2, 3.10–4	3.1	
Phonics: Vowels		3.2	
Word Patterns and Word Building	3.10–1	3.3	
Structural Analysis		3.4	
Basic Sight Words		3.5	
Sight Vocabulary	3.11	3.6	
Using Context to Predict Known Words	3.13–1	3.7	
Dictionary: Word Pronunciation		3.8	
Lack of Flexible Word-Identification Strategies	3.13	3.9	
Ineffective Use of Word-Identification Strategies	3.13	3.10	
Oral Reading Behaviors			
Lack of Fluency	3.14	4.1	
Lack of Fluency: Incorrect Phrasing	3.14	4.2	
Failure to Attempt Unknown Words		4.3	
Meaning-Changing Substitutions		4.4	
Nonmeaning-Changing Substitutions		4.5	
Nonword Substitutions		4.6	
Repetitions of Words or Phrases		4.7	
Meaning-Changing Omissions		4.8	
Nonmeaning-Changing Omissions		4.9	
Excessive Use of Phonics		4.10	
Excessive Use of Background Knowledge		4.11	
Developing Vocabulary			
Extending Meaning Vocabulary		5.1	3.1, 3.3
Using Context Cues to Predict Meanings for Unknown Words		5.2	3.2
Compound Words and Affixes		5.3	
Dictionary: Word Meanings		5.4	
Interest in Words		5.5	

(continued)

Instructional Interventions Grid for Responsive Instruction (CONTINUED)

General Area Specific Interventions	Resource Books		
	Early Literacy Assessments & Teaching Strategies	Improving Reading: Strategies and Resources	Reading & Learning Strategies for Middle & High School Students
Promoting Comprehension			
Previewing Text		6.1	
Activating Prior Knowledge	3.2–3	6.2	4.1, 5.3
Lack of Clear Purpose(s) for Reading		6.3	
Main Point	3.12–4	6.4	5.4
Facts or Details	3.12–4	6.5	
Sequence		6.6	
Making Predictions	3.12–2	6.7	
Making Inferences		6.8	6.4
Visualizing		6.9	
Drawing Conclusions		6.10	
Expanding Comprehension			
Understanding Fictional Text Structure		7.1	4.2
Understanding Nonfiction Text Structure		7.2	4.2
Charts and Graphs		7.3	
Inflexible Rate of Reading		7.4	
Monitoring Reading	3.12–1, 3.15	7.5	4.3
Summarizing Ideas	3.12–3	7.6	
Making Connections		7.7	5.3, 6.2
Processing Text		7.8	4.4, 6.3
Evaluating Written Materials		7.9	6.1
Remembering		7.10	
Motivating Students			
Lack of Motivation	3.1	1.1	2.1–2.4
Negative Attitude Toward Reading		1.2	
Limited Reading Interests		1.3	
Low Confidence in Reading Ability		1.4	
Reluctant to Set Goals		1.5	
Involving Parents			
Experiences with Books		8.1	
Word-Solving Skills		8.2	
Reading Fluency		8.3	
Understanding While Reading		8.4	
Motivation for Reading		8.5	
Reading Outside of School		8.6	
Schoolwork		8.7	
School and Home Literacies		8.8	

more strategies than earlier editions and has many resource materials that can be duplicated and readily used with students.

Reading & Learning Strategies for Middle & High School Students (Lenski, Wham, and Johns, 1999) contains more than 100 content-relevant teaching strategies to strengthen students' reading. The easy-to-adapt format of the book permits teachers to readily use the strategies. In addition to the general areas indicated in the interventions grid, this resource contains helpful chapters on studying, preparing for tests, and conducting research.

All three of these books contain many more ideas than are noted in the grid. The grid is intended to merely provide a departure point for ideas to help teachers respond effectively to students' needs in reading.

WHAT DOES THE BASIC READING INVENTORY DO FOR YOUR STUDENTS?

The results of the Basic Reading Inventory can be used as tentative guidelines for instruction. The insights can be used to inform instruction and to prepare strategy lessons. The *total* results from the Basic Reading Inventory must be used to help plan effective instruction, taking into account each student's *specific* strengths and needs in word identification and/or comprehension.

Tests like the Basic Reading Inventory play a substantial role in providing data for

- ▶ placing students in appropriate instructional materials,
- ▶ assessing reading behavior, and
- ▶ developing reading strategy lessons.

Unless test results are used in conjunction with observation, cumulative records, portfolios, and other evaluative techniques, serious errors may result. One should not underestimate the importance of the Basic Reading Inventory for classroom and clinical use; however, the results should be used to *guide* teachers' responses to a student's reading. They should not be used to dictate teachers' actions, thereby dominating their professional knowledge and experience. Professionals who use the Basic Reading Inventory as suggested in this manual will help ensure that students are placed in appropriate reading materials and taught needed reading strategies.

The teacher who places students in reading materials at the appropriate instructional levels and provides responsive instruction for specific areas of need will help students acquire greater competence in reading.

Timesaving Administration Procedures

Note: This section is intended for teachers, specialists, and others who understand the typical administration and scoring procedures of reading inventories and who desire to shorten the normal administration time. The recommended procedure is presented in a series of steps for easy reference. If further details are required or desired, refer to Section 2.

ESSENTIALS FOR ASSESSMENT

What is needed for assessment? There are four basic items:

1. This manual.

2. A piece of heavy paper to cover the passage when necessary.

3. A performance booklet in which the teacher will record the student's responses.

4. A desk or table and two chairs. It is recommended that right-handed teachers seat the student on their left. Left-handed teachers should do the opposite.

GRADED WORD LISTS

Overview: The graded word lists range in difficulty from the pre-primer through the twelfth-grade level. Form A is recommended.

Purpose: To estimate the starting level at which the student begins to read the graded passages.

> **Note:** If the teacher already has a rough estimate of the student's reading ability based on previous data and classroom observation, there is no need to administer the graded word lists. Proceed directly to the graded passages and begin with a passage at least one year below the student's estimated reading ability. If the graded word lists are to be administered, use the following steps.

Procedure

1. Select one form of the graded word lists from Part Two in this book. Form A's graded word list is recommended.

2. Duplicate the corresponding form of a performance booklet in which to record the student's responses. All performance booklets are found in Part Two of this book.

3. Begin with a word list that should be easy for the student and give the word list to the student.

4. Have the student pronounce the words rapidly. Record the words that are not pronounced correctly in the sight columns of the performance booklet. Ignore the analysis column. Self-corrections are scored as correct. Do not return to any words the student mispronounced. Examples of recorded responses are shown in Figure 5-1.

5. Stop the test when the student does not know or is unable to pronounce 7 or more words on a given list (a score of 13 or less).

6. Proceed to the graded reading passages and begin at the highest grade level at which the student correctly pronounced 19 or 20 words on a graded word list.

	Sight	Analysis	Meaning of Recording
8. she	_____	_____	Word pronounced correctly
9. but	_*bed*_	_____	Word mispronounced
10. ask	_D.K._	_____	Don't know
11. run	_*ran*_	_____	Word mispronounced
12. sleep	_sl-_	_____	Partial pronunciation

Figure 5-1   Examples of Recorded Responses on a Graded Word List

GRADED PASSAGES:
ORAL READING AND COMPREHENSION

Overview: The graded reading passages for Forms A, B, C, and D range in difficulty from the pre-primer through the eighth-grade level. Forms LN and LE range in difficulty from grade three through grade twelve. **Form A is recommended for oral reading.**

Purpose: To estimate the student's independent, instructional, and frustration levels. Section 1 contains more in-depth information on these levels. In addition, the teacher can also diagnose the student's strengths and weaknesses in word identification and comprehension. See Section 4 for a discussion of several ways to evaluate word identification and comprehension.

Procedure

1. Use the graded passages from the same form used for the graded word lists. If the graded word lists were not used, select Form A from Part Two in this book.

2. Duplicate the corresponding form of a performance booklet in which to record the student's responses. All performance booklets are found in Part Two of this book.

3. Begin with a graded passage that is at the highest level at which the student correctly pronounced 19 or 20 words on a graded word list. If the word lists were not used, begin with a passage at least one year below the student's estimated instructional level.

4. Cover the passage with heavy paper so only the title shows. Have the student read the title of the passage and predict what it might be about. Mentally note or write the student's predictions on the appropriate place in the performance booklet. Then tell the student to read the passage out loud and to think about the story, because comprehension questions will be asked.

Passage	Type of Miscue
It was the first time Bill went *in* to	insertion
camp. He was ~~very~~ happy to be there.	omission
Then Soon he went for a walk in the woods to	substitution
look for many kinds of ⓒ *leaf* leaves. He	corrected miscue
found leaves <u>from some</u> maple and oak	repetition

Figure 5-2   Examples of Recorded Responses on a Graded Passage

5. As the student reads, record the student's miscues (substitutions, omissions, insertions, and so on) on the appropriate page in the performance booklet. A suggested method for recording miscues can be found in Figure 2-3. An example for recording selected miscues is also shown in Figure 5-2.

6. After the student finishes reading the passage, remove or cover the graded passage before asking the comprehension questions. The comprehension questions deal with topics (T), facts (F), inferences (I), evaluation (E), and vocabulary (V). The answers following each question should *guide* the teacher in evaluating the student's responses. Other appropriate responses may also be fully acceptable.

7. Evaluate the student's response to each question with a plus (+) for a correct response or a minus (–) for an incorrect response. Partial credit (¹/₂) may also be given. If desired, have the student react to predictions he or she made prior to reading the passage.

8. Continue administering graded passages until the student is unable to answer half of the comprehension questions or makes so many miscues that a frustration level is apparent. Also, observe the student's general reactions during reading. As soon as the student exhibits finger pointing, word-by-word reading, considerable tension, or other behavior associated with frustration, stop reading.

9. To obtain the student's word recognition in context score, decide whether to count total miscues (all miscues) or significant miscues (those that affect meaning). Record the number of miscues in the appropriate box (total or significant) on the teacher's copy. Then consult the appropriate set of criteria in the scoring guide at the bottom of the teacher's copy of each graded passage. Circle the reading level (Independent, Ind./Inst., and so on) that corresponds to the number of miscues the student made. A sample scoring guide for word recognition is shown on the next page.

Word Recognition Scoring Guide		
Total Miscues	Level	Significant Miscues
0–1	Independent	0–1
2–4	Ind./Inst.	2
5	Instructional	3
6–9	Inst./Frust.	4
10+	Frustration	5+

10. To obtain the student's comprehension score, count the number of questions answered incorrectly. Record that numeral in the box labeled "Questions Missed" at the bottom of the comprehension questions. Consult the Comprehension Scoring Guide at the bottom of the teacher's copy, and circle the reading level that corresponds to the number of comprehension questions the student missed. At the pre-primer level, teachers must exercise their judgment, because there are only five comprehension questions.

PREPARING A SUMMARY SHEET

Record the student's scores and reading levels from each word list (if given) and the scores and reading levels for word recognition in context and comprehension from each passage on the summary sheet of the performance booklet. In the sample in Figure 5-3, the teacher counted total miscues. It appears that Joe's independent levels would be first and second grade. Because the independent level is the *highest* level at which Joe can read books by himself, the second-grade level would be his independent level. The third-grade level appears to be his instructional level, because word recognition in context is good and comprehension is satisfactory. The fourth-grade level ap-

	SUMMARY OF STUDENT'S PERFORMANCE							
	Word Recognition						Comprehension	
Grade	Isolation (Word Lists)				Context (Passages)		Oral Reading Form A	
	Flash	Analysis	Total	Level	Miscues	Level	Questions Missed	Level
PP								
P								
1					0	Ind.	1	Ind.
2					2	Ind./Inst.	0	Ind.
3					5	Inst.	2	Ind./Inst.
4					9	Inst./Frust.	5	Frust.

Figure 5-3 Example of Completed Summary Sheet for Joe

pears to be Joe's frustration level because word recognition in context is near the frustration level and his comprehension is minimal. In summary, estimates of Joe's three reading levels are independent—second grade, instructional—third grade, and frustration—fourth grade.

GRADED PASSAGES: SILENT READING (OPTIONAL)

Overview: The graded reading passages for Forms A, B, C, and D range in difficulty from the pre-primer through the eighth-grade level. Forms LN and LE range in difficulty from grade three through grade twelve. **Form D is recommended for silent reading.**

Purpose: To assess the student's silent reading ability and to gain additional information about the student's independent, instructional, and frustration levels. In addition, the teacher can also assess the student's strengths and weaknesses in comprehension and oral rereading to locate specific information.

> **Note:** It is important that students above the primary grades engage in silent reading so that their reading ability may be assessed more accurately.

Procedure

1. Use the graded passages from a form that was not used for oral reading. Form D in Part Two of this book is especially designed for silent reading.

2. Duplicate the corresponding form of a performance booklet in which to record the student's responses. All performance booklets are found in Part Two of this book.

3. Begin with a silent graded passage that is at the student's highest independent reading level in oral reading.

4. Cover the passage with heavy paper so only the title shows. Have the student read the title of the passage and predict what it might be about. Mentally note or write the student's predictions. Then tell the student to read the passage silently and think about the passage, because comprehension questions will be asked. While the student reads silently, note and record any lip movement (LM), finger pointing (FP), vocalization (V) or words pronounced (P) for the student.

5. If an assessment of reading rate is desired, time the student's reading and record the number of seconds it takes the student to read the passage. Further information is found in Section 3, Determining Rate of Reading.

6. After the student finishes the passage, cover or remove the graded passage before asking the comprehension questions.

7. Evaluate the student's response to each question with a plus (+) for a correct response or a minus (–) for an incorrect response. Partial credit ($^1/_2$) may also be given.

8. After the comprehension questions have been asked, do an oral rereading of a portion of the passage. Have the student locate and orally reread the sentence containing the requested information. Note the student's oral reading performance by recording miscues.

9. Continue administering graded passages until the student is unable to answer half of the comprehension questions or exhibits behavior associated with frustration (finger pointing, facial expressions, considerable tension, anxiety, and so on).

10. To obtain the student's comprehension score, count the number of questions answered incorrectly. Record that numeral in the box labeled "Questions Missed" at the bottom of the comprehension questions. Consult the Comprehension Scoring Guide at the bottom of the teacher's copy and circle the reading level that corresponds to the number of comprehension questions the student missed. At the pre-primer level, teachers must exercise their judgment, because there are only five comprehension questions. A sample scoring guide for comprehension is shown below.

Comprehension Scoring Guide	
Questions Missed	Level
0–1	Independent
1½–2	Ind./Inst.
2½	Instructional
3–4½	Inst./Frust.
5+	Frustration

11. Record the score and reading level from each passage on the summary sheet of the performance booklet.

LONGER GRADED PASSAGES: FORMS LN AND LE

Two additional forms (LN and LE) range in difficulty from grade three through grade twelve and have passages that each contain approximately 250 words. LN denotes longer narrative passages; LE denotes longer expository passages. Kibby (1995) notes that it is important to assess the student's ability to read both narrative and expository passages. Oral or silent reading can be used with either form. The teacher should follow the general procedures outlined earlier for oral reading or silent reading. These passages can help the teacher:

1. estimate or verify the student's independent, instructional, and frustration levels.

2. assess the student's strengths and weaknesses in word identification and comprehension.

3. compare the student's reading of longer passages with shorter passages.

4. compare the student's ability to read narrative and expository passages.

SECTION SIX

Helping Students Monitor Their Reading

The Student Repeats Words, Phrases, or Sentences

Scenario 1

Repetitions may help the student understand what he or she has read. The teacher must decide whether the student is anticipating a "hard" word, making a legitimate effort to have the reading make sense, or merely repeating from habit. Consider the following:

📖 If the student's repetitions are frequent, it is possible that the reading materials are too difficult. If this is the case, provide the student with reading materials at his or her instructional level.

📖 Repetitions that are "stalls" may provide additional time to unlock an unknown word. This may be a normal part of the reading process. Excessive use of the "stall" technique, however, may indicate that the reading material is too difficult and/or more effective reading strategies are needed. It may also indicate a need to teach how context and language cues can be used to anticipate words (see Johns and Lenski, 2001).

📖 Praise the student when a word, phrase, or sentence is repeated to preserve ongoing meaning. Tell the student that such behavior is fully acceptable when reading doesn't make sense. Provide examples from students' reading similar to the following that a student and/or class could discuss and evaluate.

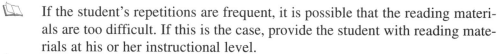

     Ⓒ <u>They grew</u>
     He <u>knew</u> he must try to save the woods he loved so much.

     Ⓒ   *in*
     He <u>jumped on the high wall</u> perfectly.

📖 If repetitions are merely a habit, it may be helpful to have the student record his or her reading on a tape recorder and then discuss it with the teacher. The student should realize that the majority of the repetitions are a habit that generally detracts from effective reading.

📖 Sometimes a student repeatedly overcorrects to ensure word-for-word accuracy. Such students should be encouraged not to repeat and break the flow when the miscue does not significantly alter the meaning (such as substituting *the* for *a*). Have the student follow along as you read and model the process.

The Student Waits to Be Told Unknown Words

Scenario 2

The reluctance of some students to attempt unknown words may be due to several factors. First, students may not have been taught a functional strategy for word identification, or they do not have a variety of strategies to use when confronted with an unknown word. Although students may have been taught phonics and the use of context, they do not realize that these strategies may be used during reading. Second, the teacher may often tell students unknown words, thereby reducing their need to acquire or use an internal strategy for word identification. Third, students who are poor readers may be reluctant to take risks. Instead, they frequently manipulate teachers or other students to tell them unknown words. The following strategies may be helpful:

- Wait 5 or 10 seconds and see whether this will suggest to the student that you expect him or her to attempt to pronounce the word.
- Discuss what the student thinks should be done when confronted with an unknown word.
- Have the student continue reading to see whether subsequent textual information will help with the unknown word.
- Ask the student to go back a line and see whether the preceding sentence and the words around the "unknown" word suggest the word. If the student does not suggest a word, ask him or her to reread the sentence until a good guess is made.
- Ask the student to reread the sentence and try to guess a word that begins with the initial sound of the "unknown" word and makes sense.
- Provide oral examples where the student uses the information provided to anticipate the missing word.

> I saw a _____.
>
> I would like to play _____.
>
> It's time to go _____.
>
> I found a _____ in the lawn.

- Use easy cloze exercises where the student is asked to write in a word that makes sense. Discuss various choices offered by a group of students. Gradually include some graphic information about the exact word the author used.

> I like _____.
>
> I like to go to the _____.
>
> I like to go to the s_____.

- If the student encounters several unknown words in a line of print, it is probable that the reading material is too difficult. Provide reading material at the student's instructional level.
- Teach a functional set of strategies for word identification. The following chart might be adapted and taught.

Figuring Out Unknown Words

1. Use the words around the unknown word to help think of a word that makes sense in the sentence.
2. Use the letters, and the sounds associated with the letters, along with the words around the unknown word to say a word that makes sense in the sentence.
3. Look for root words, prefixes, suffixes, and endings. Try to pronounce the various word parts to see whether you have heard it before. Try various pronunciations, especially for the vowels.
4. Continue reading. Later sentences may help you figure out the unfamiliar word.
5. As a last resort, use the dictionary, ask someone, or skip the unknown word.

The Student Produces a Nonword or Omits Unknown Words

Scenario 3

The student must be helped to realize that reading is a meaningful process and words pronounced should make sense. In short, reading should sound like oral language. Try the following strategies:

📖 Ask the student what the nonword means. It is possible that the student knows the meaning but has mispronounced the word.

📖 Provide oral and written examples where the student attempts to predict the appropriate word that has been omitted. Discuss the student's choices.

I will mail the _____.

The horse _____ over the fence.

📖 Provide examples that contain a nonword and ask the student to tell what the nonword could mean. Have the student share clues in the sentence that are helpful.

He drank a glass of *fax*.

The *zop* bought some candy.

📖 Place opaque white tape over certain words in the student's reading material that can be easily predicted. Encourage the student to supply a real word that makes sense. Then compare the student's word to the word in the reading material. If the words are different, encourage the student to evaluate his or her choice in light of the actual word. Help the student to transfer this prediction strategy to identifying unknown words when reading.

📖 Many nonwords may indicate that the reading material is too difficult. Provide materials at the student's independent or instructional level.

📖 If the student omits an unknown word, ask questions such as:

Does that sound like language to you?

What word do you think could go in this spot?

Why do you think so?

What word do you know that begins like _____ that would make sense?

If the student is unable to produce a word with the same beginning sound, ask the student to try a word that he or she thinks would make sense.

The goal should be to have the reader aim at producing a word or nonword rather than omitting the word. Remember, however, that there are times when a word can be omitted without a loss in meaning.

Scenario 4

The Student Substitutes Words That Make Sense

The most important strategy must be enacted by the teacher: Remain silent. Try to keep other students from breaking the thought line. You might tell students that readers will sometimes substitute words that make sense. Only substitutions that do not make sense or alter the meaning should be corrected. To help students decide whether substitutions do or do not make sense, try the following strategies:

📖 Provide sentences that contain a substituted word written above the text. Have students discuss whether or not the substituted word makes sense. You could also read a text and make substitution miscues that students could evaluate.

They went to the zoo because they there were many things to see.

📖 Provide exercises that contain substitutions two different readers made in the same sentence. Discuss which substitution, if either, appears to be closer to the author's intended meaning.

Billy decided to ride along the a little road.

Billy decided to ride along walk a little road.

📖 Develop lessons where students can discuss the subtle differences in words even though such differences are unlikely to significantly influence the author's intended meaning. For example, what is the difference between street and road, house and home, tall and big, little and small?

NOTE: Similar strategies may also be used with omissions. For example:

He knew that there were ~~so~~ many things to see. He remembered how bare and black it ~~had~~ looked.

He gave the boy twenty-~~five~~ cents.

He found leaves from ~~some~~ maple and oak trees.

Scenario 5

The Student Substitutes Words That Do Not Make Sense

Remind the student that reading is a process of reconstructing meaning. (Did that sound right to you?) The student must be taught to use semantic (contextual) cues. Try the following strategies:

📖 Remind the student to think while reading so that he or she will stop and re-read the material if it is not making sense. This student may view reading as a "word-calling" process. You may need to help the student develop a concept of reading that involves meaning as the crucial element.

Give the student oral exercises in which he or she identifies words that do not make sense in the context of the sentences or the story. Discuss why the word or words do not make sense. Do similar written exercises. For example:

> I like to drink apples.
>
> The postman delivered the groceries.
>
> He set his calendar so he would wake up at seven o'clock.
>
> Bill went to the store to buy some candy for her sister.

Give the student oral and written exercises containing closure tasks in which the student anticipates omitted words that make sense. Use the cloze procedure as a teaching technique. Develop the notion that language dictates that only certain types of words can be placed after certain language structures.

> After playing, the children _____.
>
> I will see you after _____.
>
> He was reading a _____.
>
> "I lost my money," _____ Bill.
>
> The _____ climbed the tree.

Use small group activities where certain key words in a story are covered. Elicit responses from the group and have students evaluate the responses. The ultimate criterion is: "Does the word you suggest make sense in the phrase (sentence, paragraph)?" Demonstrate how the flow of the story helps the reader to predict certain words. Think out loud so students can "see" you model the process.

Keep track of substitutions to see whether certain words are habitually associated with other words. Write selections where the grammatical structures make it highly unlikely for the habitual associations to occur. For example:

> was and saw

Once upon a time there <u>was</u> a girl named Ebony. Her hair <u>was</u> long and black. Ebony liked to wear beads in her hair. One day, while she <u>was</u> walking downtown, she <u>saw</u> some beads in a store window. She <u>saw</u> blue, yellow, and pink beads.

> in and on

Jim liked to collect insects. He kept the spiders <u>in</u> a jar <u>on</u> top of his dresser. One Friday, his mother invited some friends to come over for coffee. They were talking <u>in</u> the kitchen. Jim took his jar of spiders <u>into</u> the kitchen and set it <u>on</u> the table. When one lady reached for a cup <u>on</u> the table, she bumped the jar. It landed <u>on</u> the floor. What do you think happened next?

> when and then

José and his mother had some errands to do. His mother said, "I will get my coat; <u>then</u> I will be ready to go. <u>When</u> you find your jacket, come out to the car. First, we will go to the supermarket; <u>then</u> we can go to the pet shop to find out <u>when</u> the puppy will be ready to come home. <u>When</u> we bring the puppy home you will get the basket out of the closet. <u>Then</u> the puppy will have a nice place to sleep."

📖   Provide sentences that contain a substituted word written above the text. Have students discuss whether the substituted word makes sense. For example:

they
They went to the zoo because there were many things to see.

📖   Provide exercises that contain substitutions two different readers made in the same sentence. Discuss which substitution appears to be closer to the author's intended meaning. For example:

the
Billy decided to ride along a little road.

walk
Billy decided to ride along a little road.

📖   Tape-record the student's reading. Have the student listen to the reading and note substitutions that resulted in a partial or total loss of meaning. Discuss and use some of the appropriate strategies already presented. In addition, encourage the student to monitor his or her reading by asking, "Does that make sense?"

📖   If there are many substitutions that distort the author's intended meaning, the book may be too difficult. Choose materials at the student's instructional level. Books at this level should contain words that are usually within the student's meaning vocabulary. In other words, the student should have the necessary background, experiences, and concepts to understand the words.

NOTE: Similar strategies may also be used with omissions that distort the meaning.

Scenario 6   The Student Habitually Tries to Sound Out Unknown Words

Some students may have been taught that the only appropriate strategy is to sound out words when they are unknown. Other students may not have been taught any strategies that can be applied in such a situation. In either case, teachers must help students use their knowledge of language (syntax) and teach the value of context (semantic) cues. The following strategies represent a meager but appropriate beginning:

📖   Show the student that a word in oral language can often be predicted correctly before it is heard. Then, help the student use this same knowledge in reading. For example:

He gave the kitten some _____.

Put a stamp on the _____.

Five pennies make a _____.

📖   Provide examples where two readers have come across the same unknown word. Discuss the responses of the two readers in an attempt to decide which reader has been most effective and why.

Text:	The car went down the old *street*.
Reader 1:	The car went down the old *road*.
Reader 2:	The car went down the old *stream*.

 Provide words that the student is probably able to pronounce but that are not familiar in meaning. Then provide a sentence that builds meaning for the word. For example:

kingcups	He picked some kingcups for his mother because she likes flowers.
kipper	The kipper is not usually caught by fishermen.

 The teacher might then provide words in the student's meaning vocabulary that he or she is unable to pronounce. Such words can then be placed in a context that builds meaning for the words. Through such exercises the student should realize that meaning can be achieved without always sounding out words.

 Teach the student a set of strategies for word identification. A chart or bookmark could be adapted from the following:

Figuring Out Unknown Words

1. What makes sense here?
2. What sound does it start with?
3. Are there root words, prefixes, or endings?
4. Keep reading to try to figure it out.
5. Use these last:
    ▾ dictionary
    ▾ someone's help
    ▾ skip it

The Student Ignores Punctuation, Adds Punctuation, or Uses Inappropriate Intonation

Scenario 7

Try the following strategies to rectify misuses of punctuation and intonation:

 The student should be shown examples where punctuation is ignored or substituted. In some cases meaning may not be disturbed; in other cases a change in meaning may occur. Discuss whether or not the reader should have paid attention to the punctuation. The following examples may be useful:

He woke up ̶a̶n̶d̶ .He got ready for school.

Billy looked ahead ̶a̶n̶d̶ .He saw smoke coming out of a pile of dry brush.

at

Even as Billy looked, the flames burst out.

with

But Blaze scrambled up the bank, and Billy held on somehow, his arms around the pony's neck.

Down Blaze went to his knees, ~~and~~ Billy slipped out of the saddle.

Similar oral examples could also be modeled by the teacher using classroom materials.

- Read plays and write experience stories or journals. Help the student see the role of punctuation.
- Teach the basic marks of punctuation, as needed, in a natural writing situation.
- Discuss reading that has been tape recorded, and ask the student to point out areas where it can be improved.
- Remember that some intonation patterns may be the result of the student's dialect. In such cases no strategy lessons are necessary.
- Use slash marks to indicate appropriate phrasing (for instance, Bill,/my brother,/ has gone away.). Reduce the number of slash marks as the student's phrasing and attention to punctuation improve.
- Use pattern books. Each time the pattern is repeated, ask the student to read it. Stress that the pattern should sound like speech.
- List phrases on cards and have the student read the phrases as they would sound naturally.

    at school   at home   near my house

    on the table   by my house   in the box

- Model correct phrasing and punctuation in a passage that is easy for the student. Then have the student read along. Finally, have the student read the passage independently.

Scenario 8   The Student Overrelies on Context While Reading

Some students read fluently, but they often add a number of words that were not written by the author. These same students may also omit a number of words. The result is often an interesting story that is quite different from the one in print. These students seem to rely heavily on their background knowledge to the partial exclusion of graphophonic knowledge. Because effective reading requires the use of context, language cues, and graphophonic cues, the teacher may wish to consider the following strategies.

- Tell the student that background knowledge is important to help predict words while reading, but other cues should also be used. Model how initial sounds along with context clues can be used to help pronounce words.

The leaves on the tree are g_____.

To write, you need p_____ and p_____.

Jamie is my best f_____.

The h_____ has a roof and ch_____.

📖 Tape-record the student's reading, listen to it, and mark any miscues. Then review selected miscues with the student and discuss how meaning is changed even though the miscue may make sense in the sentence. Model how graphic cues can be used along with the context to determine the actual word used by the author.

quietly
She quickly dashed down the hill.

perplexed
The soft buzz of the computer relaxed Anthony.

📖 Present sentences where the student can make initial predictions of a missing word. Then provide a series of graphic cues to help the student correctly identify the word used by the author.

I must put the _____ away.

I must put the d_____ away.

I must put the de_____s away.

I must put the decor_____s away.

I must put the decorations away.

📖 Tell the student that readers make miscues, but stress the importance of trying to pay attention to the words written by the author. Relate the situation to a piece of the student's writing. The expectation is that the reader will read the words that were written.

The Student's Oral Reading Lacks Fluency

Scenario 9

Students at the beginning stages of reading are seldom fluent readers (National Reading Panel, 2000). This situation is to be expected and no intervention is required. Such students are beginning to acquire a sight vocabulary and learn strategies such as phonics so they can identify unknown words. Such is the case for most beginning readers, whatever their age. If, however, students remain in a stage where they continue to read word for word, the following strategies may be considered.

📖 Be sure students are placed in materials at an appropriate instructional level. At the instructional level, the student will generally miss no more that one word in twenty.

📖 Recognize that reading is a developmental process. Fluency will usually improve as sight vocabularies and word-identification strategies develop.

📖 Encourage the repeated readings of pattern books and books at the student's independent and instructional levels.

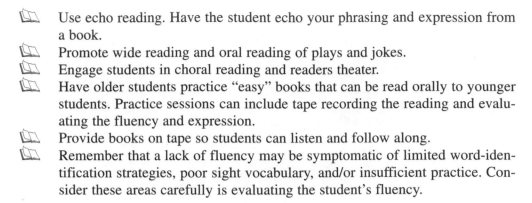

Use echo reading. Have the student echo your phrasing and expression from a book.

Promote wide reading and oral reading of plays and jokes.

Engage students in choral reading and readers theater.

Have older students practice "easy" books that can be read orally to younger students. Practice sessions can include tape recording the reading and evaluating the fluency and expression.

Provide books on tape so students can listen and follow along.

Remember that a lack of fluency may be symptomatic of limited word-identification strategies, poor sight vocabulary, and/or insufficient practice. Consider these areas carefully is evaluating the student's fluency.

SECTION SEVEN

History of the Informal Reading Inventory*

*Based on Jerry L. Johns and Mary K. Lunn, "The Informal Reading Inventory: 1910–1980," *Reading World*, 23 (October 1983), 8–19. Copyright © 1983 by the College Reading Association. Used with permission.

The informal reading inventory (IRI), an individually administered reading test, is composed of a series of graded word lists and graded passages. During the student's oral reading of the passages, the test administrator notes reading miscues such as mispronunciations, omissions, insertions, and substitutions. After the oral reading, the test administrator asks the student comprehension questions. Silent reading passages, accompanied by comprehension checks, are also usually included.

Emmett A. Betts is generally considered to be the originator of the IRI. The oft used word recognition and comprehension percentages for the independent, instructional, and frustration reading levels, referred to as the *Betts criteria*, are evidence of the major contributions he made to the development of the IRI. Betts, however, was not the sole creator of the IRI. Several other individuals made important contributions to the development of the IRI.

BEGINNINGS OF INFORMAL ASSESSMENT

The Early 1900s

At the beginning of the twentieth century, there was no IRI as we know it today. Waldo (1915) seems to be one of the first professionals who promoted the informal assessment of *both* oral and silent reading ability. While superintendent of the Sycamore Public Schools in Illinois, Waldo attempted to keep records of students' oral reading ability and to compare teaching methods for their effectiveness. He initially used oral expression during the reading as the sole means for evaluating comprehension. After completing this informal study, Waldo did more investigative work "to test the silent rather than the oral reading, for the former is of much greater importance, not only in school, but in future life" (Waldo, 1915, p. 251). It was not his purpose to formulate a series of standard tests. A major reason Waldo cited for using informal tests was to help teachers and administrators assess students' reading as a means to ultimately improve instruction.

Waldo's assessment of silent reading and comprehension was based on five minutes of reading for students in grades three through eight. Tests were administered by the same individual to ensure uniformity in administration. Students marked their place after five minutes and their silent reading rate was determined. Students were then asked to write a reproduction or complete account of what they had just read. A set of 10 questions about the reading material was also given to the students, who were asked to write brief answers to the questions. Scores for rate and reproduction as well as percentages of correct answers were recorded for each student. This test was administered in the early part of the school year. Six months later another test was given using selections of the same relative difficulty from the same reading material. Data from the second test were compared with data from the first test to determine whether the students made any gains in silent reading rate and/or comprehension.

Trends in assessing reading at this time centered mainly on oral reading and rate. Waldo's study is important because it appears to be one of the earliest attempts to informally assess *silent* reading rate and *comprehension*.

William S. Gray was another professional whose work probably influenced the development of the IRI. Although Gray's tests were standardized, they were similar to many of today's IRIs. His tests were called "Standard Tests" (Gray, 1916, p. 281), and appear to be the forerunner of what came to be known as the *Standardized Oral Reading Paragraphs*. The *Oral-Reading Test* consisted of 11 paragraphs arranged in order of increasing difficulty, and the *Silent-Reading Test* consisted of three paragraphs intended for designated grade levels. The purpose of the *Oral-Reading Test* was to determine oral reading rate and the ability to pronounce words at sight. Gray listed specific directions for the administration of these tests. The tests were administered individually and a record was kept of the time required to read each paragraph and the errors made.

No evaluation of comprehension was made on the oral reading. After compiling data from 3,000 students, Gray established the criteria for discontinuing the oral reading as follows:

▶ A paragraph is not successfully read if it requires 30 or more seconds for the reading, and if four or more errors are made.

▶ A paragraph is not successfully read if it is read in less than 30 seconds and five or more errors are made (Gray, 1916, p. 292).

The *Silent-Reading Test* was then administered to determine rate and comprehension. After the students read each paragraph silently, they were asked to reproduce it. Second- and third-grade students were asked to retell the story; older students were asked to write the story as well as they could. Following this reproduction, the students were given 10 questions to answer about the story. Again, the younger students were allowed to dictate their answers; the older students wrote their answers. Silent reading rate was calculated in words read per second. A quality of silent reading score was also obtained using the student's reproduction and answers to the questions.

Gray's test of silent reading reflects characteristics similar to those found in Waldo's test. The comprehension assessment is identical except the younger students who read Gray's tests were allowed to dictate their answers. The method of calculating the quality of silent reading using the reproductions and comprehension questions is also similar in both tests. Gray, however, used individual testing, whereas Waldo's assessment involved the group or class as a whole.

It is interesting to note that several characteristics of today's IRIs are present in Gray's tests: paragraphs increasing in difficulty; individual testing by a trained person; an error marking system; comprehension assessment of silent reading through questions; and criteria for evaluation. The beginnings of the IRI can be seen in the tests of this period; however, many refinements and contributions were made before the IRI reached its present state.

The 1920s

Professional publications at this time suggested the need to improve informal assessment of reading ability, to improve reading instruction, and to make provisions for individual differences in reading ability (Whipple, 1925).

In regard to informal assessment, a study by McLeod (cited in Beldin, 1970) identified the most common types of errors made by students in grades one through eight in their oral reading: mispronunciations and substitutions. Wheat (1923) stressed the importance of teachers knowing the level of achievement for each student in oral and silent reading, and offered suggestions for informal classroom testing using the students' readers. He suggested testing students individually with readers from the current year and the two previous years. A paragraph from each reader was selected. Records were kept of the rate and number of errors made in oral reading. Comprehension was tested informally. Wheat also made reference to standards suggested by Bolenius (1919) for silent reading rate and comprehension in grades four through eight. The criterion for rate was given in words read per minute, with increasing rates suggested for each successive grade. The same standard for comprehension was intended for each grade. Another suggestion for informal assessment was a concern for reading behaviors (such as head movements, finger pointing, lip movements, vocalization, signs of eye strain, and wandering attention) that were thought to be indicative of reading difficulty (Whipple, 1925).

A number of questions were also raised regarding the need for future investigations concerning informal testing of reading: (1) What tests are appropriate for classifying students? (2) What are desirable standards for various grade levels? and (3) What are desirable variations in these standards for students who are at different capacity levels? (Whipple, 1925). Some of these questions were addressed in later decades.

The 1930s

Beldin (1970) notes that in the 1920s and 1930s there was a great deal of contemplation regarding the informal assessment of reading, but a paucity of writing about it. Some attempts were made to answer the three questions raised by Whipple. Professionals were working to develop a uniform process for informal reading assessment and to establish criteria for such assessment.

Thorndike was one whose opinions influenced the need for researched criteria in judging a student's reading performance. Thorndike (1934) discussed the fact that unknown words students are unable to guess at, and/or locate the meaning of, may cause frustration. He stated, "Two or three frustrations per page from unintelligible words may make the difference between enjoyment and discomfort" (Thorndike, 1934, p. 125). Thus, the need for some sort of criteria was apparent.

Gates (1935) suggested that tests of reading achievement should include word recognition, sentence reading, silent paragraph reading, oral reading, techniques of reading context, and techniques of working out recognition and pronunciation of isolated words. No criteria, however, were suggested by Gates for the attainment of these skills.

Betts (1936) discussed three main areas (educational factors, physical factors, and social attitudes) that could offer insights into student behaviors observable during test administration. Betts also listed some of the behavioral symptoms evident in poor oral reading. Still, there were no specific criteria established and no references were made to the three levels of reading.

Durrell (1937) further emphasized the paragraph or passage aspect of the IRI that was not yet formally developed, and suggested a basic criterion for word recognition. For primary students, Durrell suggested using a paragraph approximately 100 words long from their basal reader or another book of similar difficulty. He also related that material which contained more than one difficult word in every 20 running words would usually be difficult for students to master. No empirical study or evidence was offered to support Durrell's statement regarding this criterion for word recognition. The need for standard criteria in the informal assessment of reading, recognized in previous decades, was still a concern.

The 1940s

In the previous decade, attempts were made to find solutions for many of the problems dealing with the informal assessment of reading. At the beginning of the 1940s efforts were being made to develop standard criteria. The 1940s can be viewed as the era in which these efforts came to fruition.

Early in this decade, Betts (1941) used his "subjective reading inventory" in the Reading Clinic at Pennsylvania State College. By 1942, the IRI was a valuable test used in this clinic. Betts set up three reading levels for the IRI: independent, instructional, and frustration. He also assigned criteria for each reading level. There is no clear statement or empirical evidence regarding the manner in which Betts established these criteria. A study by Killgallon (1942), who was a doctoral student working with Betts at Pennsylvania State College, offered evidence to support some of the criteria established by Betts. It should be kept in mind, however, that the actual sample Killgallon used for his study comprised only 41 students. Many questions have been raised with regard to the size of the sample used in this study.

In regard to the IRI criteria, Betts (1946) stated, "While research has validated most of the items included in the criteria for appraising reading performance by means of an informal reading inventory, total criteria for this purpose are in need of further study" (p. 439). The establishment of criteria for the IRI reading levels, whether empirically supported or not, was an addition that enhanced its use by professionals in the field of reading.

The increasing popularity of the IRI and of informal assessment can be viewed as trends of this period. Betts (1949) made several important statements with regard to these trends:

> In general, teachers interpret standardized test scores in a manner that tends to place children above their instructional levels. This is especially true for children at the lower end of the distribution . . . Two types of appraisal devices are used to identify needs: standardized measures and informal inventories . . . These informal appraisals complement rather than supplement the findings on standardized tests (pp. 269, 273).

It is clear that Betts advocated the use of both standardized and informal means of reading assessment, and it is possible that he regarded informal assessment as a more accurate indicator of a student's reading ability. His efforts in the development and propagation of the IRI made it possible for the IRI to be used in a variety of educational settings.

The 1950s

If the advances of the 1940s are viewed as efforts to establish the IRI as a valuable tool for use in reading clinics and classrooms, the 1950s can be characterized as the beginnings of research that examined the criteria for the independent, instructional, and frustration reading levels. The major study in this area was conducted by Cooper (1952). He appears to be the first individual to present another set of criteria for the instructional level after the Betts criteria were established. For students in grades two and three, Cooper's criteria for word recognition and comprehension were 98 percent and 70 percent, respectively. Students in grades four through six made the greatest amount of progress in reading when their word recognition was 96 percent and comprehension was at least 60 percent. Despite the experimental nature of Cooper's investigation, his criteria have been "virtually ignored" (Kender, 1970, p. 165), possibly because of methodological problems (Powell, 1970). Although the findings from the Cooper study may be questioned, there is little doubt that it served as a stimulus for further research in subsequent years. Harris and Sipay (1990, p. 226) note that, "to date the best study for determining IRI criteria has been conducted by Cooper."

The 1960s

During the 1960s there was a continuation of research on criteria for the instructional level. In addition, a number of studies compared IRIs to standardized tests. Informal reading inventories began to be commercially published (for example, Botel, 1966; McCracken, 1966; Silvaroli, 1969). The first monograph devoted exclusively to the topics of IRIs was also published (Johnson and Kress, 1965).

The period is also notable because at least seven doctoral dissertations dealt with IRIs. In general, the dissertations supported the contention that standardized tests overestimated students' instructional levels. Research by Brown (1963) and Patty (1965), in particular, noted that it was not possible to generalize whether standardized tests or IRIs more accurately assessed students' reading levels.

Important studies by Kender (1966) and Powell (1970) seriously questioned the traditional criteria used for the instructional level. Other research (Emans, 1965; Ladd, 1961; and Millsap, 1962) explored whether teachers were able to consistently administer and interpret the results of the IRI. Unfortunately, the research findings were inconsistent. The available literature seems to lead to the conclusion that reading authorities valued the IRI but were concerned with how reading levels were determined and the consistency with which teachers could administer IRIs.

Of the published inventories that appeared in the 1960s, McCracken (1963) reported one of the most thorough studies to establish the validity and reliability of the *Standard Reading Inventory*. In a review of that inventory in the *Seventh Mental Measurements Yearbook* (Buros, 1972), Robinson noted that "it is useful as a rough, semidiagnostic tool when an examiner wants to learn more about a given learner and how he reads certain kinds of materials" (p. 1126). McCracken's study remains one of the most ambitious and thorough efforts to establish the validity and reliability of an IRI.

In an attempt to help teachers and diagnosticians, Johnson and Kress (1965) presented procedures for developing and using IRIs. This practical volume may be considered a handbook for professionals who wish to understand the nature of IRIs and the procedures to follow in developing, scoring, and using IRIs. The response to this publication by professionals has been considerable; it was one of the largest-selling publications of the International Reading Association.

The 1970s

The 1970s continued some of the emphases of the 1960s and opened new avenues of inquiry. Commercially published IRIs continued to grow in number (for example, Johns, 1978; Sucher and Allred, 1973). Reviews of the history and development of the IRI were published (Beldin, 1970; Walter, 1974), a critical review of IRIs appeared (Pikulski, 1974), and an annotated bibliography on IRIs was published (Johns et al., 1977). This bibliography contains more than 100 articles and research studies pertaining to IRIs—further evidence of the important role IRIs have had in the assessment of reading.

A concern for criteria was still in evidence (Dunkeld, 1970; Ekwall, 1976; Hays, 1975; Lowell, 1970; Pikulski, 1974; Powell, 1971). Although much research was reported, no consensus was reached on the criteria for the three reading levels. Research on the ability of teachers to use IRIs to determine a student's instructional level (Windell, 1975) was also a concern. Research began to focus on such areas as the influence of student interest and motivation on reading levels (Brittain, 1970; Estes and Vaughan, 1973; Hunt, 1970). Johns (1976) noted problem areas perceived by professionals who used IRIs (for example, the number and type(s) of comprehension questions, counting miscues, and the passages used at the beginning reading levels). In addition, Froese (1974) questioned the use of graded word lists.

Perhaps the greatest influence on the thinking concerning informal assessment of reading came about as a result of insights from psycholinguists. In earlier decades, deviations from the printed page that the student made while reading orally were called "errors." Accuracy in word recognition was determined by counting the number of errors. Psycholinguistic insights into reading errors led to the term "miscues" to more accurately describe misreadings (Burke and Goodman, 1970; Goodman, 1973). Gradually, a growing number of professionals became interested in trying to understand the reasons why a particular miscue occurred. The publication of the *Reading Miscue Inven-*

tory (Goodman and Burke, 1972) stimulated further interest in the qualitative (understanding of miscues) aspect of a student's word recognition performance on an IRI.

The interest in miscue analysis added a new dimension to IRIs: efforts to synthesize some of the traditional aspects of the IRI with the concept of miscue analysis (Smith and Weaver, 1978; Williamson and Young, 1974). For example, combining the qualitative aspects of miscue analysis with the quantitative aspects provides powerful clues to students' strengths and weaknesses in reading.

The 1980s

At the beginning of this decade, some new IRIs were published. The *Advanced Reading Inventory* (Johns, 1981) was designed for grades seven through college. Rinsky and de Fossard (1980) developed an IRI for grades two through nine that contained passages in the content areas of science and social studies. By the middle or end of this decade, several previously published IRIs appeared in new editions (such as Burns and Roe, 1989; Ekwall, 1986; Johns, 1985, 1988; Woods and Moe, 1985, 1989).

The computer became more prominent in classrooms, and the adaptation of informal assessment strategies to computers was developed for both elementary (Blanchard, 1985) and secondary (Johns, 1986) students. In addition, Alvermann (1985) developed a program for teaching IRIs by interfacing microcomputers with video cassettes for use in school systems, colleges, and universities where competence with IRIs is desired.

With advances in the analysis of text structures, traditional IRIs were studied to determine the nature of the passages they contained and how well the passages were formed (Gillis and Olson, 1985; Olson and Gillis, 1985). In addition to text structure, Caldwell (1985) examined IRIs in light of recent research findings in the areas of schema theory and metacognition. Based on her analysis, authors of IRIs were encouraged to assess topic familiarity, provide uniform and coherent structure of reading passages, use consistent text structures (narrative or expository), and explore unaided recall for assessing comprehension.

The question of word-recognition criteria at the instructional level continued to be an area of focus for research. Homan and Klesius (1985) investigated this issue by administering IRIs to 10 students in each grade, one through five. The results of their analysis of IRI results indicated that "at no grade level could students tolerate less than 94 percent word recognition performance" (p. 56) and still maintain an adequate level of comprehension (at least 70 percent). The investigators concluded that the word-recognition criterion should be set at about 95 percent for students in grades one through six. Although the Homan and Klesius study supported the traditional criteria (95 percent), the investigators also urged teachers to consider other variables (for example, topic familiarity, concept density, and type and wording of comprehension questions) that may influence reading performance.

In related studies, Anderson and Joels (1986) found that first graders could maintain 70 percent comprehension with oral reading accuracy of 90 percent. For students in grades two through four, 94 percent oral reading accuracy with 70 percent comprehension was achieved. Johns and Magliari (1989) examined IRI word recognition scores of 83 students in grades one through six. Students in the primary grades averaged approximately 91 percent oral reading accuracy with 70 percent comprehension. Students in grades four through six achieved word-recognition scores of 93 to 94 percent. It would seem that Powell's (1970) claim that the traditional Betts criteria appear to be too stringent for primary-grade students is at least partially supported by these studies; nevertheless, the issue of the appropriate word-recognition criterion for the instructional level is still subject to debate.

Johns and Magliari also reported word-recognition criteria when only significant miscues were counted. Students in the primary grades achieved average word recognition scores approximately one percent above the Betts criterion of 95 percent. Students in the intermediate grades achieved an average of 98 percent in word recognition.

One of the most noteworthy happenings in this decade was the publication of an updated version of *Informal Reading Inventories* (Johnson, Kress, and Pikulski, 1987). This volume updates the research and theory related to IRIs. It also provides much useful and basic information to help teachers construct, administer, and interpret IRIs. Numerous textbooks on reading (such as Leu and Kinzer, 1987; McCormick, 1987; Vacca, Vacca, and Gove, 1987) gave attention to how teachers and other professionals could use IRIs.

The 1990s

IRIs continued to be refined and developed. Several previously published inventories (such as Bader, 1998; Burns and Roe, 1993, 1999; Ekwall and Shanker, 1993; Johns, 1990b, 1994, 1997; Silvaroli, 1994, 1998; Woods and Moe, 1995, 1999) were updated. In addition, new IRIs were developed by Flynt and Cooter (1993, 1995), Leslie and Caldwell (1990, 1995), Manzo, Manzo, and McKenna (1995), and Stieglitz (1992, 1997). Professional textbooks in literacy (such as Barr, Blachowicz, and Wogman-Sadow, 1995; Burns, Roe, and Ross, 1996; Gunning, 1998; Leu and Kinzer, 1999; McCormick, 1999; Vacca, Vacca, and Gove, 1995; Walker, 1996) discussed the value and use of IRIs. After a half-century, IRIs appear to have evolved as a valuable and useful way to help assess a student's reading (Johns, 1996). IRIs are used in classrooms, resource rooms, clinical situations, and teacher training.

Ackland (1994) documented reasons teachers and aides in a professional development program valued IRIs. Among the thirteen reasons were the following: assessing reading (comprehension, word identification, miscues, fluency), gaining understanding of a standardized test score and the student's classroom performance, informing the teacher about the strategies the student currently uses, determining reading levels to assign appropriate materials or to design a personalized program, screening for a possible referral, and communicating with parents.

A number of educators use portfolios to chronicle the literacy development of students within their classrooms. Surveys by Johns and VanLeirsburg (1990, 1992) and a summary by VanLeirsburg and Johns (1995) found a growing awareness and use of portfolios among educators; moreover, IRIs have been identified among those items included in literacy portfolios. Some teachers reported recording the student's reading on audio tape and then having the student engage in self-reflection after listening to the recording. Other teachers had students read the same IRI passages at various times during the school year as one way to help document changes in fluency, word identification, and other reading behaviors.

There are a number of unresolved issues relating to IRIs. Perhaps the longest lasting and most perplexing issue concerns the appropriate criteria for the instructional level. Although a considerable amount of research has been done in this area, there are no universally accepted and empirically validated criteria for the independent, instructional, or frustration levels. With the growth of miscue analysis, the question about which miscues to count as significant continued to cloud research on the appropriate word-recognition criterion for the instructional level. The question of appropriate criteria remained an area of controversy and debate.

Some research addressed these issues. Using average readers in second and fourth grade, Morris (1990) found that students' word-recognition percentages generally supported the Betts criteria. When only significant miscues were counted, second graders achieved 98 percent accuracy and fourth graders obtained 99 percent accuracy. Morris also found no significant differences in miscue percentages between shorter (100 word) and longer passages.

Johns (1990a) reported data from 88 students in first through fifth grade. The students in primary grades averaged approximately 97 percent accuracy in word recognition when significant miscues were counted; intermediate students averaged approximately 98 percent in word recognition. The percentages were 92 and 94 percent respectively when all miscues were counted. Based on the data from his study and a review of six previous studies, Johns (1990, p. 139) noted that 92 to 95 percent in word recognition "seems to be a reasonable expectation for students in the intermediate grades. The available research does not consistently support a specific percentage." For students in the primary grades, the traditional criteria of 95 percent appears to be too stringent for the instructional level.

The notion of frustration level was challenged by Pehrsson (1994) who used Vygotsky's theory about the zone of proximal development. Applied to reading, this level is achieved through "problem solving under adult guidance or in collaboration with more capable peers" (Vygotsky, 1978, p. 86). To the extent that teachers are able to provide such guidance consistently, it is possible that students might be able to achieve success with more difficult materials. In any event, a key point to be kept in mind is that reading levels are estimates of student's reading ability and should be regarded as a place to begin instruction. The dynamic nature of the interactions among the student, text, teacher, and situation during reading can impact the student in positive or negative ways. Scaffolding and other support from a teacher may facilitate the reading and help the student extend and build more effective reading strategies (Kragler, 1996).

Questions regarding the validity and reliability of IRIs continued to be raised. Many users of IRIs have dealt with the questions of validity and reliability as they have used the IRI with their students by making modifications so that the IRI fits their curriculum, theoretical orientation, and student population. Although the IRI, by definition, is an informal assessment procedure, the growing number of commercially published IRIs led to a re-evaluation of validity and reliability issues raised earlier (Klesius and Homan, 1985; Pikulski and Shanahan, 1982). In addition, teachers in the Ackland (1994) study identified concerns about possible gender or culture bias, the use of readability formulas, interrater reliability, and numerous areas relating to the administration of IRIs. An annotated bibliography on IRIs (Johns, 1993) provides a useful guide to explore many of these and other areas in greater depth.

Richek, Caldwell, Jennings, and Lerner (1996, p. 47) note that "IRIs provide one of the best tools for observing and analyzing reading performance and for gathering information about how a student uses a wide range of reading strategies." The 1990s had some controversy and debate regarding IRIs; nevertheless, they remained a valuable way for a diverse group of professionals to assess their students' reading and to study students' reading behavior.

A New Century

Revisions of previously published IRIs have appeared in new editions (Flynt and Cooter, 2001; Johns, 2001; Leslie and Caldwell, 2001). Professional texts in reading continue to include sections or chapters that promote the use of IRIs to assess students' reading and to provide a means for determining instructional needs in reading (Gillet and Temple, 2000; Vacca, Vacca, and Gove, 2000; Walker, 2000). As educators enter a new century, the 1990s have given growth to three important trends with respect to IRIs.

▶ First, there has been a growing acceptance of the important role IRIs play in the initial training of teachers and in graduate programs where professionals specialize in reading. Revised editions of numerous IRIs offer evidence that there is a continuing need for informal tools to help assess students' reading in programs designed for prospective teachers and professionals who seek advanced training in reading and allied areas. In addition, several IRIs have a videotape or audio tape available to assist in the administration and scoring of IRIs.

▶ Second, there has been a resurgence of interest in IRIs for use in classrooms. Individual teachers and school districts seeking ways to help students become better readers have brought about some of this interest. The major trend influencing this newfound interest in IRIs, however, has been state mandates or laws that require school districts to use multiple measures to assess and track students' reading. IRIs are often selected as an informal means for evaluating students' reading. One positive outcome of such mandates has been a greater awareness of the wide range of reading abilities in most classrooms. This awareness has led to staff development programs that focus on ways to help teachers make their instruction more responsive to students' reading needs. Unfortunately, the state mandates have also, intentionally or unintentionally, made the IRI a high-stakes assessment in some instances. IRIs, by their very nature, are intended to help teachers study their students' reading so instructional adjustments can be made. IRIs were not developed to be used as high-stakes assessments. IRIs can be used along with other tests, teacher observations, and samples of students' work to make informed decisions about students' reading. The use of any single source of information for making important decisions is not warranted. In a recent position statement, the International Reading Association (2000) notes that students "deserve assessments that map a path toward their continued literacy growth" (p. 7). The whole area of high-stakes assessments is likely to produce considerable debate among educators, parents, and politicians in the next several years.

▶ Third, there has been a growing awareness of the need for assessments that can be used with students who enter schools speaking languages other than English. Since 1997 at least two IRIs have been published for use with students to assess their ability to read Spanish (Flynt and Cooter, 1999; Johns, 1997, 2001). Hispanics will be the largest United States minority by 2005 and will represent nearly one-quarter of the population in the United States by 2050. There is likely to be a need for additional informal assessments in Spanish as well as other languages.

"Increasingly, classroom teachers are administering informal reading inventories" (Gunning, 2000, p. 492). If teachers want to make a difference in students' reading achievement, it is likely that IRIs will be a valuable tool to use for reading assessment. The teacher can determine the student's instructional level, study the student's word recognition and comprehension, and conduct an analysis of the student's miscues. The information can then be used by the teacher to help select materials for instruction and plan lessons that are responsive to the student's needs. Technology may impact the form IRIs will take in the years ahead; nevertheless, thoughtful and reflective teachers will continue to use this long-standing method of reading assessment.

EMMETT A. BETTS: A BIOGRAPHICAL SKETCH*

Emmett A. Betts' career as an educator and theorist in the teaching of reading began in the 1920s, a time when both psychology and the hard sciences established themselves as essential factors in education. Betts began his teaching career in 1922 as a director of industrial arts and agriculture in Orient, Iowa. He also served as superintendent of schools in Northboro, Iowa. In 1925, he became a school psychologist and principal in Shaker Heights, Ohio. There he brought his psychological training to bear on the development of the Betts Ready to Read Tests, which were designed to determine the preparedness of young children to read.

In 1934 Betts was named director of teacher education at State Teacher's College in Oswego, New York, and pursued research in reading instruction as the head of the college's reading clinic. It was at this time that he conducted his first weeklong national institute on reading, which he continued to provide at various locations until 1963. Appointed a research professor and director of the reading clinic at Pennsylvania State University in 1937, he continued his study of visual readiness for reading and developed a series of courses leading to advanced degrees in reading education. Betts always placed heavy emphasis on laboratory demonstrations and a clinical approach to reading instruction while stressing the psychology of the reading process.

In 1945 Betts became professor of psychology at Temple University and founded the reading clinic in the university's department of psychology. During his tenure at Temple, he was instrumental in helping to organize the International Council for the Improvement of Reading Instruction (which later became the International Reading Association). At the same time, he was beginning his inquiry into word perception and the psychological processing of graphic symbols. In 1954 Betts opened the Betts Reading Clinic in Haverford, Pennsylvania, and directed its operations until 1961, when he became professor of education at the University of Miami, Coral Gables, Florida. At this university Betts worked to enhance the doctoral program in reading and in psychology and to establish a research center for a multidisciplinary approach to the study of reading processes.

Besides being one of the most prolific of contributors to educational journals throughout his career, having published in excess of 1,300 papers and articles, and an editor for many years of *Highlights for Children* and *My Weekly Reader*, Betts is also known for such books as *Prevention and Correction of Reading Difficulties* (1936), *Visual Problems of School Children* (1941), and *Foundations of Reading Instruction* (1957). Betts placed primary emphasis on the visual and physiological aspects of reading and did much to bring scientific and psychological methodology to the teaching of reading. As director of various university reading clinics, he worked to expand laboratory and research facilities to bring greater professionalism to schools and education. He is probably best known for his insistence on the need for gearing reading instruction to the needs and the reading levels of particular students and in overcoming what he called the "vicious tendency in the schools to do little about individual differences" (Betts, Everett, and Rodewald, 1936, p. 89).

*Special thanks are extended to Jeffrey Willis for his assistance in preparing this biographical sketch.

The idea of informal reading inventories came to Betts in the 1920s when he was working on his master's thesis on students' solving of long division problems. Betts used many of the ideas brought forth from his research into the development of the informal reading inventory (IRI), and by 1935 this method was already being used in his reading clinic.

Prior to his death in 1987, Betts commented on the main purpose of the IRI, which he believed to be a means to train teachers to be perceptive about student reading behavior (Johns, 1991). This is noteworthy because, according to Betts, 40 percent of students are expected to read books that are too difficult. His devising of informal reading inventories to help determine reading levels, especially an appropriate instructional level for each student, has perhaps been his most important contribution to reading education.

Development of the Basic Reading Inventory

BASIS FOR THE GRADED WORD LISTS

The word lists were selected from two sources: *EDL Core Vocabularies in Reading, Mathematics, Science, and Social Studies* (Taylor et al., 1979) and *Basic Skills Word List: Grades 1–12* (IOX, 1980). These two word lists and their development are described here.

▶ The first source was the Reading Core Vocabulary portion from the *EDL Core Vocabularies*. Fourteen graded word lists, from pre-primer through grade thirteen, are included. The lists are composed of words "introduced in the more widely used basal reading series and/or found on frequency lists" (p. 1). Originally published in 1949, the EDL Reading Core Vocabulary was revised in 1951, 1955, 1969, and 1979. In the 1979 revision, several procedures were used to select words for the 14 graded word lists.

The lists through grade three were developed by determining the level at which words were introduced in nine different basal reader series. A word was included if it was introduced at the same level in at least three of the nine basal series.

In selecting words for the fourth-, fifth-, and sixth-grade lists, words occurring in at least three basals on the same level or below were judged to be suitable for that level. In addition, words occurring in two readers at the same level were checked against the Rinsland (1945) list and the Thorndike and Lorge (1944) list. The Rinsland list was used to confirm student knowledge of the word at that particular level. The Thorndike-Lorge list was used to determine whether a word occurred with sufficient frequency to justify its inclusion.

For grades seven and eight, words used in basal readers in grades four through six that did not occur with sufficient frequency to be included in earlier lists were checked against the Rinsland and Thorndike-Lorge lists for frequency. If warranted, these words were included in the Reading Core Vocabulary. The remaining words for grades seven and eight were derived, for the most part, from frequency on these same two word lists.

Nine of the Reading Core Vocabulary graded lists were used for the graded word lists on the Basic Reading Inventory: pre-primer through grade eight. The pre-primer list contained 68 different words; the eighth-grade word list contained over 700 different words.

▶ The second source, *Basic Skills Word List: Grades 1–12* (IOX, 1980), contains lists of words for grades one through twelve.* The graded word lists contain key words that students need to master in each grade and were designed as a resource for reading teachers and for the development of tests.

To select the words for the Basic Skills Word List, three criteria were used:

1. the frequency of words in basal readers

2. the frequency of words in general reading materials

3. students' demonstrated familiarity with particular words.

The initial source of words, the *EDL Core Vocabularies*, was described earlier. All the words on the *EDL Core Vocabularies* were checked for their familiarity to children by using *The Living Word Vocabulary—The Words We Know* (Dale & O'Rourke, 1976). To determine students' knowledge of commonly encountered words, Dale and O'Rourke administered three-option, multiple-choice test items to students. Students were given a word and asked to choose the correct definition for it. *The Living Word Vocabulary* provides a "familiarity percentage" for each word listed. This index reflects

---

*The description of the word list has been adapted with permission of the publisher.

the percentage of students who answered that word's multiple-choice test item correctly. In order to assign a word to a particular grade level, Dale and O'Rourke aimed for each tested word to have a familiarity percentage for a given grade level that was within the range of 67 percent to 84 percent. Therefore, if a word was tested at the sixth grade and only 66 percent of the students at that grade were familiar with it, then the word was retested at the eighth grade. Conversely, if a word tested at the eighth grade received a familiarity score higher than 84 percent, it was retested at the sixth grade. The familiarity percentage supplied with each word in *The Living Word Vocabulary* reflects the percentage of correct student responses at the grade level to which the word was ultimately assigned.

The authors of *The Living Word Vocabulary* did not begin testing words until the fourth grade; after that, they tested words only at alternate grades. Thus, familiarity percentages appear only for grades four, six, eight, and so on. Therefore, EDL words through grade four were checked for their familiarity to students according to the fourth-grade Dale-O'Rourke familiarity percentages. Fifth-grade EDL words were checked against both fourth- and sixth-grade familiarity percentages. Words in all subsequent grade lists were checked for familiarity ratings at either the grade level at which they appeared in EDL or at a lower grade.

Words that were not familiar to at least 65 percent of students at a given grade on the basis of the Dale-O'Rourke study were moved to a higher grade level in the Basic Skills Word List. The exact familiarity percentages necessary for an EDL word to be retained at the same grade level on the Basic Skills Word List varied slightly from grade to grade. These percentages were adjusted in order to meet the requirements of a predetermined word load for each grade. (This word load factor will be described subsequently.) Table 8.1 contains the minimum familiarity percentages used through the tenth grade.

The rationale for employing a stringent familiarity criterion was straightforward: even if a word is found in several reading series at a given grade level, it may still be unfamiliar to many students and therefore should not be assigned to that grade level. The effect of this student familiarity screen was to move some words from each of the graded EDL word lists to higher grade levels.

For instructional purposes, it is desirable to allocate words to grade levels on a proportional basis. It would make little sense to assign 200 words to one grade level and 2,000 words to another. One of the best guides to the determination of an appropriate word load per grade level is the average number of words introduced per grade level by publishers of reading textbook series. These commercially published textbooks, many of them revised more than once, provide an experience-based estimate of how many new words can be reasonably introduced at each grade level. In the process of researching the background for their core vocabularies, developers of the EDL word lists calculated the average number of words introduced at grades one through six for nine different textbook series. These textbook-derived word loads were the following:

Grade	1	2	3	4	5	6
Word Load	341	440	708	787	1,063	1,077

The word loads for the Basic Skills Word List at grades one through four were designed to coincide as closely as possible with these textbook-derived word loads. The word loads for the Basic Skills Word List at grades one through four are as follows:

Grade	1	2	3	4
Word Load	341	439	708	785

Table 8.1　Minimum Familiarity Percentages: Pre-Primer Through Twelfth Grade

Grade at Which Word Appeared in EDL	Grade to Which Word Was Assigned in Dale-O'Rourke Study*	Minimum Familiarity Percentage Required for Retention in Same Grade Level as EDL on Basic Skills Word List
Pre-Primer and First	Fourth	80%
Second	Fourth	83%
Third	Fourth	76%
Fourth	Fourth	65%
	Sixth	75%
Fifth	Fourth	65%
	Sixth	75%
Sixth	Fourth	65%
	Sixth	84%
Seventh	Fourth and Sixth	65%
Eighth	Fourth and Sixth	65%
	Eighth	80%
Ninth	Sixth and Eighth	65%
Tenth	Sixth and Eighth	65%
	Tenth	75%
Eleventh	Eighth and Tenth	65%
Twelfth	Eighth and Tenth	65%
	Twelfth	75%

*This study did not include words from the pre-primer through third grade.

In grades five through twelve, students' familiarity with words, as reflected by the Dale-O'Rourke study, became a major determinant of grade level word load for the Basic Skills Word List. Students at these grade levels displayed insufficient familiarity with many potentially includable words, thus reducing the word loads—particularly in grades nine through twelve. The word loads for the Basic Skills Word List in grades five through twelve are as follows:

Grade	5	6	7	8	9	10	11	12
Word Load	971	846	884	874	325	407	393	345

The final step in the selection of words for the Basic Skills Word List was based on a massive study by Carroll, Davies, and Richman (1971). This study analyzed 5,000,000 running words of text. These 5,000,000 words were taken from approximately 10,000 samples of 500 words excerpted from textbooks in 17 different curriculum areas in grades three through nine, plus magazines, books, newspapers, and poetry. The result of the study is a list of 87,000 words, accompanied by the frequency with which each of those words appears in print. Unfortunately, this enormous set of words is listed alphabetically rather than in the order of each word's frequency of usage. Hence, one cannot readily determine the most frequently encountered words. Sakiey and Fry (1979), however, have drawn on the 87,000 words to provide a list of the 3,000 most frequently occurring words ranked according to their frequency of usage in print. These words, in order of decreasing frequency of appearance, were added at each grade level of the Basic Skills Word List if they were not already listed. This ensured that words appearing very frequently in general reading materials were not overlooked because they did not have a high enough familiarity percentage.

SELECTION OF THE GRADED WORD LISTS

Fourteen graded word lists accompany Forms A, B, and C of the Basic Reading Inventory. Each list contains 20 words. The lists range in difficulty from pre-primer through the twelfth-grade level.

The general rule for selecting words for inclusion in the graded word lists for grades one through eight was that the word had to be assigned to the same grade on both the Reading Core Vocabulary and the Basic Skills Word List. Words from an earlier edition of the Basic Reading Inventory were used when they met the criterion. The remaining words to complete each list were selected at random within each grade level designation of the published word lists. Once a word was selected, it was checked for inclusion on the other list. If the word appeared on both lists it was included; otherwise, another word was randomly selected and the checking procedure was repeated until 20 words were secured for each word list.

A slight modification was used to select words for the pre-primer and primer graded word lists because neither published word list used the term *primer*. Words selected at the pre-primer and primer levels had to appear on either the pre-primer or first-grade list of the Reading Core Vocabulary *and* on the first-grade level of the Basic Skills Word List. After the words were selected, they were assigned to one of the three forms of the Basic Reading Inventory.

Fieldtesting the pre-primer through grade eight word lists involved 309 students in grades one through eight from the United States and Canada. The vast majority of the students were identified as average readers by their teachers. As the students pronounced the words on the graded word lists, examiners marked the words that were mispronounced. The major change resulting from fieldtesting the graded word lists was moving some of the words from one form to another form. Equivalence of forms was accomplished by the initial selection of words from large scale vocabulary studies and fieldtesting to help ensure that the more difficult words were evenly distributed among the three forms of word lists at each grade level. In addition, the words on each list are arranged from easier to more difficult based on fieldtest results.

A three-phase process was used to develop the graded word lists for grades nine through twelve. First, all words common to both the Reading Core Vocabulary and the Basic Skills Word List for grades nine through twelve were listed. A total of 66 words was randomly selected from each graded list.

Next, the 66 words were randomly divided into three forms and fieldtested with 334 students in ninth grade, 544 students in tenth grade, 301 students in eleventh grade, and 207 students in twelfth grade. The students attended schools in Washington, South Carolina, and Illinois. The students marked each word they could read with a plus sign (+) and used a minus sign (–) for each word they thought they couldn't read. Students were instructed not to mark a word if they were in doubt. All words marked with a minus sign were tallied across forms for each grade level. Then, using the student responses, three new forms were devised. Words were ranked and distributed among the three forms. Six words were deleted from each grade level because students' responses indicated that the words were either very easy or very difficult.

Finally, the revised forms were given to 330 students in grade nine, 276 students in grade ten, 231 students in grade eleven, and 263 students in grade twelve who crossed out any words they were unable to pronounce. The students attended high schools in New York or Illinois. Research assistants then asked 65 students in grade nine, 61 students in grade ten, 75 students in grade eleven, and 157 students in grade twelve to respond individually to the words that were not crossed out. Based on an analysis of student responses, several words were rearranged so the words at the end of each list were the most difficult.

STRENGTHENING THE GRADED PASSAGES AND COMPREHENSION QUESTIONS

The passages in the Basic Reading Inventory were evaluated by one or more readability formulas. The same passages, with the exception of the new form (B), were used in the previous edition. A readability computer program (Hardy and Jerman, 1985; Micro Power & Light Co., 1995) was used to help assess the appropriateness of passages for assigned grade levels.

To revise the graded passages for the eighth edition of the Basic Reading Inventory, data and input were gathered from a wide variety of sources. First, users of the inventory in the United States and Canada were invited to share reactions based on use of the inventory in their particular educational setting. Second, undergraduate and graduate students at Northern Illinois University who used the inventory in classroom and clinical situations critiqued the passages and questions. Third, letters and e-mails sent to the author that contained suggestions for improving the passages and questions were given careful consideration. Fourth, relevant articles and research studies pertaining to informal reading inventories, and the Basic Reading Inventory in particular, were critically reviewed. Fifth, several reading professionals who used the Basic Reading Inventory provided input for revision of the manual, word lists, passages, questions, and related features. Finally, the author's use of the Basic Reading Inventory with students at a wide variety of grade levels provided still more input.

DEVELOPMENT OF FORMS LN AND LE

In late 1987, the development of two new forms for grades three through eight was begun. In 1990, the development of longer passages for grades nine and ten was undertaken. The longer passages for grades eleven and twelve used in the seventh edition were adapted from an inventory developed by Johns (1990b). The forms were developed to (1) provide additional passages for initial assessment, (2) provide for assessment of the student's ability to read longer narrative and expository passages, (3) allow post-testing with different passages, and (4) give teachers greater flexibility in using the Basic Reading Inventory.

Written or adapted drafts of the initial passages were based on topics that would be interesting and appropriate for average readers in grades three through eight. The initial passages were analyzed by a readability program (Hardy and Jerman, 1985) to help assess their appropriateness for a particular grade level. Comprehension questions were prepared for each passage. Numerous changes in the passages and questions were made based on an initial limited fieldtesting and critical reviews of the passages and questions by 26 teachers and graduate students enrolled in an advanced reading course.

Fieldtesting for grade three through grade eight passages began in 1989 and continued into 1990. Classroom teachers, reading teachers, and research assistants participated in the fieldtests. The fieldtests took place in Illinois, Missouri, and Michigan. Average, above-average, and below-average students in grades three through eight participated in the fieldtesting. A total of 537 students read Form LN and LE passages.

In 1990, two new grade levels (nine and ten) were developed for forms LN and LE using the general procedures just described. Both comprehension questions and passages underwent numerous revisions based on limited fieldtesting and the critical analysis by several reading professionals.

Actual fieldtesting was carried out early in 1993 with the cooperation of a local high school and two research assistants. Table 8.2 contains the number of students who read each passage in grades three through ten. As mentioned earlier, the passages for grades eleven and twelve were adapted from Johns (1990b).

Table 8.2   Number of Students Involved in Fieldtesting Forms LN and LE

Passage	Form	
	LN	LE
3	51	47
4	47	50
5	48	55
6	41	48
7	36	40
8	34	40
9	48	50
10	51	49
Totals	356	379

During the process of fieldtesting, a number of changes were suggested. These changes were incorporated into subsequent fieldtests. The nature of the changes involved some changes in the vocabulary used in the passages and, in one instance, modification in the organization of the passage. Other changes included revisions in the wording of comprehension questions. Students initially responded to more than 10 questions, and their answers were very useful in the selection of the final comprehension questions.

The Basic Reading Inventory has existed, in one form or another, for over three decades. It has been used with thousands of students in a wide variety of educational settings. Informal and published reports (Bristow, Pikulski, and Pelosi, 1983; Cunningham, Hall, and Defee, 1991; Helgren-Lempesis and Mangrum, 1986; Pikulski and Shanahan, 1982) have provided evidence of its usefulness to a diverse group of professionals who are interested in the informal assessment of students' reading.

PART TWO

Basic Reading Inventory Forms

FORM A

Oral Reading

Form A is intended for oral reading. When administering the inventory, the student reads from the student copy while the teacher records responses in the performance booklet.

Form A may be used as a pretest.

Performance Booklet
(Teacher Copy)

 Note: This Performance Booklet is on the CD-ROM that accompanies the Basic Reading Inventory.

BASIC READING INVENTORY PERFORMANCE BOOKLET

Jerry L. Johns, Ph.D.

Student _____   Grade _____ Sex   M   F   Date of Test _____

School _____   Examiner _____   Date of Birth _____

Address _____   Current Book/Level _____   Age _____

SUMMARY OF STUDENT'S READING PERFORMANCE

| Grade | Word Recognition | | | | | | Comprehension | | | |
| | Isolation (Word Lists) | | | | Context (Passages) | | Oral Reading Form A Questions | | Silent Reading Form D Questions | |
	Sight	Analysis	Total	Level	Miscues	Level	Missed	Level	Missed	Level
PP										
P										
1										
2										
3										
4										
5										
6										
7										
8										
9										
10										
11										
12										

ESTIMATE OF READING LEVELS

Independent _____   Instructional _____   Frustration _____

LISTENING LEVEL

Grade	Form _____ Questions Missed	Level
PP		
P		
1		
2		
3		
4		
5		
6		
7		
8		

ESTIMATED LEVEL: _____

GENERAL OBSERVATIONS

INFORMAL MISCUE ANALYSIS SUMMARY

| Types of Miscues | Frequency of Occurrence | | | General Impact of Miscues on Meaning | | |
	Seldom	Sometimes	Frequently	No Change	Little Change	Much Change
Substitutions						
Insertions						
Omissions						
Reversals						
Repetitions						

QUALITATIVE ANALYSIS OF BASIC READING INVENTORY INSIGHTS

General Directions: Note the degree to which the student shows behavior or evidence in the following areas. Space is provided for additional items.

	Seldom Weak Poor				Always Strong Excellent

COMPREHENSION

Seeks to construct meaning

Makes predictions

Activates background knowledge

Possesses appropriate concepts
   and vocabulary

Monitors reading

Varies reading rate as needed

Understands topic and major ideas

Remembers facts or details

Makes and supports appropriate
   inferences

Evaluates ideas from passages

Understands vocabulary used

Provides appropriate definitions
   of words

Engagement with passages

WORD IDENTIFICATION

Possesses numerous strategies

Uses strategies flexibly

Uses graphophonic information

Uses semantic information

Uses syntactic information

Knows basic sight words
   automatically

Possesses sight vocabulary

ORAL AND SILENT READING

Reads fluently

Reads with expression

Attends to punctuation

Keeps place while reading

Appropriate rate

Reads silently without vocalization

ATTITUDE AND CONFIDENCE

Enjoys reading

Demonstrates willingness to risk

Possesses positive self-concept

Chooses to read

Regards himself/herself as a reader

Exhibits persistence

Form A • Graded Word Lists • Performance Booklet • Student Copy is on page 124.

List A-A (Pre-Primer)	Sight	Analysis	List A (Primer)	Sight	Analysis
1. me*			1. show		
2. get*			2. play*		
3. home			3. be*		
4. not*			4. eat*		
5. he*			5. did*		
6. tree			6. brown		
7. girl			7. is*		
8. take*			8. boat		
9. book			9. call*		
10. milk			10. run*		
11. dog			11. what*		
12. all*			12. him*		
13. apple			13. wagon		
14. like*			14. over*		
15. go*			15. but*		
16. farm			16. on*		
17. went*			17. had*		
18. friend			18. this*		
19. about*			19. around*		
20. some*			20. sleep		

*denotes basic sight word from Revised Dolch List   *denotes basic sight word from Revised Dolch List

Number Correct _____ _____   Number Correct _____ _____

Total _____   Total _____

Scoring Guide for Graded Word Lists

Independent	Instructional	Frustration
20 19	18 17 16 15 14	13 or less

List A 7141 (Grade 1)	Sight	Analysis	List A 8224 (Grade 2)	Sight	Analysis
1. here*	_____	_____	1. ten*	_____	_____
2. down*	_____	_____	2. poor	_____	_____
3. then*	_____	_____	3. city	_____	_____
4. how*	_____	_____	4. teacher	_____	_____
5. saw*	_____	_____	5. turn*	_____	_____
6. pocket	_____	_____	6. fight	_____	_____
7. hello	_____	_____	7. because*	_____	_____
8. aunt	_____	_____	8. soft	_____	_____
9. never*	_____	_____	9. open*	_____	_____
10. puppy	_____	_____	10. winter	_____	_____
11. could*	_____	_____	11. joke	_____	_____
12. after*	_____	_____	12. different	_____	_____
13. hill	_____	_____	13. say*	_____	_____
14. men	_____	_____	14. quiet	_____	_____
15. gone*	_____	_____	15. sister	_____	_____
16. ran*	_____	_____	16. above	_____	_____
17. gave*	_____	_____	17. seed	_____	_____
18. or*	_____	_____	18. thought*	_____	_____
19. way	_____	_____	19. such	_____	_____
20. coat	_____	_____	20. chase	_____	_____

*denotes basic sight word from Revised Dolch List   *denotes basic sight word from Revised Dolch List

Number Correct _____ _____   Number Correct _____ _____

Total _____   Total _____

Scoring Guide for Graded Word Lists

Independent	Instructional	Frustration
20 19	18 17 16 15 14	13 or less

List A 3183 (Grade 3)	Sight	Analysis	List A 5414 (Grade 4)	Sight	Analysis
1. trail			1. stove		
2. stream			2. government		
3. beach			3. program		
4. snake			4. grape		
5. lift			5. favorite		
6. cabin			6. blizzard		
7. bless			7. noon		
8. rooster			8. greet		
9. journey			9. sport		
10. treasure			10. rumble		
11. hero			11. tropical		
12. beyond			12. language		
13. moan			13. expert		
14. glitter			14. nervous		
15. impossible			15. starve		
16. shot			16. voyage		
17. island			17. silence		
18. manage			18. scamper		
19. receive			19. prairie		
20. automobile			20. moccasin		
Number Correct			Number Correct		
Total			Total		

Scoring Guide for Graded Word Lists

Independent	Instructional	Frustration
20 19	18 17 16 15 14	13 or less

List A 8595 (Grade 5)	Sight	Analysis	List A 6867 (Grade 6)	Sight	Analysis
1. lizard			1. bleed		
2. double			2. accomplishment		
3. scarlet			3. whimper		
4. helmet			4. marriage		
5. dusk			5. frisky		
6. bandit			6. seam		
7. loyal			7. backward		
8. choice			8. location		
9. furnish			9. nightmare		
10. century			10. gently		
11. kindergarten			11. employ		
12. entrance			12. broadcast		
13. dentist			13. kennel		
14. celebration			14. pulp		
15. blister			15. satisfaction		
16. symbol			16. cushion		
17. drowsy			17. graduate		
18. attach			18. harmonica		
19. rehearse			19. definite		
20. terrace			20. yacht		
Number Correct			Number Correct		
Total			Total		

Scoring Guide for Graded Word Lists

Independent	Instructional	Frustration
20 19	18 17 16 15 14	13 or less

List A 3717 (Grade 7)	Sight	Analysis		List A 8183 (Grade 8)	Sight	Analysis
1. dwell				1. quote		
2. slogan				2. ventilate		
3. knapsack				3. surgeon		
4. administration				4. analyze		
5. gangster				5. masterpiece		
6. flatter				6. pollute		
7. incredible				7. extraordinary		
8. algebra				8. camouflage		
9. bachelor				9. ruthless		
10. vocabulary				10. perpendicular		
11. longitude				11. juvenile		
12. saliva				12. vacancy		
13. peninsula				13. dictator		
14. monarch				14. negative		
15. feminine				15. honorary		
16. quench				16. custody		
17. competition				17. maneuver		
18. disinfectant				18. faculty		
19. ambitious				19. pneumonia		
20. orchid				20. embassy		
Number Correct				Number Correct		
Total				Total		

Scoring Guide for Graded Word Lists

Independent	Instructional	Frustration
20 19	18 17 16 15 14	13 or less

List A 4959 (Grade 9)	Sight	Analysis	List A 1047 (Grade 10)	Sight	Analysis
1. random			1. displacement		
2. disrupt			2. heritage		
3. autobiography			3. exponent		
4. expire			4. variable		
5. contestant			5. preliminary		
6. strategy			6. embryo		
7. crave			7. sterile		
8. detach			8. gratify		
9. apprehend			9. maternity		
10. idolize			10. incorporate		
11. consecutive			11. gore		
12. vacate			12. illogical		
13. debatable			13. radiate		
14. combustion			14. forum		
15. famished			15. predominant		
16. detract			16. fictitious		
17. crochet			17. cuticle		
18. insomnia			18. panorama		
19. siesta			19. inquisitive		
20. bayonet			20. artisan		
Number Correct			Number Correct		
Total			Total		

Scoring Guide for Graded Word Lists

Independent	Instructional	Frustration
20 19	18 17 16 15 14	13 or less

List A 1187 (Grade 11)	Sight	Analysis	List A 1296 (Grade 12)	Sight	Analysis
1. insensible	_____	_____	1. denote	_____	_____
2. beneficiary	_____	_____	2. hallowed	_____	_____
3. spectrum	_____	_____	3. transcend	_____	_____
4. idealism	_____	_____	4. affiliate	_____	_____
5. epic	_____	_____	5. obtuse	_____	_____
6. composite	_____	_____	6. recipient	_____	_____
7. informant	_____	_____	7. consensus	_____	_____
8. ransack	_____	_____	8. concentric	_____	_____
9. interlude	_____	_____	9. postulate	_____	_____
10. suede	_____	_____	10. impel	_____	_____
11. renaissance	_____	_____	11. collateral	_____	_____
12. dissociate	_____	_____	12. repugnant	_____	_____
13. commemorate	_____	_____	13. promissory	_____	_____
14. populous	_____	_____	14. meticulous	_____	_____
15. fraudulent	_____	_____	15. flippant	_____	_____
16. inquisition	_____	_____	16. sardonic	_____	_____
17. dexterity	_____	_____	17. indemnity	_____	_____
18. lenient	_____	_____	18. adamant	_____	_____
19. dilapidated	_____	_____	19. effigy	_____	_____
20. disheveled	_____	_____	20. tithe	_____	_____
Number Correct	_____	_____	Number Correct	_____	_____
Total		_____	Total		_____

Scoring Guide for Graded Word Lists

Independent	Instructional	Frustration
20 19	18 17 16 15 14	13 or less

Student Copy is on page 130.

A-A (Pre-Primer) Activity Background: Look at the picture and read the title to yourself. Then tell me what you think will happen.

Background: Low |———+———| High

Walk in the Fall

	MISCUES						
	Substitution	Insertion	Omission	Reversal	Repetition	Self-Correction of Unacceptable Miscue	Meaning Change (Significant Miscue)
It was fall. Pat went for a walk. She							
took her dog Sam. They liked to walk.							
They walked for a long time. They saw							
trees. Some were red. Some were green.							
They were pretty. Pat and Sam saw birds							
too. Sam did not run after them. He was							
nice.							
TOTAL							

Word Recognition Scoring Guide		
Total Miscues	Level	Significant Miscues
0	Independent	0
1–2	Ind./Inst.	1
3	Instructional	2
4	Inst./Frust.	3
5 +	Frustration	4

Total Miscues ☐   Significant Miscues ☐

WPM
)3000

A-A (Pre-Primer)
Comprehension Questions

F 1. _____ What time of the year or season
           was it?
           (fall)

F 2. _____ What did Pat do?
           (went for a walk; took her dog for
           a walk)

E 3. _____ Why do you think Pat took her
           dog on the walk?
           (any logical response; for
           company; she liked him)

I 4. _____ Why do you think Sam didn't run
           after the birds?
           (any logical response)

V 5. _____ What does "pretty" mean?
           (nice; any logical response)

Retelling Notes

☐ Questions
   Missed

Comprehension Scoring Guide	
Questions Missed	Level
0	Independent
1	Ind./Inst.
1½	Instructional
2	Inst./Frust.
2½ +	Frustration

Retelling
Excellent
Satisfactory
Unsatisfactory

Student Copy is on page 131.

A (Primer) Activating Background: Read the title to yourself; then tell me what you think will happen.

Background: Low ├──────┼──────┤ High

The First Snow

	MISCUES						
	Substitution	Insertion	Omission	Reversal	Repetition	Self-Correction of Unacceptable Miscue	Meaning Change (Significant Miscue)
Jack woke up Saturday morning. He							
looked out of the window. The ground was							
white. The trees were white.							
"Oh boy," said Jack, "snow."							
"What did you say?" asked Tom,							
opening his eyes.							
"It snowed last night. Get up and							
see," said Jack.							
Both boys ran to the window.							
"Look at that!" said Tom. "Come on.							
Let's get dressed."							
Jack and Tom ran into the kitchen.							
"Mom!" they said. "It snowed last							
night."							
"Yes," said Mom. "Dad went out to							
get your sleds. First we will eat breakfast.							
Then we can have some fun. The first snow							
is the best!"							
TOTAL							

Word Recognition Scoring Guide		
Total Miscues	Level	Significant Miscues
0–1	Independent	0–1
2–4	Ind./Inst.	2
5	Instructional	3
6–9	Inst./Frust.	4
10 +	Frustration	5 +

Total Miscues ☐   Significant Miscues ☐

WPM
)6000

A (Primer)
Comprehension Questions

T   1. _____ What is this story about?
(boys getting ready to play in the snow)

F   2. _____ What day of the week does the story take place?
(Saturday)

F   3. _____ What happened when the boys woke up?
(they ran to the window; they saw snow)

F   4. _____ Who woke up first?
(Jack)

F   5. _____ What was Dad doing?
(getting the sleds)

F   6. _____ How did the trees look in this story?
(white)

F   7. _____ What did the boys have to do before playing in the snow?
(eat breakfast)

I   8. _____ Why do you think the boys were so excited?
(any logical response; they will play in the snow)

E   9. _____ What things do you think the family will do outside?
(any logical response; make snowballs; go sledding, and so on)

V   10. _____ What is "ground"?
(dirt; something you walk on; any logical response)

Retelling Notes

☐ Questions Missed

Comprehension Scoring Guide	
Questions Missed	Level
0–1	Independent
1½–2	Ind./Inst.
2½	Instructional
3–4½	Inst./Frust.
5 +	Frustration

Retelling
Excellent
Satisfactory
Unsatisfactory

Student Copy is on page 132.

A 7141 (Grade 1) Activating Background: Read the title to yourself; then tell me what you think will happen.

Background: Low ├────────┼────────┤ High

Spotty Swims

	Substitution	Insertion	Omission	Reversal	Repetition	Self-Correction of Unacceptable Miscue	Meaning Change (Significant Miscue)
	MISCUES						
One day Spotty went for a walk.							
The sun was warm. Spotty walked to							
the pond. There he saw a frog. The							
frog was on a log. Spotty wanted to							
play. Spotty began to bark. The frog							
jumped into the water.							
Then Spotty jumped into the water.							
But poor Spotty did not know what to							
do. The water was very deep. The water							
went way over his head. Spotty moved							
his legs. Soon his head came out of the							
water. He kept on moving. He came to							
the other side of the pond. That is how							
Spotty learned to swim.							
TOTAL							

Word Recognition Scoring Guide		
Total Miscues	Level	Significant Miscues
0–1	Independent	0–1
2–4	Ind./Inst.	2
5	Instructional	3
6–9	Inst./Frust.	4
10 +	Frustration	5 +

Total Miscues ☐   Significant Miscues ☐

WPM
)6000

155

A 7141 (Grade 1)
Comprehension Questions

<table>
<tr><td>T</td><td>1. _____</td><td>What is this story about?
(Spotty and a frog; how Spotty
learned to swim)</td></tr>
<tr><td>F</td><td>2. _____</td><td>Where did Spotty go?
(to the pond; for a walk)</td></tr>
<tr><td>F</td><td>3. _____</td><td>What did Spotty see?
(a frog)</td></tr>
<tr><td>F</td><td>4. _____</td><td>What happened when Spotty saw
the frog?
(he barked; he wanted to play; he
jumped into the water [any 1])</td></tr>
<tr><td>F</td><td>5. _____</td><td>What did the frog do when Spotty
barked?
(the frog jumped into the water)</td></tr>
<tr><td>F</td><td>6. _____</td><td>What did Spotty do when the
water went over his head?
(moved his legs; he didn't know
what to do)</td></tr>
<tr><td>F</td><td>7. _____</td><td>What did Spotty learn in this
story?
(how to swim)</td></tr>
<tr><td>I</td><td>8. _____</td><td>Who was Spotty?
(any logical response; a dog)</td></tr>
<tr><td>E</td><td>9. _____</td><td>Why do you think Spotty wanted
to play with the frog?
(any logical response; he was
lonesome)</td></tr>
<tr><td>V</td><td>10. _____</td><td>What is a "pond"?
(like a lake, and so on)</td></tr>
</table>

Retelling Notes

☐ Questions
Missed

Comprehension Scoring Guide	
Questions Missed	Level
0–1	Independent
1½–2	Ind./Inst.
2½	Instructional
3–4½	Inst./Frust.
5 +	Frustration

Retelling
Excellent
Satisfactory
Unsatisfactory

156

Student Copy is on page 133.

A 8224 (Grade 2) Activating Background: Read the title to yourself; then tell me what you think will happen.

Background: Low ├──────┼──────┤ High

Bill at Camp

	MISCUES						
	Substitution	Insertion	Omission	Reversal	Repetition	Self-Correction of Unacceptable Miscue	Meaning Change (Significant Miscue)
It was the first time Bill went to							
camp. He was very happy to be there. Soon							
he went for a walk in the woods to look for							
many kinds of leaves. He found leaves							
from some maple and oak trees. As Bill							
walked in the woods, he saw some animal							
tracks. At that moment, a mouse ran into							
a small hole by a tree. Bill wondered if the							
tracks were made by the mouse. He looked							
around for other animals. He did not see							
any. The last thing Bill saw was an old							
bird nest in a pine tree.							
TOTAL							

Word Recognition Scoring Guide		
Total Miscues	Level	Significant Miscues
0–1	Independent	0–1
2–4	Ind./Inst.	2
5	Instructional	3
6–9	Inst./Frust.	4
10 +	Frustration	5 +

Total Miscues ☐   Significant Miscues ☐

_____ WPM

)6000

Retelling Notes

T   1. _____   What is this story about?
(a boy at camp; Bill's walk in the woods)

F   2. _____   Did Bill enjoy going to camp?
How do you know?
(yes, the story said he was happy there)

F   3. _____   Why did Bill go walking in the woods?
(to look for leaves)

F   4. _____   What kinds of leaves did Bill find in the woods?
(maple and oak leaves)

F   5. _____   What else did Bill see besides the mouse?
(a bird nest; animal tracks)

F   6. _____   Where did the mouse go?
(into a small hole by or in a tree)

F   7. _____   What other animals did Bill see?
(none; he didn't see any)

I   8. _____   Do you think Bill went on this walk by himself? What makes you think so?
(any logical response)

E   9. _____   What other animals might Bill see if he goes for another walk?
(any logical response)

V   10. _____   What are "tracks"?
(footprints made in the dirt; something made by animals when they walk or run)

☐ Questions Missed

Comprehension Scoring Guide	
Questions Missed	Level
0–1	Independent
1½–2	Ind./Inst.
2½	Instructional
3–4½	Inst./Frust.
5 +	Frustration

Retelling
Excellent
Satisfactory
Unsatisfactory

Student Copy is on page 134.

A 3183 (Grade 3) Activating Background: Read the title to yourself; then tell me what you think will happen.

Background: Low ├─────┼─────┤ High

The Hungry Bear

	MISCUES						
	Substitution	Insertion	Omission	Reversal	Repetition	Self-Correction of Unacceptable Miscue	Meaning Change (Significant Miscue)
The busy bees had been making honey all							
day. That night it was cool and damp. I had							
slept well until I heard a loud noise near my							
window. It sounded as if someone were							
trying to break into my cabin. As I moved							
from my cot, I could see something black							
standing near the window. In fright I knocked							
on the window. Very slowly and quietly the							
great shadow moved back and went away.							
The next day we found huge bear tracks.							
The bear had come for the honey the bees							
were making in the attic of the cabin.							
TOTAL							

Word Recognition Scoring Guide		
Total Miscues	Level	Significant Miscues
0–1	Independent	0–1
2–4	Ind./Inst.	2
5	Instructional	3
6–9	Inst./Frust.	4
10 +	Frustration	5 +

Total Miscues ☐

Significant Miscues ☐

_____ WPM
)6000

Comprehension Questions

T   1. _____   What is this story about?
                (a bear trying to get honey; being
                scared)

F   2. _____   What had the bees been doing?
                (making honey)

F   3. _____   Where were the bees making
                honey?
                (in the attic of the cabin)

F   4. _____   Who or what woke the person in
                this story?
                (a bear; a loud noise at the
                window)

F   5. _____   What was near the window?
                (blackness; a shadow; a bear)

F   6. _____   What was found the next day?
                (bear tracks)

F   7. _____   What did the bear want?
                (honey)

I   8. _____   Why do you think the bear
                walked away?
                (any logical response; it heard the
                knock)

E   9. _____   What might you do to keep the
                bear away?
                (any logical response; remove the
                honey)

V 10. _____   What is an "attic"?
                (a place way upstairs in your
                house where you put junk and
                stuff)

Retelling Notes

☐ Questions
   Missed

Comprehension Scoring Guide	
Questions Missed	Level
0–1	Independent
1½–2	Ind./Inst.
2½	Instructional
3–4½	Inst./Frust.
5 +	Frustration

Retelling
Excellent
Satisfactory
Unsatisfactory

Student Copy is on page 135.

A 5414 (Grade 4) Activating Background: Read the title to yourself; then tell me what you think will happen.

Background: Low ├────┼────┤ High

Fire and Animals

	MISCUES						
	Substitution	Insertion	Omission	Reversal	Repetition	Self-Correction of Unacceptable Miscue	Meaning Change (Significant Miscue)
The summer was a dry one, unusual							
for this area. Trees and bushes in the forest							
wilted and died. One afternoon a storm							
came to the forest. Thunder was heard and							
lightning was seen. Then it began to							
rain. A spark touched the leaves and a							
fire began. The fire spread quickly. The							
animals warned each other as they hurried							
to escape the flames. As the fire came							
closer, trees fell to the ground. Their							
branches were yellow, orange, and red.							
The smoke was so thick that the animals							
could hardly breathe. Many couldn't							
escape the danger of the flames.							
TOTAL							

Word Recognition Scoring Guide		
Total Miscues	Level	Significant Miscues
0–1	Independent	0–1
2–4	Ind./Inst.	2
5	Instructional	3
6–9	Inst./Frust.	4
10 +	Frustration	5 +

Total Miscues ☐   Significant Miscues ☐

_____ WPM

)6000

A 5414 (Grade 4)
Comprehension Questions

<table>
<tr><td>T</td><td>1. _____</td><td>What is this story about?
(a forest fire)</td></tr>
<tr><td>F</td><td>2. _____</td><td>What did the animals try to do?
(escape; warn each other)</td></tr>
<tr><td>F</td><td>3. _____</td><td>What was unusual about this summer?
(it had been a dry one)</td></tr>
<tr><td>F</td><td>4. _____</td><td>What was heard and seen in the woods before the fire began?
(thunder and lightning)</td></tr>
<tr><td>F</td><td>5. _____</td><td>What started the fire?
(a spark; lightning)</td></tr>
<tr><td>F</td><td>6. _____</td><td>What colors were the trees in this story?
(yellow, orange, and red [any 2])</td></tr>
<tr><td>F</td><td>7. _____</td><td>Why was it difficult for the animals to breathe?
(smoke filled the air; the fire)</td></tr>
<tr><td>I</td><td>8. _____</td><td>Why do you think the fire spread quickly?
(any logical response; it had been a dry summer)</td></tr>
<tr><td>E</td><td>9. _____</td><td>What problems do you think the animals that survived the fire might have?
(any logical response)</td></tr>
<tr><td>V</td><td>10. _____</td><td>What does "escape" mean?
(get away; any logical response)</td></tr>
</table>

Retelling Notes

☐ Questions Missed

Comprehension Scoring Guide	
Questions Missed	Level
0–1	Independent
1½–2	Ind./Inst.
2½	Instructional
3–4½	Inst./Frust.
5 +	Frustration

Retelling
Excellent
Satisfactory
Unsatisfactory

Student Copy is on page 136.

A 8595 (Grade 5) Activating Background: Read the title to yourself; then tell me what you think will happen.

Background: Low ├────┼────┤ High

The Mystery

	MISCUES						
	Substitution	Insertion	Omission	Reversal	Repetition	Self-Correction of Unacceptable Miscue	Meaning Change (Significant Miscue)
Everyone turned to stare as a black							
hooded figure whizzed by on a skateboard.							
It was a mystery because no one knew							
who the talented person was. Ken saw							
the skateboarder slide down the library							
railing and disappear into the alley. Nita							
followed the person from school and							
watched as a curb was jumped and a							
three hundred sixty degree turn was							
completed with ease. One day Ken							
noticed a skateboard and a black hooded							
jacket next to Rose's house. He also saw							
a library book called *Skate Board Tips*							
in her desk at school. Ken had solved							
the mystery.							
TOTAL							

Word Recognition Scoring Guide		
Total Miscues	Level	Significant Miscues
0–1	Independent	0–1
2–4	Ind./Inst.	2
5	Instructional	3
6–9	Inst./Frust.	4
10 +	Frustration	5 +

Total Miscues ☐   Significant Miscues ☐

WPM
$)6000$

A 8595 (Grade 5)
Comprehension Questions

T 1. _____ What is this story about?
(a skateboarder; finding out who
the skateboarder was)

F 2. _____ What did the mystery person look
like?
(wore a black hood; rode a
skateboard)

F 3. _____ Why was this person such a
mystery?
(no one knew who it was)

F 4. _____ Who saw the skateboarder?
(everyone; Ken and Nita)

F 5. _____ What kind of stunts did the
mystery person do?
(slide down a railing; three
hundred sixty degree turn; jump
a curb [any 1])

F 6. _____ Who solved the mystery?
(Ken)

F 7. _____ What items did Ken see that
helped him solve the mystery?
(hooded jacket, skateboard, book
[any 2])

I 8. _____ Who was the mystery person?
(Rose)

E 9. _____ If you were Ken, how might you
have solved the mystery differently?
(any logical response)

V 10. _____ What does "talented" mean?
(good at something; gifted)

	Retelling Notes

☐ Questions Missed

Comprehension Scoring Guide	
Questions Missed	Level
0–1	Independent
1½–2	Ind./Inst.
2½	Instructional
3–4½	Inst./Frust.
5 +	Frustration

Retelling
Excellent
Satisfactory
Unsatisfactory

Student Copy is on page 137.

A 6867 (Grade 6) Activating Background: Read the title to yourself; then tell me what you think will happen.

Background: Low |———|———| High

Keep Your Distance

	MISCUES						
	Substitution	Insertion	Omission	Reversal	Repetition	Self-Correction of Unacceptable Miscue	Meaning Change (Significant Miscue)
Elwood was considered a tough							
guy at Anderson School. Everybody							
called him Sky. They didn't dare							
call him by his full name because							
that riled him. He was colossal in							
size. From far away Elwood looked							
like Mr. Wilson, a teacher, but the							
moment you saw Elwood's shoes							
and faded, torn jeans, you knew it							
could only be Elwood. He felt							
inferior because of his clothing, so							
he tried to make up for it by							
shocking people with his rude							
behavior and toughness. Elwood							
didn't have many friends, except for							
Bob who lived in the same old							
apartment building.							
TOTAL							

Word Recognition Scoring Guide		
Total Miscues	Level	Significant Miscues
0–1	Independent	0–1
2–4	Ind./Inst.	2
5	Instructional	3
6–9	Inst./Frust.	4
10 +	Frustration	5 +

Total Miscues ☐   Significant Miscues ☐

WPM

)6000

A 6867 (Grade 6)
Comprehension Questions

T   1. _____   What is this story about?
(a boy named Elwood)

F   2. _____   What was Elwood considered?
(a tough guy)

F   3. _____   What school did he attend?
(Anderson School)

F   4. _____   What did Elwood look like?
(a teacher; colossal in size; big;
tough)

F   5. _____   What kind of clothes did Elwood
wear?
(faded, torn jeans; old clothes)

F   6. _____   What did everybody call him?
(Sky)

F   7. _____   How did Elwood shock people?
(rude behavior; toughness)

I   8. _____   Why do you think Bob was
Elwood's friend?
(any logical response; he lived in
the same apartment building)

E   9. _____   Would you be Elwood's friend if
you went to Anderson School?
Why?
(any logical response)

V 10. _____   What does "riled" mean?
(irritated; made angry)

Retelling Notes

☐ Questions
Missed

Comprehension Scoring Guide	
Questions Missed	Level
0–1	Independent
1½–2	Ind./Inst.
2½	Instructional
3–4½	Inst./Frust.
5 +	Frustration

Retelling
Excellent
Satisfactory
Unsatisfactory

Student Copy is on page 138.

A 3717 (Grade 7) Activating Background: Read the title to yourself; then tell me what you think will happen.

Background: Low ├────┼────┤ High

Guerilla Soldiers

	MISCUES						
	Substitution	Insertion	Omission	Reversal	Repetition	Self-Correction of Unacceptable Miscue	Meaning Change (Significant Miscue)
The foreheads of the people glistened							
with sweat as they struggled forward under							
the hot sun of the tropics. These people							
were guerillas who sincerely felt that							
their leader was the salvation of their							
country. Their goal was to reach a							
distant army fort where they hoped to fire							
a rocket into the storeroom of the							
fort. This would cause the gunpowder to							
erupt like a tinderbox. A huge person							
bellowed an order from the leader as they							
trudged across the uninhabited land. The							
guerillas hoped their attack would							
scare army soldiers and impress more							
local people to join them.							
TOTAL							

Word Recognition Scoring Guide		
Total Miscues	Level	Significant Miscues
0–1	Independent	0–1
2–4	Ind./Inst.	2
5	Instructional	3
6–9	Inst./Frust.	4
10 +	Frustration	5 +

Total Miscues [ ]   Significant Miscues [ ]

_____ WPM
)6000

A 3717 (Grade 7)
Comprehension Questions

T   1. _____   What is this story about?
(a guerilla raid on an army fort; life among guerilla fighters; fighting between guerillas and army soldiers)

F   2. _____   What was the weather like?
(hot; tropical; hot and sunny [any 1])

F   3. _____   How did the guerillas feel about their leader?
(they felt the leader was the salvation of their country; they liked him)

F   4. _____   What kind of land were they traveling in?
(uninhabited; tropics)

F   5. _____   What was the guerillas' goal?
(to destroy the gunpowder of the army fort)

F   6. _____   What would be used to destroy the storeroom?
(a rocket)

F   7. _____   What did they hope their attack would accomplish?
(scare army soldiers; impress local people to join them)

I   8. _____   In what country do you think this story took place? Why?
(any logical response that suggests a tropical climate)

E   9. _____   What dangers do you think might be involved for the guerillas in their attack?
(any logical response)

V   10. _____   What does "glistened" mean?
(to shine; to sparkle)

[ ] Questions Missed

Comprehension Scoring Guide	
Questions Missed	Level
0–1	Independent
1½–2	Ind./Inst.
2½	Instructional
3–4½	Inst./Frust.
5 +	Frustration

Retelling
Excellent
Satisfactory
Unsatisfactory

Retelling Notes

Student Copy is on page 139.

A 8183 (Grade 8) Activating Background: Read the title to yourself; then tell me what you think will happen.

Background: Low ⊢——————⊣ High

A Scientist's Search

	MISCUES						
	Substitution	Insertion	Omission	Reversal	Repetition	Self-Correction of Unacceptable Miscue	Meaning Change (Significant Miscue)
Chris, a scientist, worked hard at							
the lab bench. Chris had been given a							
very stimulating suggestion in a letter							
from an unknown person. The key to							
success was in the radium reaction that							
would activate the needed medicine.							
From that point, it was simply a matter							
of reducing different compounds to find							
the right one. Ultimately, it would be							
found, and then Chris would have a							
monopoly on the medicine that could							
make people immortal. Only Chris would							
know the correct amount in each tablet.							
The disappearance of death and disease							
would make Chris the most powerful							
person alive.							
TOTAL							

Word Recognition Scoring Guide		
Total Miscues	Level	Significant Miscues
0–1	Independent	0–1
2–4	Ind./Inst.	2
5	Instructional	3
6–9	Inst./Frust.	4
10 +	Frustration	5 +

Total Miscues ☐   Significant Miscues ☐

$\frac{}{6000}$ WPM

T   1. _____   What is this story about?
(a scientist is searching for a
medicine to make people
immortal)

F   2. _____   Where did the scientist get the
idea for the formula?
(in a letter from an unknown
person)

F   3. _____   What was the key to the
experiment?
(the radium reaction)

F   4. _____   What would the radium reaction
do?
(activate the medicine)

F   5. _____   What would the medicine do?
(make people immortal)

F   6. _____   Why would Chris be powerful?
(only he or she would know the
right amount in each tablet)

F   7. _____   What would disappear because of
the medicine?
(death and disease)

I   8. _____   How do you think people would
react to this discovery? Why?
(any logical response)

E   9. _____   Do you think Chris might be
placed in a dangerous position?
Why?
(any logical response)

V   10. _____   What does "immortal" mean?
(to live forever; not to die)

☐	Questions Missed

Retelling Notes

Comprehension Scoring Guide	
Questions Missed	Level
0–1	Independent
1½–2	Ind./Inst.
2½	Instructional
3–4½	Inst./Frust.
5 +	Frustration

Retelling
Excellent
Satisfactory
Unsatisfactory

FORM B

Oral Reading

Form B is intended for oral reading. When administering the inventory, the student reads from the student copy while the teacher records responses in the performance booklet.

Form B may be used as a posttest.

Form B
Graded Word Lists
(Student Copy)

List B-B	List B	List B 7141	List B 8224
1. we	1. they	1. little	1. feel
2. and	2. she	2. next	2. drink
3. house	3. will	3. reads	3. wave
4. the	4. of	4. my	4. gray
5. duck	5. blue	5. make	5. start
6. one	6. it	6. old	6. horn
7. street	7. are	7. mother	7. across
8. happy	8. his	8. bed	8. warm
9. lost	9. now	9. grow	9. bad
10. first	10. dress	10. laugh	10. even
11. do	11. if	11. near	11. feed
12. at	12. from	12. before	12. always
13. very	13. morning	13. lamb	13. round
14. find	14. father	14. ride	14. country
15. out	15. ask	15. store	15. enough
16. party	16. back	16. high	16. able
17. goat	17. green	17. began	17. should
18. wish	18. time	18. made	18. bottom
19. know	19. who	19. cry	19. crawl
20. sing	20. cookie	20. her	20. machine

List B 3183	**List B 5414**	**List B 8595**	**List B 6867**
1. star	1. bike	1. science	1. painful
2. net	2. castle	2. blush	2. raspberry
3. doctor	3. jungle	3. marvelous	3. medical
4. spoon	4. bullet	4. index	4. label
5. trap	5. factory	5. panther	5. household
6. valley	6. stripe	6. grace	6. foreman
7. shirt	7. problem	7. boss	7. catalog
8. meet	8. target	8. emergency	8. solar
9. chuckle	9. capture	9. blond	9. unexpected
10. gaze	10. sleeve	10. nugget	10. beggar
11. rib	11. pump	11. terrific	11. thermometer
12. discover	12. sausage	12. effort	12. portable
13. hundred	13. electric	13. observe	13. distrust
14. reason	14. business	14. mammoth	14. dandelion
15. conductor	15. instant	15. transportation	15. charity
16. coast	16. balance	16. liberty	16. graduation
17. escape	17. surround	17. balcony	17. species
18. thirty	18. invention	18. scar	18. variety
19. prepare	19. accident	19. confidence	19. contribute
20. nation	20. rifle	20. admiral	20. jagged

List B 3717	List B 8183	List B 4959	List B 1047
1. focus	1. skyscraper	1. disapprove	1. immature
2. turnpike	2. reaction	2. data	2. reorganize
3. harmony	3. horsepower	3. texture	3. evaluate
4. uranium	4. justify	4. disqualify	4. visualize
5. merchandise	5. garlic	5. compress	5. grim
6. irregular	6. omit	6. slur	6. patronize
7. humidity	7. divorce	7. gruesome	7. rupture
8. enlarge	8. survival	8. deceased	8. chronic
9. expel	9. flounder	9. transaction	9. exploit
10. remainder	10. comedian	10. misconduct	10. obituary
11. industrious	11. nomination	11. sarcasm	11. saturate
12. pamphlet	12. barbarian	12. momentary	12. induce
13. geologist	13. molecule	13. ingenious	13. recuperate
14. rayon	14. recruit	14. mechanism	14. pictorial
15. novel	15. imperfect	15. audible	15. phenomenal
16. exception	16. upholster	16. embezzle	16. portal
17. meteorite	17. authentic	17. robust	17. centennial
18. dormitory	18. variation	18. luminous	18. silhouette
19. mahogany	19. mortgage	19. heathen	19. boisterous
20. chauffeur	20. brigade	20. ecstasy	20. impertinent

List B 1187

1. discredit
2. habitat
3. profane
4. intern
5. intimidate
6. inseparable
7. binder
8. bilingual
9. jurisdiction
10. stilt
11. metropolis
12. preposterous
13. pollinate
14. patronage
15. reminiscent
16. secede
17. knoll
18. promenade
19. catechism
20. cavalcade

List B 1296

1. invalidate
2. metabolism
3. metamorphosis
4. advert
5. impotent
6. predatory
7. protocol
8. prodigy
9. derivative
10. zealous
11. debase
12. pretentious
13. regurgitate
14. herbivorous
15. maritime
16. aesthetic
17. blasphemy
18. extemporaneous
19. agrarian
20. colloquial

Form B
Graded Passages
(Student Copy)

Birds

I can look for birds. I look up in a tree. I see a big bird. It is brown. I see a baby bird. It is little. It is brown too.

The big bird can fly. The baby bird can not fly. It is little. I like to see birds.

The Box

Ben went to see his friend Nan. He had a blue box. Nan saw the box. She said, "What is in the blue box?"

"I can not tell you," said Ben. Nan asked, "Is it a ball?"

"No, it is not a ball," said Ben. "Is it a car?" asked Nan.

"No, it is not a car," said Ben. "I know, it is an apple," said Nan.

Ben looked in the box. There were two apples. One apple was green. One apple was red. He gave the red apple to Nan. Nan liked the apple. Ben was a good friend.

Up a Tree

Jeff likes to play with his cat Boots. One day a dog walked by. Boots ran up a big tree.

Jeff said, "Come down Boots." The cat did not come down. Jeff did not know what to do. He called his mom.

His mom said, "Here Boots. Come here." The cat did not come.

Then Jeff went home. He came back with a bag. He put the bag down. He took out some milk. He walked to the tree with the milk. He said, "Here Boots. Come get some milk." Boots came down and had some milk. Jeff was happy.

The Strange Object

It was a breezy day in March. I was walking home thinking about my day at school. In the sky I saw a strange object. At first, I thought it was an airplane.

I climbed up a hill to get a better view. As I got closer, I saw it diving through the air in a strange way. It was brown and had wings. Maybc it was a bird.

Then the wind stopped, and the object came crashing toward me. I ran to get away. Then I heard a friendly laugh. My friend Max came to get his hawk kite.

The Noise

Fred was lying in bed trying to go to sleep. He had a big test the next day. He kept hearing a soft whistle, so he went into the kitchen and checked the tea kettle. The stove was off. Then he stood outside his parents' room to listen for snoring. Everyone was sleeping quietly. He returned to his room and noticed some wind. It wasn't the fan. It was off. He heard a dog bark outside and saw that his window was open a little. He closed it and the noise stopped. He climbed into bed and fell asleep quickly.

The Detectives

It had been raining. Kate and her brother Michael were looking for something entertaining to do. Aunt Sue came into the living room and announced, "I can't find my purse."

The children looked for the missing purse in various parts of the house. Michael looked in the den where his aunt wrote checks, but no purse. Kate searched the bedroom carefully because the purse was last seen there. It wasn't there, but Kate recalled that her aunt had been shopping earlier that day. She ran outside. Just as she arrived, Michael was opening the trunk and Kate saw the purse.

The Strange Gift

Cheryl sat quietly, staring at the tiny black and green slip of paper in her hand. She was remembering how moved she had been when Marlene first gave it to her. Cheryl knew her best friend was poor. Marlene couldn't afford even a small gift for Cheryl's twelfth birthday. She was surprised when Marlene pulled her aside and timidly handed her a pretty, gift-wrapped box with a bow on it. Inside there was a ticket. Cheryl was touched by her friend's gesture. She never imagined that the slip of paper would be the winning ticket for their classroom drawing.

Stranger at Willowbrook

Phil entered Willowbrook School for the first time. The five-minute bell rang. As he hurried to math class, an unfamiliar voice asked, "How's it going, Phil?" Startled, Phil responded with a quick wave and continued on to room 203. During lunch, Phil saw the stranger in the cafeteria, but he pretended not to notice. During the last period, Mr. Nichols was taking attendance when Phil heard a familiar name called. "Zack Wilson," thought Phil. "I remember when we used to build block houses in kindergarten." Phil turned to find Zack and realized that the stranger was a forgotten friend.

Black Out

The soft buzz of the computer relaxed
Anthony as he worked on his yearly report
for his anxious employer. He typed the
final sentence, sighed in relief, and saved
the computer file. The office lights
flickered, the computer screen went black,
and New York City was silent. Sirens
sounded in the area. Flashlights guided the
impatient crowd to sunlight twenty floors
down. An hour later, the police chief
announced through his loud speaker, "All
is clear." The workers filed into the
elevators like clockwork, returning to their
projects. One observer commented, "All
in a day's work in New York City."

Sunset

Alix was enjoying the sunset from Daisy Hill. The magnificent display of bright orange, red, and yellow appeared to be a sweet, ripe mango slowly sinking into the earth. Alix was again surrounded by the beautiful colors of falling leaves as she reluctantly headed home for dinner. Turning east toward the house, she witnessed a horrible sight; her greenhouse was enveloped in flames! She quickly dashed down the hill and across a field of drying corn stalks. A few yards before she arrived, she realized the fire was only a reflection of the sunset on the glass of the greenhouse.

B 8183

Performance Booklet
(Teacher Copy)

 Note: This Performance Booklet is on the CD-ROM that accompanies the Basic Reading Inventory.

BASIC READING INVENTORY PERFORMANCE BOOKLET
Jerry L. Johns, Ph.D.

Student _____ Grade _____ Sex   M   F   Date of Test _____

School _____ Examiner _____ Date of Birth _____

Address _____ Current Book/Level _____ Age _____

SUMMARY OF STUDENT'S READING PERFORMANCE

| Grade | Word Recognition | | | | | | Comprehension | | | |
| | Isolation (Word Lists) | | | | Context (Passages) | | Oral Reading Form B Questions | | Silent Reading Form D Questions | |
	Sight	Analysis	Total	Level	Miscues	Level	Missed	Level	Missed	Level
PP										
P										
1										
2										
3										
4										
5										
6										
7										
8										
9										
10										
11										
12										

ESTIMATE OF READING LEVELS

Independent _____   Instructional _____   Frustration _____

LISTENING LEVEL

Form _____

Grade	Questions Missed	Level
PP		
P		
1		
2		
3		
4		
5		
6		
7		
8		

ESTIMATED LEVEL: ____

GENERAL OBSERVATIONS

INFORMAL MISCUE ANALYSIS SUMMARY

| Types of Miscues | Frequency of Occurrence | | | General Impact of Miscues on Meaning | | |
	Seldom	Sometimes	Frequently	No Change	Little Change	Much Change
Substitutions						
Insertions						
Omissions						
Reversals						
Repetitions						

QUALITATIVE ANALYSIS OF BASIC READING INVENTORY INSIGHTS

General Directions: Note the degree to which the student shows behavior or evidence in the following areas. Space is provided for additional items.

	Seldom Weak Poor				Always Strong Excellent

COMPREHENSION

Seeks to construct meaning
Makes predictions
Activates background knowledge
Possesses appropriate concepts
   and vocabulary
Monitors reading
Varies reading rate as needed
Understands topic and major ideas
Remembers facts or details
Makes and supports appropriate
   inferences
Evaluates ideas from passages
Understands vocabulary used
Provides appropriate definitions
   of words
Engagement with passages

WORD IDENTIFICATION

Possesses numerous strategies
Uses strategies flexibly
Uses graphophonic information
Uses semantic information
Uses syntactic information
Knows basic sight words
   automatically
Possesses sight vocabulary

ORAL AND SILENT READING

Reads fluently
Reads with expression
Attends to punctuation
Keeps place while reading
Appropriate rate
Reads silently without vocalization

ATTITUDE AND CONFIDENCE

Enjoys reading
Demonstrates willingness to risk
Possesses positive self-concept
Chooses to read
Regards himself/herself as a reader
Exhibits persistence

List B-B (Pre-Primer)	Sight	Analysis	List B (Primer)	Sight	Analysis
1. we*	_____	_____	1. they*	_____	_____
2. and*	_____	_____	2. she*	_____	_____
3. house	_____	_____	3. will*	_____	_____
4. the*	_____	_____	4. of*	_____	_____
5. duck	_____	_____	5. blue*	_____	_____
6. one*	_____	_____	6. it*	_____	_____
7. street	_____	_____	7. are*	_____	_____
8. happy	_____	_____	8. his*	_____	_____
9. lost	_____	_____	9. now*	_____	_____
10. first*	_____	_____	10. dress	_____	_____
11. do*	_____	_____	11. if*	_____	_____
12. at*	_____	_____	12. from*	_____	_____
13. very*	_____	_____	13. morning	_____	_____
14. find*	_____	_____	14. father	_____	_____
15. out*	_____	_____	15. ask*	_____	_____
16. party	_____	_____	16. back	_____	_____
17. goat	_____	_____	17. green*	_____	_____
18. wish	_____	_____	18. time	_____	_____
19. know*	_____	_____	19. who*	_____	_____
20. sing	_____	_____	20. cookie	_____	_____

*denotes basic sight word from Revised Dolch List   *denotes basic sight word from Revised Dolch List

Number Correct _____ _____   Number Correct _____ _____

Total _____   Total _____

Scoring Guide for Graded Word Lists

Independent	Instructional	Frustration
20 19	18 17 16 15 14	13 or less

Form B • Graded Word Lists • Performance Booklet • Student Copy is on page 174.

List B 7141 (Grade 1)	Sight	Analysis	List B 8224 (Grade 2)	Sight	Analysis
1. little*	_____	_____	1. feel	_____	_____
2. next*	_____	_____	2. drink	_____	_____
3. reads	_____	_____	3. wave	_____	_____
4. my*	_____	_____	4. gray	_____	_____
5. make*	_____	_____	5. start*	_____	_____
6. old*	_____	_____	6. horn	_____	_____
7. mother	_____	_____	7. across*	_____	_____
8. bed	_____	_____	8. warm*	_____	_____
9. grow*	_____	_____	9. bad	_____	_____
10. laugh	_____	_____	10. even*	_____	_____
11. near*	_____	_____	11. feed	_____	_____
12. before*	_____	_____	12. always*	_____	_____
13. lamb	_____	_____	13. round*	_____	_____
14. ride	_____	_____	14. country	_____	_____
15. store	_____	_____	15. enough*	_____	_____
16. high*	_____	_____	16. able	_____	_____
17. began*	_____	_____	17. should*	_____	_____
18. made*	_____	_____	18. bottom	_____	_____
19. cry	_____	_____	19. crawl	_____	_____
20. her*	_____	_____	20. machine	_____	_____

*denotes basic sight word from Revised Dolch List

*denotes basic sight word from Revised Dolch List

Number Correct _____ _____   Number Correct _____ _____

Total _____   Total _____

Scoring Guide for Graded Word Lists

Independent	Instructional	Frustration
20 19	18 17 16 15 14	13 or less

Form B • Graded Word Lists • Performance Booklet • Student Copy is on page 175.

List B 3183 (Grade 3)	Sight	Analysis	List B 5414 (Grade 4)	Sight	Analysis
1. star			1. bike		
2. net			2. castle		
3. doctor			3. jungle		
4. spoon			4. bullet		
5. trap			5. factory		
6. valley			6. stripe		
7. shirt			7. problem		
8. meet			8. target		
9. chuckle			9. capture		
10. gaze			10. sleeve		
11. rib			11. pump		
12. discover			12. sausage		
13. hundred			13. electric		
14. reason			14. business		
15. conductor			15. instant		
16. coast			16. balance		
17. escape			17. surround		
18. thirty			18. invention		
19. prepare			19. accident		
20. nation			20. rifle		
Number Correct			Number Correct		
Total			Total		

Scoring Guide for Graded Word Lists

Independent	Instructional	Frustration
20 19	18 17 16 15 14	13 or less

List B 8595 (Grade 5)	Sight	Analysis	List B 6867 (Grade 6)	Sight	Analysis
1. science	_____	_____	1. painful	_____	_____
2. blush	_____	_____	2. raspberry	_____	_____
3. marvelous	_____	_____	3. medical	_____	_____
4. index	_____	_____	4. label	_____	_____
5. panther	_____	_____	5. household	_____	_____
6. grace	_____	_____	6. foreman	_____	_____
7. boss	_____	_____	7. catalog	_____	_____
8. emergency	_____	_____	8. solar	_____	_____
9. blond	_____	_____	9. unexpected	_____	_____
10. nugget	_____	_____	10. beggar	_____	_____
11. terrific	_____	_____	11. thermometer	_____	_____
12. effort	_____	_____	12. portable	_____	_____
13. observe	_____	_____	13. distrust	_____	_____
14. mammoth	_____	_____	14. dandelion	_____	_____
15. transportation	_____	_____	15. charity	_____	_____
16. liberty	_____	_____	16. graduation	_____	_____
17. balcony	_____	_____	17. species	_____	_____
18. scar	_____	_____	18. variety	_____	_____
19. confidence	_____	_____	19. contribute	_____	_____
20. admiral	_____	_____	20. jagged	_____	_____
Number Correct	_____	_____	Number Correct	_____	_____
Total		_____	Total		_____

Scoring Guide for Graded Word Lists

Independent	Instructional	Frustration
20 19	18 17 16 15 14	13 or less

List B 3717 (Grade 7)	Sight	Analysis	List B 8183 (Grade 8)	Sight	Analysis
1. focus	_____	_____	1. skyscraper	_____	_____
2. turnpike	_____	_____	2. reaction	_____	_____
3. harmony	_____	_____	3. horsepower	_____	_____
4. uranium	_____	_____	4. justify	_____	_____
5. merchandise	_____	_____	5. garlic	_____	_____
6. irregular	_____	_____	6. omit	_____	_____
7. humidity	_____	_____	7. divorce	_____	_____
8. enlarge	_____	_____	8. survival	_____	_____
9. expel	_____	_____	9. flounder	_____	_____
10. remainder	_____	_____	10. comedian	_____	_____
11. industrious	_____	_____	11. nomination	_____	_____
12. pamphlet	_____	_____	12. barbarian	_____	_____
13. geologist	_____	_____	13. molecule	_____	_____
14. rayon	_____	_____	14. recruit	_____	_____
15. novel	_____	_____	15. imperfect	_____	_____
16. exception	_____	_____	16. upholster	_____	_____
17. meteorite	_____	_____	17. authentic	_____	_____
18. dormitory	_____	_____	18. variation	_____	_____
19. mahogany	_____	_____	19. mortgage	_____	_____
20. chauffeur	_____	_____	20. brigade	_____	_____
Number Correct	_____	_____	Number Correct	_____	_____
Total	_____		Total	_____	

Scoring Guide for Graded Word Lists

Independent	Instructional	Frustration
20 19	18 17 16 15 14	13 or less

List B 4959 (Grade 9)	Sight	Analysis	List B 1047 (Grade 10)	Sight	Analysis
1. disapprove			1. immature		
2. data			2. reorganize		
3. texture			3. evaluate		
4. disqualify			4. visualize		
5. compress			5. grim		
6. slur			6. patronize		
7. gruesome			7. rupture		
8. deceased			8. chronic		
9. transaction			9. exploit		
10. misconduct			10. obituary		
11. sarcasm			11. saturate		
12. momentary			12. induce		
13. ingenious			13. recuperate		
14. mechanism			14. pictorial		
15. audible			15. phenomenal		
16. embezzle			16. portal		
17. robust			17. centennial		
18. luminous			18. silhouette		
19. heathen			19. boisterous		
20. ecstasy			20. impertinent		
Number Correct			Number Correct		
Total			Total		

Scoring Guide for Graded Word Lists

Independent	Instructional	Frustration
20 19	18 17 16 15 14	13 or less

List B 1187 (Grade 11)	Sight	Analysis	List B 1296 (Grade 12)	Sight	Analysis
1. discredit	_____	_____	1. invalidate	_____	_____
2. habitat	_____	_____	2. metabolism	_____	_____
3. profane	_____	_____	3. metamorphosis	_____	_____
4. intern	_____	_____	4. advert	_____	_____
5. intimidate	_____	_____	5. impotent	_____	_____
6. inseparable	_____	_____	6. predatory	_____	_____
7. binder	_____	_____	7. protocol	_____	_____
8. bilingual	_____	_____	8. prodigy	_____	_____
9. jurisdiction	_____	_____	9. derivative	_____	_____
10. stilt	_____	_____	10. zealous	_____	_____
11. metropolis	_____	_____	11. debase	_____	_____
12. preposterous	_____	_____	12. pretentious	_____	_____
13. pollinate	_____	_____	13. regurgitate	_____	_____
14. patronage	_____	_____	14. herbivorous	_____	_____
15. reminiscent	_____	_____	15. maritime	_____	_____
16. secede	_____	_____	16. aesthetic	_____	_____
17. knoll	_____	_____	17. blasphemy	_____	_____
18. promenade	_____	_____	18. extemporaneous	_____	_____
19. catechism	_____	_____	19. agrarian	_____	_____
20. cavalcade	_____	_____	20. colloquial	_____	_____
Number Correct	_____	_____	Number Correct	_____	_____
Total	_____		Total	_____	

Scoring Guide for Graded Word Lists

Independent	Instructional	Frustration
20 19	18 17 16 15 14	13 or less

Student Copy is on page 180.

B-B (Pre-Primer) Activating Background: Look at the picture and read the title to yourself. Then tell me what you think will happen.

Background: Low |———+———| High

Birds

	MISCUES						
	Substitution	Insertion	Omission	Reversal	Repetition	Self-Correction of Unacceptable Miscue	Meaning Change (Significant Miscue)
I can look for birds. I look up in							
a tree. I see a big bird. It is brown.							
I see a baby bird. It is little. It is							
brown too.							
The big bird can fly. The baby							
bird can not fly. It is little. I like to							
see birds.							
TOTAL							

Total Miscues ☐   Significant Miscues ☐

_____ WPM

)3000

B-B (Pre-Primer)
Comprehension Questions

F 1. _____ Where did the person in the story look for the birds?
(in a tree)

F 2. _____ What kind of birds did the person see?
(big bird; baby bird; brown; little [any 2])

E 3. _____ Besides being too little, why do you think the baby bird could not fly?
(any logical response)

I 4. _____ Why do you think the person looked up in a tree to find birds?
(any logical response; birds live there)

V 5. _____ What does "little" mean?
(small; tiny; baby)

```
┌─────────────────────────┐
│     Retelling Notes      │
├─────────────────────────┤
│                         │
│                         │
│                         │
│                         │
│                         │
│                         │
│                         │
│                         │
│                         │
└─────────────────────────┘
```

☐ Questions Missed

Comprehension Scoring Guide	
Questions Missed	Level
0	Independent
1	Ind./Inst.
1½	Instructional
2	Inst./Frust.
2½ +	Frustration

Retelling
Excellent
Satisfactory
Unsatisfactory

Student Copy is on page 181.

B (Primer) Activating Background: Read
the title to yourself; then tell me what you think
will happen.

Background: Low ├────┼────┤ High

The Box

	MISCUES						
	Substitution	Insertion	Omission	Reversal	Repetition	Self-Correction of Unacceptable Miscue	Meaning Change (Significant Miscue)
Ben went to see his friend Nan. He							
had a blue box. Nan saw the box. She							
said, "What is in the blue box?"							
"I can not tell you," said Ben.							
Nan asked, "Is it a ball?"							
"No, it is not a ball," said Ben.							
"Is it a car?" asked Nan.							
"No, it is not a car," said Ben.							
"I know, it is an apple," said Nan.							
Ben looked in the box. There were							
two apples. One apple was green. One							
apple was red. He gave the red apple to							
Nan. Nan liked the apple. Ben was a							
good friend.							
TOTAL							

Word Recognition Scoring Guide		
Total Miscues	Level	Significant Miscues
0–1	Independent	0–1
2–4	Ind./Inst.	2
5	Instructional	3
6–9	Inst./Frust.	4
10 +	Frustration	5 +

Total Miscues ☐   Significant Miscues ☐

_____ WPM
$\overline{)6000}$

B (Pre-Primer)
Comprehension Questions

T 1. _____ What is this story about?
       (Ben's box; Nan guessing about the box)

F 2. _____ Who did Ben see?
       (Nan)

F 3. _____ What did Ben have with him?
       (a box; apples)

F 4. _____ What color was the box?
       (blue)

F 5. _____ What did Nan think was in the box?
       (ball, car, apple [any 2])

F 6. _____ How many apples were in the box?
       (two)

F 7. _____ How did Nan feel about the apple?
       (she liked it)

I 8. _____ What color was the apple that Ben kept?
       (green)

E 9. _____ Would you like Ben as your friend? Why?
       (any logical response)

V 10. _____ What does "good" mean?
       (nice; friendly; kind)

Retelling Notes

☐ Questions Missed

Comprehension Scoring Guide	
Questions Missed	Level
0–1	Independent
1½–2	Ind./Inst.
2½	Instructional
3–4½	Inst./Frust.
5 +	Frustration

Retelling
Excellent
Satisfactory
Unsatisfactory

Student Copy is on page 182.

B 7141 (Grade 1) Activating Background: Read the title to yourself; then tell me what you think will happen.

Background: Low ├────────┼────────┤ High

Up a Tree

	MISCUES						
	Substitution	Insertion	Omission	Reversal	Repetition	Self-Correction of Unacceptable Miscue	Meaning Change (Significant Miscue)
Jeff likes to play with his cat Boots.							
One day a dog walked by. Boots ran up a							
big tree.							
Jeff said, "Come down Boots." The cat							
did not come down. Jeff did not know what							
to do. He called his mom.							
His mom said, "Here Boots. Come							
here." The cat did not come.							
Then Jeff went home. He came back							
with a bag. He put the bag down. He took							
out some milk. He walked to the tree with							
the milk. He said, "Here Boots. Come get							
some milk." Boots came down and had							
some milk. Jeff was happy.							
TOTAL							

Word Recognition Scoring Guide		
Total Miscues	Level	Significant Miscues
0–1	Independent	0–1
2–4	Ind./Inst.	2
5	Instructional	3
6–9	Inst./Frust.	4
10 +	Frustration	5 +

Total Miscues ☐   Significant Miscues ☐

_____ WPM
)6000

B 7141 (Grade 1)
Comprehension Questions

<table>
<tr><td>T</td><td>1. _____</td><td>What is this story about?
(Boots; getting Boots down from a tree; a cat)</td></tr>
<tr><td>F</td><td>2. _____</td><td>Why did Boots run up the tree?
(a dog walked by; the dog scared the cat)</td></tr>
<tr><td>F</td><td>3. _____</td><td>At first, how did Jeff try to get Boots down?
(called the cat; called mom)</td></tr>
<tr><td>F</td><td>4. _____</td><td>Where did Jeff go after mom came?
(home)</td></tr>
<tr><td>F</td><td>5. _____</td><td>What did he bring from home?
(a bag; milk)</td></tr>
<tr><td>F</td><td>6. _____</td><td>How did Jeff finally get Boots down?
(he brought milk and told Boots to get the milk)</td></tr>
<tr><td>F</td><td>7. _____</td><td>How did Jeff feel at the end of the story?
(happy)</td></tr>
<tr><td>I</td><td>8. _____</td><td>Why didn't Boots come down when Jeff and his mom called?
(any logical response; it was scared of the dog; it didn't want to)</td></tr>
<tr><td>E</td><td>9. _____</td><td>How would you feel if your cat ran up a tree?
(any logical response; sad; scared)</td></tr>
<tr><td>V</td><td>10. _____</td><td>What is a "bag?"
(a sack; something to put things in)</td></tr>
</table>

Retelling Notes

☐ Questions Missed

Comprehension Scoring Guide	
Questions Missed	Level
0–1	Independent
1½–2	Ind./Inst.
2½	Instructional
3–4½	Inst./Frust.
5 +	Frustration

Retelling
Excellent
Satisfactory
Unsatisfactory

Student Copy is on page 183.

B 8224 (Grade 2) Activating Background: Read the title to yourself; then tell me what you think will happen.

Background: Low ├───────┼───────┤ High

The Strange Object

	MISCUES						
	Substitution	Insertion	Omission	Reversal	Repetition	Self-Correction of Unacceptable Miscue	Meaning Change (Significant Miscue)
It was a breezy day in March. I was							
walking home thinking about my day at							
school. In the sky I saw a strange object.							
At first, I thought it was an airplane.							
I climbed up a hill to get a better view.							
As I got closer, I saw it diving through the							
air in a strange way. It was brown and had							
wings. Maybe it was a bird.							
Then the wind stopped, and the object							
came crashing toward me. I ran to get away.							
Then I heard a friendly laugh. My friend							
Max came to get his hawk kite.							
TOTAL							

Word Recognition Scoring Guide		
Total Miscues	Level	Significant Miscues
0–1	Independent	0–1
2–4	Ind./Inst.	2
5	Instructional	3
6–9	Inst./Frust.	4
10 +	Frustration	5 +

Total Miscues ☐

Significant Miscues ☐

___ WPM
)6000

B 8224 (Grade 2)
Comprehension Questions

T   1. _____   What is this story about?
(a kite in the sky; a strange object)

F   2. _____   What month was it?
(March)

F   3. _____   What was the person thinking about
before seeing the object?
(the day at school)

F   4. _____   What did the person think the
object was?
(an airplane; a large bird)

F   5. _____   What did the person do to get a
better view?
(climbed a hill)

F   6. _____   How did the object look?
(like a hawk; brown and had wings)

F   7. _____   To whom did the object belong?
(Max)

I   8. _____   Why was the breeze important in
this passage?
(any logical response; it kept the
kite in the air)

E   9. _____   How do you think the person felt
when he saw Max and his kite?
Why?
(any logical response; angry;
happy; relieved)

V   10. _____   What does "strange" mean?
(unusual; different; weird)

[ ]   Questions
Missed

Comprehension Scoring Guide	
Questions Missed	Level
0–1	Independent
1½–2	Ind./Inst.
2½	Instructional
3–4½	Inst./Frust.
5 +	Frustration

Retelling
Excellent
Satisfactory
Unsatisfactory

Student Copy is on page 184.

B 3183 (Grade 3) Activating Background: Read the title to yourself; then tell me what you think will happen.

Background: Low |———|———| High

The Noise

	MISCUES						
	Substitution	Insertion	Omission	Reversal	Repetition	Self-Correction of Unacceptable Miscue	Meaning Change (Significant Miscue)
Fred was lying in bed trying to go to sleep.							
He had a big test the next day. He kept hearing							
a soft whistle, so he went into the kitchen and							
checked the tea kettle. The stove was off.							
Then he stood outside his parents' room to							
listen for snoring. Everyone was sleeping							
quietly. He returned to his room and noticed							
some wind. It wasn't the fan. It was off. He							
heard a dog bark outside and saw that his							
window was open a little. He closed it and the							
noise stopped. He climbed into bed and fell							
asleep quickly.							
TOTAL							

Word Recognition Scoring Guide		
Total Miscues	Level	Significant Miscues
0–1	Independent	0–1
2–4	Ind./Inst.	2
5	Instructional	3
6–9	Inst./Frust.	4
10 +	Frustration	5 +

Total Miscues ☐   Significant Miscues ☐

WPM
)6000

T   1. _____   What is this story about?
(a noise that kept Fred awake; Fred looking for a noise)

F   2. _____   What was Fred trying to do at the beginning of the story?
(sleep)

F   3. _____   What did Fred have to do the next day?
(take a test)

F   4. _____   How did the noise sound?
(like a soft whistle)

F   5. _____   Where did Fred look for the noise?
(the tea kettle; his parents' room [either 1])

F   6. _____   What did Fred hear from the window?
(a dog barking)

F   7. _____   How did Fred make the noise go away?
(he closed the window)

I   8. _____   What was probably causing the soft whistle?
(any logical response; the wind)

E   9. _____   How would you feel if you heard a soft whistle when you were trying to sleep? Why?
(any logical response; scared; frustrated; mad)

V   10. _____   What does "listen" mean?
(try to hear)

Retelling Notes

☐ Questions Missed

Comprehension Scoring Guide	
Questions Missed	Level
0–1	Independent
1½–2	Ind./Inst.
2½	Instructional
3–4½	Inst./Frust.
5 +	Frustration

Retelling
Excellent
Satisfactory
Unsatisfactory

Student Copy is on page 185.

B 5414 (Grade 4) Activating Background: Read the title to yourself; then tell me what you think will happen.

Background: Low ├────┼────┤ High

The Detectives

	MISCUES						
	Substitution	Insertion	Omission	Reversal	Repetition	Self-Correction of Unacceptable Miscue	Meaning Change (Significant Miscue)
It had been raining. Kate and her brother							
Michael were looking for something							
entertaining to do. Aunt Sue came into the							
living room and announced, "I can't find my							
purse."							
The children looked for the missing							
purse in various parts of the house. Michael							
looked in the den where his aunt wrote							
checks, but no purse. Kate searched the							
bedroom carefully because the purse was							
last seen there. It wasn't there, but Kate							
recalled that her aunt had been shopping							
earlier that day. She ran outside. Just as she							
arrived, Michael was opening the trunk and							
Kate saw the purse.							
TOTAL							

Word Recognition Scoring Guide		
Total Miscues	Level	Significant Miscues
0–1	Independent	0–1
2–4	Ind./Inst.	2
5	Instructional	3
6–9	Inst./Frust.	4
10 +	Frustration	5 +

Total Miscues ☐   Significant Miscues ☐

_____ WPM
)6000

B 5414 (Grade 4)
Comprehension Questions

T 1. _____ What is this story about?
          (looking for Aunt Sue's purse)

F 2. _____ What were Kate and Michael doing
          at the beginning of the story?
          (thinking of something entertaining
          to do)

F 3. _____ Why were Kate and Michael inside?
          (it had been raining)

F 4. _____ Where did Kate and Michael look
          for the purse?
          (den; bedroom; trunk [any 2])

F 5. _____ Why did Michael go into the den to
          look for the purse?
          (that is where his aunt wrote checks)

F 6. _____ Besides the house, where had Aunt
          Sue been that day?
          (shopping)

F 7. _____ Where was the purse found?
          (in Aunt Sue's trunk)

I 8. _____ Why do you think this story is called
          "The Detectives"?
          (any logical response)

E 9. _____ What qualities made Kate and
          Michael good detectives? Why?
          (any logical response)

V 10. _____ What does "various" mean?
          (several; different; many)

Retelling Notes

☐ Questions Missed

Comprehension Scoring Guide	
Questions Missed	Level
0–1	Independent
1½–2	Ind./Inst.
2½	Instructional
3–4½	Inst./Frust.
5 +	Frustration

Retelling
Excellent
Satisfactory
Unsatisfactory

Student Copy is on page 186.

B 8595 (Grade 5) Activating Background: Read the title to yourself; then tell me what you think will happen.

Background: Low |———+———| High

The Strange Gift

	Substitution	Insertion	Omission	Reversal	Repetition	Self-Correction of Unacceptable Miscue	Meaning Change (Significant Miscue)
	MISCUES						
Cheryl sat quietly, staring at the tiny							
black and green slip of paper in her hand.							
She was remembering how moved she had							
been when Marlene first gave it to her.							
Cheryl knew her best friend was poor.							
Marlene couldn't afford even a small gift for							
Cheryl's twelfth birthday. She was surprised							
when Marlene pulled her aside and timidly							
handed her a pretty, gift-wrapped box with a							
bow on it. Inside there was a ticket. Cheryl							
was touched by her friend's gesture. She							
never imagined that the slip of paper would							
be the winning ticket for their classroom							
drawing.							
TOTAL							

Word Recognition Scoring Guide		
Total Miscues	Level	Significant Miscues
0–1	Independent	0–1
2–4	Ind./Inst.	2
5	Instructional	3
6–9	Inst./Frust.	4
10 +	Frustration	5 +

Total Miscues ☐   Significant Miscues ☐

WPM

)6000

B 8595 (Grade 5)
Comprehension Questions

T   1. _____   What is this story about?
(a birthday gift; a winning ticket)

F   2. _____   Who is Cheryl's best friend?
(Marlene)

F   3. _____   How old is Cheryl?
(eleven or twelve)

F   4. _____   Why did Cheryl receive a gift?
(it was her birthday)

F   5. _____   Why was Cheryl surprised?
(She didn't think Marlene could
afford a gift)

F   6. _____   What was the ticket for?
(a classroom drawing)

F   7. _____   What color was the ticket?
(black and green)

I   8. _____   Why do you think Marlene pulled
her aside to give her the gift?
(any logical response; she was
embarrassed)

E   9. _____   How would you feel if you were
Cheryl?
(any logical response; happy;
surprised)

V   10. _____   What does "timidly" mean?
(shy)

Retelling Notes

▢ Questions
Missed

Comprehension Scoring Guide	
Questions Missed	Level
0–1	Independent
1½–2	Ind./Inst.
2½	Instructional
3–4½	Inst./Frust.
5 +	Frustration

Retelling
Excellent
Satisfactory
Unsatisfactory

Student Copy is on page 187.

B 6867 (Grade 6) Activating Background: Read the title to yourself; then tell me what you think will happen.

Background: Low ├────┼────┤ High

Stranger at Willowbrook

	Substitution	Insertion	Omission	Reversal	Repetition	Self-Correction of Unacceptable Miscue	Meaning Change (Significant Miscue)
	MISCUES						
Phil entered Willowbrook School							
for the first time. The five-minute bell							
rang. As he hurried to math class, an							
unfamiliar voice asked, "How's it							
going, Phil?" Startled, Phil responded							
with a quick wave and continued on to							
room 203. During lunch, Phil saw the							
stranger in the cafeteria, but he							
pretended not to notice. During the last							
period, Mr. Nichols was taking							
attendance when Phil heard a familiar							
name called. "Zack Wilson," thought							
Phil. "I remember when we used to							
build block houses in kindergarten."							
Phil turned to find Zack and realized							
that the stranger was a forgotten friend.							
TOTAL							

Word Recognition Scoring Guide		
Total Miscues	Level	Significant Miscues
0–1	Independent	0–1
2–4	Ind./Inst.	2
5	Instructional	3
6–9	Inst./Frust.	4
10 +	Frustration	5 +

Total Miscues ☐   Significant Miscues ☐

WPM

)6000

B 6867 (Grade 6)
Comprehension Questions

<table>
<tr><td></td><td>Retelling Notes</td></tr>
</table>

*T 1. _____ What is this passage about?
(Phil meets a forgotten friend; Phil figures out who the stranger is)

F 2. _____ What was the name of Phil's school?
(Willowbrook)

F 3. _____ What startled Phil?
(an unfamiliar voice; someone saying "How's it going?")

F 4. _____ Where was Phil going when he first heard the stranger?
(math class; room 203)

F 5. _____ Where else did Phil see the stranger?
(in the cafeteria; in the last period)

F 6. _____ When did Phil recognize the stranger?
(during last hour; during Mr. Nichols' class; during attendance)

F 7. _____ What did Phil and Zack do in kindergarten?
(build block houses)

I 8. _____ Why do you think Phil had trouble remembering Zack?
(any logical response; he hadn't seen him since kindergarten)

E 9. _____ How would you feel if you met a forgotten friend? Why?
(any logical response; happy)

V 10. _____ What does "familiar" mean?
(known; accustomed to; friendly)

[ ] Questions Missed

Comprehension Scoring Guide	
Questions Missed	Level
0–1	Independent
1½–2	Ind./Inst.
2½	Instructional
3–4½	Inst./Frust.
5 +	Frustration

Retelling
Excellent
Satisfactory
Unsatisfactory

216

Student Copy is on page 188.

B 3717 (Grade 7) Activating Background: Read the title to yourself; then tell me what you think will happen.

Background: Low ├────┼────┤ High

	MISCUES						
Black Out	Substitution	Insertion	Omission	Reversal	Repetition	Self-Correction of Unacceptable Miscue	Meaning Change (Significant Miscue)
The soft buzz of the computer relaxed							
Anthony as he worked on his yearly report							
for his anxious employer. He typed the							
final sentence, sighed in relief, and saved							
the computer file. The office lights							
flickered, the computer screen went black,							
and New York City was silent. Sirens							
sounded in the area. Flashlights guided the							
impatient crowd to sunlight twenty floors							
down. An hour later, the police chief							
announced through his loud speaker, "All							
is clear." The workers filed into the							
elevators like clockwork, returning to their							
projects. One observer commented, "All							
in a day's work in New York City."							
TOTAL							

Word Recognition Scoring Guide		
Total Miscues	Level	Significant Miscues
0–1	Independent	0–1
2–4	Ind./Inst.	2
5	Instructional	3
6–9	Inst./Frust.	4
10 +	Frustration	5 +

Total Miscues ☐

Significant Miscues ☐

WPM

)6000

B 3717 (Grade 7)
Comprehension Questions

T   1. _____ What is this passage about?
(the electricity going off in a building; people
leaving a building after the electricity went off)

F   2. _____ What relaxed Anthony?
(the soft buzz of the computer; the computer
noises; having finished his report)

F   3. _____ What was Anthony working on for his employer?
(a yearly report; paper; report)

F   4. _____ Where did the story take place?
(New York City; office building; skyscraper)

F   5. _____ Who announced that it was safe to enter the
building?
(the police chief; police)

F   6. _____ How many floors did the workers have to go
down?
(twenty)

F   7. _____ How long did the workers wait before they heard
the all clear announcement?
(an hour)

I   8. _____ What time of day did the story take place? How
do you know?
(any logical response; morning or afternoon
because sunlight was outside)

E   9. _____ How do you think you would feel if you were in
a large building when the electricity went off?
Why?
(any logical response)

V   10. _____ What is an "observer?"
(someone who watches or notices something)

☐ Questions
Missed

Comprehension Scoring Guide	
Questions Missed	Level
0–1	Independent
1½–2	Ind./Inst.
2½	Instructional
3–4½	Inst./Frust.
5 +	Frustration

Retelling
Excellent
Satisfactory
Unsatisfactory

Student Copy is on page 189.

B 8183 (Grade 8) Activating Background: Read the title to yourself; then tell me what you think will happen.

Background: Low ├────────┼────────┤ High

Sunset

	MISCUES						
	Substitution	Insertion	Omission	Reversal	Repetition	Self-Correction of Unacceptable Miscue	Meaning Change (Significant Miscue)
Alix was enjoying the sunset from							
Daisy Hill. The magnificent display of							
bright orange, red, and yellow appeared to							
be a sweet, ripe mango slowly sinking into							
the earth. Alix was again surrounded by							
the beautiful colors of falling leaves as she							
reluctantly headed home for dinner.							
Turning east toward the house, she							
witnessed a horrible sight; her greenhouse							
was enveloped in flames! She quickly							
dashed down the hill and across a field of							
drying corn stalks. A few yards before she							
arrived, she realized the fire was only a							
reflection of the sunset on the glass of the							
greenhouse.							
TOTAL							

Word Recognition Scoring Guide		
Total Miscues	Level	Significant Miscues
0–1	Independent	0–1
2–4	Ind./Inst.	2
5	Instructional	3
6–9	Inst./Frust.	4
10 +	Frustration	5 +

Total Miscues ☐   Significant Miscues ☐

_____ WPM
)6000

B 8183 (Grade 8)
Comprehension Questions

<table>
<tr><td>T</td><td>1. ____</td><td>What is this passage about?
(an exciting sunset; Alix being fooled by a sunset; a greenhouse that appears to be on fire)</td></tr>
<tr><td>F</td><td>2. ____</td><td>Where was Alix enjoying the sunset?
(Daisy Hill)</td></tr>
<tr><td>F</td><td>3. ____</td><td>What did the sun resemble as it was setting?
(a mango)</td></tr>
<tr><td>F</td><td>4. ____</td><td>Why did Alix first decide to go home?
(to eat dinner)</td></tr>
<tr><td>F</td><td>5. ____</td><td>Which direction did she head to go home?
(east)</td></tr>
<tr><td>F</td><td>6. ____</td><td>How was the greenhouse described when Alix first saw it?
(enveloped in flames)</td></tr>
<tr><td>F</td><td>7. ____</td><td>Why did the greenhouse appear to be on fire?
(the glass reflected the sunset, which is the color of fire)</td></tr>
<tr><td>I</td><td>8. ____</td><td>Why didn't Alix notice the greenhouse sooner?
(any logical response; she was facing west; the sun sets in the west)</td></tr>
<tr><td>E</td><td>9. ____</td><td>How do you think Alix felt when she realized her mistake? Why?
(any logical response; relieved; embarrassed)</td></tr>
<tr><td>V</td><td>10. ____</td><td>What does "reluctantly" mean?
(hesitated; not sure at first; cautiously)</td></tr>
</table>

Retelling Notes

☐ Questions Missed

Comprehension Scoring Guide	
Questions Missed	Level
0–1	Independent
1½–2	Ind./Inst.
2½	Instructional
3–4½	Inst./Frust.
5 +	Frustration

Retelling
Excellent
Satisfactory
Unsatisfactory

FORM C

Optional

*Use Optional **Form C***

- *as a posttest*
- *to determine the student's listening level*
- *for additional oral or silent reading passages*

Form C
Graded Word Lists
(Student Copy)

List C-C	List C	List C 7141	List C 8224
1. see	1. red	1. ball	1. brave
2. you	2. day	2. new	2. top
3. school	3. in	3. fast	3. it's
4. to	4. for	4. has	4. follow
5. can	5. have	5. with	5. gold
6. good	6. walk	6. children	6. front
7. soon	7. boy	7. work	7. family
8. into	8. cake	8. pet	8. knock
9. up	9. your	9. ready	9. count
10. big	10. again	10. much	10. smell
11. man	11. bee	11. came	11. afraid
12. look	12. come	12. parade	12. done
13. away	13. picture	13. hen	13. silver
14. stop	14. said	14. live	14. face
15. that	15. put	15. hear	15. visit
16. yard	16. word	16. far	16. mountain
17. train	17. baby	17. thing	17. track
18. truck	18. car	18. year	18. pile
19. black	19. no	19. hurry	19. been
20. white	20. funny	20. met	20. through

List C 3183	List C 5414	List C 8595	List C 6867
1. pack	1. thunder	1. brag	1. youngster
2. matter	2. friendship	2. college	2. activity
3. hang	3. crickets	3. tend	3. research
4. center	4. yesterday	4. ditch	4. grizzly
5. chew	5. dozen	5. bully	5. tornado
6. rule	6. telescope	6. journal	6. ruffle
7. pound	7. whiskers	7. public	7. judgment
8. danger	8. skunk	8. goblin	8. nylon
9. force	9. amount	9. ransom	9. fable
10. history	10. nature	10. remarkable	10. exact
11. spend	11. level	11. ankle	11. decay
12. wisdom	12. husky	12. social	12. substitute
13. mind	13. sight	13. gym	13. wealthy
14. adventure	14. distance	14. education	14. communicate
15. mental	15. hunger	15. darling	15. assemble
16. harbor	16. figure	16. muscle	16. economics
17. fault	17. medicine	17. pouch	17. biscuit
18. pilot	18. ashamed	18. barley	18. forbid
19. usually	19. saddle	19. petticoat	19. attractive
20. though	20. anxious	20. invitation	20. pliers

List C 3717	List C 8183	List C 4959	List C 1047
1. jazz	1. motive	1. nationality	1. organism
2. puncture	2. function	2. complex	2. tart
3. fantastic	3. transplant	3. bleach	3. ashtray
4. publication	4. impressive	4. comparable	4. consultant
5. derby	5. encircle	5. overwhelm	5. intolerable
6. terminal	6. browse	6. contraction	6. synthetic
7. hemisphere	7. investment	7. equivalent	7. conclusive
8. paralyze	8. fortify	8. conservative	8. diverse
9. cnvironment	9. maximum	9. bewitch	9. premature
10. cantaloupe	10. detain	10. insignificant	10. insufferable
11. blockade	11. leaflet	11. earthy	11. cater
12. ornamental	12. privacy	12. monogram	12. reformatory
13. warrant	13. lubricant	13. redeem	13. demolition
14. bombard	14. oblong	14. amputate	14. disintegrate
15. typhoon	15. liberal	15. disastrous	15. hoax
16. hypnotize	16. identification	16. disband	16. granulate
17. linoleum	17. energetic	17. coronation	17. necessitate
18. nasal	18. carburetor	18. barracks	18. illegitimate
19. tuberculosis	19. antiseptic	19. abolition	19. gaseous
20. lacquer	20. infuriate	20. vestibule	20. revue

Form C • Graded Word Lists • Student Copy

List C 1187

1. nonexistent
2. recession
3. prohibition
4. collaborate
5. philosophy
6. franchise
7. essence
8. flagrant
9. replenish
10. anesthetic
11. monotone
12. instigate
13. cataract
14. sedative
15. memoir
16. dubious
17. premonition
18. libel
19. maladjustment
20. claimant

List C 1296

1. fusion
2. modulate
3. infectious
4. delusion
5. marginal
6. vulnerable
7. inalienable
8. fiscal
9. convene
10. avid
11. platitude
12. predecessor
13. amity
14. detonate
15. caste
16. atrophy
17. amenable
18. omnibus
19. arable
20. meritorious

Form C
Graded Passages
(Student Copy)

Fun

"Here it comes!" said Tom.

"I can see it," said Dan. "Here comes the band!"

Tom jumped up and down. "Look at the man. He is tall. I can see his red hat."

"Look!" said Dan. "I see a dog. The dog is big. The dog is brown and white."

Food for Birds

"See the small birds," said Jim. "They are looking in the snow. They want food."

"The snow is deep," said Sue. "They cannot find food."

Jim said, "Let's help them."
"Yes," said Sue. "We can get bread for them."

Jim and Sue ran home. They asked Mother for bread. Mother gave bread to them. Then they ran to find the birds.

"There are the birds," said Sue. "Give them the bread."
Jim put the bread on the snow.
Sue said, "Look at the birds! They are eating the bread."

"They are happy now," said Jim. "They are fat and happy."

Fun with Leaves

Bill had many leaves in his yard. He raked them into a big pile. Pat helped.

Then Bill got a very good idea. He ran and jumped in that pile of leaves.

"Wow! What fun!"
"Let me jump," said Pat. He jumped in the leaves.

Soon both boys were jumping. They threw leaves up into the air.

Mother looked out and said, "I see two boys having fun. Come in for something to eat."

"See our big pile!" said Bill.
"Where?" asked Mother.

The boys looked around. The pile was not big now. The leaves were all over the yard.

Zoo Work

Bob works at the zoo. He takes care
of all kinds of animals. The animals are
brought to the zoo from all over the world.
Bob gives hay to the elephants. He feeds
raw meat to the lions and fresh fish to the
seals. He knows just what to give every
animal. Each day Bob washes the cages in
the zoo. When an animal gets sick, Bob
takes it to the zoo doctor. He will make it
well. Bob keeps the zoo keys. When the
people go home, Bob locks the gate to the
zoo. Then he can go home.

The Pet Shop

Maria really wanted a little dog. One day she went with her parents to the pet shop. They looked at the fish, turtles, parrots, and many kinds of dogs. Maria and her parents saw one nice puppy that acted very lively. It looked like a small, bouncing, black ball of fur. The puppy was a fluffy black poodle. It jumped around in its cage. When Maria petted the puppy, it sat up and begged. Maria and her parents laughed because the poodle looked so cute. They decided to buy the poodle. After all, who could resist such a nice dog?

The Soccer Game

There were only two minutes to go in the big soccer game between the Jets and the Bombers. The score was tied. The ball was in the Jets' area dangerously close to their goal. Rosa, a Jets halfback, ran for the ball. She got to the ball and delivered a great kick. The ball went sailing over the midline into Bomber territory.

With a yell, Kim got the ball and dribbled hard for the Bomber goal. There was no time for a mistake. The shot must be true. Kim faked right. Then Kim kicked left and scored as the game ended.

Pioneer House Building

When the first pioneers came to America, there were no special people to build houses, so they did the work together. All the people in the area would come and help. Some people would cut trees. Other people would take this wood and start forming the frame of the house. The older children helped by carting bits of wood or cutting the limbs. Younger children played. The work was difficult and long and gave the people enormous appetites. Large quantities of food were prepared and set outside on long wooden tables. Then everyone gathered around the table and feasted.

Museum Visit

On our field trip we visited the new
museum. We saw different exhibits about
science and the world around us. The
telephone exhibit was definitely the most
interesting. Phones from the early days
were made of wood and metal. People
had to ring the operator to make a call.
The exhibit displayed many other types of
phones. Some had televisions so that you
could see the person you were talking to.
There were also wireless phones for people
and cars that transmit calls with radio
signals. We saw movies that showed us
how telephones help us in our everyday
lives.

Capture and Freedom

One of the most beloved tales is of the princess and a knight. The princess, shackled to a rock, caught the eye of the wandering knight. He galloped over and, with a single stroke of his sword, freed her from the iron chain. Taking her hand, he led her away from the dreadful confinement of the rock. While relaxing in a sunny meadow, he comforted her with reassuring words. The princess told him that she had been seized by pirates. These pirates had brought her to this savage island as a peace offering to the terrible monsters of the sea.

Mount Kilarma

The large mountain loomed ominously in the foreground. Many had tried to defeat this magnificent creation of nature, but to date no one had. There it was, the lonely unconquered giant, Mount Kilarma. In sheer size, there was nothing imposing about the 15,000 foot height of Mount Kilarma. The dangers rested in the skirt of glaciers around the steep sides of the mountain and in the fiercely changing winds that tore at the summit. The small band of mountaineers stared at the huge mass of ice. Could they reach the mountain's peak and do what no one had ever accomplished?

Performance Booklet
(Teacher Copy)

 Note: This Performance Booklet is on the CD-ROM that accompanies the Basic Reading Inventory.

BASIC READING INVENTORY PERFORMANCE BOOKLET

Eighth Edition

Jerry L. Johns, Ph.D.

C Optional Form

Student _____ Grade _____ Sex M F Date of Test _____

School _____ Examiner _____ Date of Birth _____

Address _____ Current Book/Level _____ Age _____

SUMMARY OF STUDENT'S READING PERFORMANCE

| Grade | Word Recognition | | | | | | Comprehension | | | |
| | Isolation (Word Lists) | | | | Context (Passages) | | Oral Reading Form ___ Questions | | Silent Reading Form D Questions | |
	Sight	Analysis	Total	Level	Miscues	Level	Missed	Level	Missed	Level
PP										
P										
1										
2										
3										
4										
5										
6										
7										
8										
9										
10										
11										
12										

ESTIMATE OF READING LEVELS

Independent _____ Instructional _____ Frustration _____

LISTENING LEVEL

Grade	Form ___ Questions Missed	Level
PP		
P		
1		
2		
3		
4		
5		
6		
7		
8		

ESTIMATED LEVEL: ____

GENERAL OBSERVATIONS

INFORMAL MISCUE ANALYSIS SUMMARY

| Types of Miscues | Frequency of Occurrence | | | General Impact of Miscues on Meaning | | |
	Seldom	Sometimes	Frequently	No Change	Little Change	Much Change
Substitutions						
Insertions						
Omissions						
Reversals						
Repetitions						

QUALITATIVE ANALYSIS OF BASIC READING INVENTORY INSIGHTS

General Directions: Note the degree to which the student shows behavior or evidence in the following areas. Space is provided for additional items.

	Seldom Weak Poor				Always Strong Excellent

COMPREHENSION

Seeks to construct meaning

Makes predictions

Activates background knowledge

Possesses appropriate concepts
and vocabulary

Monitors reading

Varies reading rate as needed

Understands topic and major ideas

Remembers facts or details

Makes and supports appropriate
inferences

Evaluates ideas from passages

Understands vocabulary used

Provides appropriate definitions
of words

Engagement with passages

_____

_____

WORD IDENTIFICATION

Possesses numerous strategies

Uses strategies flexibly

Uses graphophonic information

Uses semantic information

Uses syntactic information

Knows basic sight words
automatically

Possesses sight vocabulary

_____

_____

ORAL AND SILENT READING

Reads fluently

Reads with expression

Attends to punctuation

Keeps place while reading

Appropriate rate

Reads silently without vocalization

_____

_____

ATTITUDE AND CONFIDENCE

Enjoys reading

Demonstrates willingness to risk

Possesses positive self-concept

Chooses to read

Regards himself/herself as a reader

Exhibits persistence

_____

_____

List C-C (Pre-Primer)	Sight	Analysis	List C (Primer)	Sight	Analysis
1. see*	_____	_____	1. red*	_____	_____
2. you*	_____	_____	2. day	_____	_____
3. school	_____	_____	3. in*	_____	_____
4. to*	_____	_____	4. for*	_____	_____
5. can*	_____	_____	5. have*	_____	_____
6. good*	_____	_____	6. walk*	_____	_____
7. soon*	_____	_____	7. boy	_____	_____
8. into*	_____	_____	8. cake	_____	_____
9. up*	_____	_____	9. your*	_____	_____
10. big*	_____	_____	10. again*	_____	_____
11. man	_____	_____	11. bee	_____	_____
12. look*	_____	_____	12. come*	_____	_____
13. away*	_____	_____	13. picture	_____	_____
14. stop*	_____	_____	14. said*	_____	_____
15. that*	_____	_____	15. put*	_____	_____
16. yard	_____	_____	16. word	_____	_____
17. train	_____	_____	17. baby	_____	_____
18. truck	_____	_____	18. car	_____	_____
19. black*	_____	_____	19. no*	_____	_____
20. white*	_____	_____	20. funny	_____	_____

*denotes basic sight word from Revised Dolch List   *denotes basic sight word from Revised Dolch List

Number Correct _____ _____   Number Correct _____ _____

Total _____   Total _____

Scoring Guide for Graded Word Lists

Independent	Instructional	Frustration
20 19	18 17 16 15 14	13 or less

List C 7141 (Grade 1)	Sight	Analysis	List C 8224 (Grade 2)	Sight	Analysis
1. ball	_____	_____	1. brave	_____	_____
2. new*	_____	_____	2. top	_____	_____
3. fast*	_____	_____	3. it's	_____	_____
4. has*	_____	_____	4. follow	_____	_____
5. with*	_____	_____	5. gold	_____	_____
6. children	_____	_____	6. front	_____	_____
7. work*	_____	_____	7. family	_____	_____
8. pet	_____	_____	8. knock	_____	_____
9. ready	_____	_____	9. count	_____	_____
10. much*	_____	_____	10. smell	_____	_____
11. came*	_____	_____	11. afraid	_____	_____
12. parade	_____	_____	12. done*	_____	_____
13. hen	_____	_____	13. silver	_____	_____
14. live	_____	_____	14. face	_____	_____
15. hear	_____	_____	15. visit	_____	_____
16. far*	_____	_____	16. mountain	_____	_____
17. thing	_____	_____	17. track	_____	_____
18. year	_____	_____	18. pile	_____	_____
19. hurry	_____	_____	19. been*	_____	_____
20. met	_____	_____	20. through*	_____	_____

*denotes basic sight word from Revised Dolch List   *denotes basic sight word from Revised Dolch List

Number Correct _____ _____   Number Correct _____ _____

Total _____   Total _____

Scoring Guide for Graded Word Lists

Independent	Instructional	Frustration
20 19	18 17 16 15 14	13 or less

List C 3183 (Grade 3)	Sight	Analysis	List C 5414 (Grade 4)	Sight	Analysis
1. pack	_____	_____	1. thunder	_____	_____
2. matter	_____	_____	2. friendship	_____	_____
3. hang	_____	_____	3. crickets	_____	_____
4. center	_____	_____	4. yesterday	_____	_____
5. chew	_____	_____	5. dozen	_____	_____
6. rule	_____	_____	6. telescope	_____	_____
7. pound	_____	_____	7. whiskers	_____	_____
8. danger	_____	_____	8. skunk	_____	_____
9. force	_____	_____	9. amount	_____	_____
10. history	_____	_____	10. nature	_____	_____
11. spend	_____	_____	11. level	_____	_____
12. wisdom	_____	_____	12. husky	_____	_____
13. mind	_____	_____	13. sight	_____	_____
14. adventure	_____	_____	14. distance	_____	_____
15. mental	_____	_____	15. hunger	_____	_____
16. harbor	_____	_____	16. figure	_____	_____
17. fault	_____	_____	17. medicine	_____	_____
18. pilot	_____	_____	18. ashamed	_____	_____
19. usually	_____	_____	19. saddle	_____	_____
20. though	_____	_____	20. anxious	_____	_____
Number Correct	_____	_____	Number Correct	_____	_____
Total		_____	Total		_____

Scoring Guide for Graded Word Lists

Independent	Instructional	Frustration
20 19	18 17 16 15 14	13 or less

List C 8595 (Grade 5)	Sight	Analysis	List C 6867 (Grade 6)	Sight	Analysis
1. brag			1. youngster		
2. college			2. activity		
3. tend			3. research		
4. ditch			4. grizzly		
5. bully			5. tornado		
6. journal			6. ruffle		
7. public			7. judgment		
8. goblin			8. nylon		
9. ransom			9. fable		
10. remarkable			10. exact		
11. ankle			11. decay		
12. social			12. substitute		
13. gym			13. wealthy		
14. education			14. communicate		
15. darling			15. assemble		
16. muscle			16. economics		
17. pouch			17. biscuit		
18. barley			18. forbid		
19. petticoat			19. attractive		
20. invitation			20. pliers		
Number Correct			Number Correct		
Total			Total		

Scoring Guide for Graded Word Lists

Independent	Instructional	Frustration
20 19	18 17 16 15 14	13 or less

List C 3717 (Grade 7)	Sight	Analysis	List C 8183 (Grade 8)	Sight	Analysis
1. jazz	_____	_____	1. motive	_____	_____
2. puncture	_____	_____	2. function	_____	_____
3. fantastic	_____	_____	3. transplant	_____	_____
4. publication	_____	_____	4. impressive	_____	_____
5. derby	_____	_____	5. encircle	_____	_____
6. terminal	_____	_____	6. browse	_____	_____
7. hemisphere	_____	_____	7. investment	_____	_____
8. paralyze	_____	_____	8. fortify	_____	_____
9. environment	_____	_____	9. maximum	_____	_____
10. cantaloupe	_____	_____	10. detain	_____	_____
11. blockade	_____	_____	11. leaflet	_____	_____
12. ornamental	_____	_____	12. privacy	_____	_____
13. warrant	_____	_____	13. lubricant	_____	_____
14. bombard	_____	_____	14. oblong	_____	_____
15. typhoon	_____	_____	15. liberal	_____	_____
16. hypnotize	_____	_____	16. identification	_____	_____
17. linoleum	_____	_____	17. energetic	_____	_____
18. nasal	_____	_____	18. carburetor	_____	_____
19. tuberculosis	_____	_____	19. antiseptic	_____	_____
20. lacquer	_____	_____	20. infuriate	_____	_____
Number Correct	_____	_____	Number Correct	_____	_____
Total		_____	Total		_____

Scoring Guide for Graded Word Lists

Independent	Instructional	Frustration
20 19	18 17 16 15 14	13 or less

List C 4959 (Grade 9)	Sight	Analysis	List C 1047 (Grade 10)	Sight	Analysis
1. nationality			1. organism		
2. complex			2. tart		
3. bleach			3. ashtray		
4. comparable			4. consultant		
5. overwhelm			5. intolerable		
6. contraction			6. synthetic		
7. equivalent			7. conclusive		
8. conservative			8. diverse		
9. bewitch			9. premature		
10. insignificant			10. insufferable		
11. earthy			11. cater		
12. monogram			12. reformatory		
13. redeem			13. demolition		
14. amputate			14. disintegrate		
15. disastrous			15. hoax		
16. disband			16. granulate		
17. coronation			17. necessitate		
18. barracks			18. illegitimate		
19. abolition			19. gaseous		
20. vestibule			20. revue		
Number Correct			Number Correct		
Total			Total		

Scoring Guide for Graded Word Lists

Independent	Instructional	Frustration
20 19	18 17 16 15 14	13 or less

List C 1187 (Grade 11)	Sight	Analysis	List C 1296 (Grade 12)	Sight	Analysis
1. nonexistent	_____	_____	1. fusion	_____	_____
2. recession	_____	_____	2. modulate	_____	_____
3. prohibition	_____	_____	3. infectious	_____	_____
4. collaborate	_____	_____	4. delusion	_____	_____
5. philosophy	_____	_____	5. marginal	_____	_____
6. franchise	_____	_____	6. vulnerable	_____	_____
7. essence	_____	_____	7. inalienable	_____	_____
8. flagrant	_____	_____	8. fiscal	_____	_____
9. replenish	_____	_____	9. convene	_____	_____
10. anesthetic	_____	_____	10. avid	_____	_____
11. monotone	_____	_____	11. platitude	_____	_____
12. instigate	_____	_____	12. predecessor	_____	_____
13. cataract	_____	_____	13. amity	_____	_____
14. sedative	_____	_____	14. detonate	_____	_____
15. memoir	_____	_____	15. caste	_____	_____
16. dubious	_____	_____	16. atrophy	_____	_____
17. premonition	_____	_____	17. amenable	_____	_____
18. libel	_____	_____	18. omnibus	_____	_____
19. maladjustment	_____	_____	19. arable	_____	_____
20. claimant	_____	_____	20. meritorious	_____	_____
Number Correct	_____	_____	Number Correct	_____	_____
Total	_____		Total		_____

Scoring Guide for Graded Word Lists

Independent	Instructional	Frustration
20 19	18 17 16 15 14	13 or less

Student Copy is on page 230.

C-C (Pre-Primer) Activating Background: Look at the picture and read the title to yourself. Then tell me what you think will happen.

Background: Low |———+———| High

Fun

	MISCUES						
	Substitution	Insertion	Omission	Reversal	Repetition	Self-Correction of Unacceptable Miscue	Meaning Change (Significant Miscue)
"Here it comes!" said Tom.							
"I can see it," said Dan. "Here comes							
the band!"							
Tom jumped up and down. "Look at							
the man. He is tall. I can see his red hat."							
"Look!" said Dan. "I see a dog. The							
dog is big. The dog is brown and white."							
TOTAL							

Word Recognition Scoring Guide		
Total Miscues	Level	Significant Miscues
0	Independent	0
1–2	Ind./Inst.	1
3	Instructional	2
4	Inst./Frust.	3
5 +	Frustration	4 +

Total Miscues ☐   Significant Miscues ☐

_____ WPM
)3000

C-C (Pre-Primer)
Comprehension Questions

F   1. _____ What were the children's names?
             (Tom and Dan)

F   2. _____ What was the first thing they
             saw?
             (the band; a man)

E   3. _____ Why did Tom jump up and down?
             (any logical response; he was
             excited; he couldn't see)

I   4. _____ What were the children probably
             doing?
             (any logical response; having fun;
             listening to music; watching a
             parade)

V   5. _____ What is a "hat"?
             (something you wear; something
             you put on your head)

Retelling Notes

☐ Questions
  Missed

Comprehension Scoring Guide	
Questions Missed	Level
0	Independent
1	Ind./Inst.
1½	Instructional
2	Inst./Frust.
2½ +	Frustration

Retelling
Excellent
Satisfactory
Unsatisfactory

Student Copy is on page 231.

C (Primer) Activating Background: Read the title to yourself; then tell me what you think will happen.

Background: Low |——————|——————| High

Food for Birds	Substitution	Insertion	Omission	Reversal	Repetition	Self-Correction of Unacceptable Miscue	Meaning Change (Significant Miscue)
MISCUES							
"See the small birds," said Jim.							
"They are looking in the snow. They want							
food."							
"The snow is deep," said Sue. "They							
cannot find food."							
Jim said, "Let's help them."							
"Yes," said Sue. "We can get bread							
for them."							
Jim and Sue ran home. They asked							
Mother for bread. Mother gave bread to							
them. Then they ran to find the birds.							
"There are the birds," said Sue.							
"Give them the bread."							
Jim put the bread on the snow.							
Sue said, "Look at the birds! They							
are eating the bread."							
"They are happy now," said Jim.							
"They are fat and happy."							
TOTAL							

Word Recognition Scoring Guide		
Total Miscues	Level	Significant Miscues
0–1	Independent	0–1
2–4	Ind./Inst.	2
5	Instructional	3
6–9	Inst./Frust.	4
10 +	Frustration	5 +

Total Miscues ☐   Significant Miscues ☐

WPM
)6000

C (Primer)
Comprehension Questions

<table>
<tr><td>T</td><td>1. _____</td><td>What is this story about?
(feeding the hungry birds)</td></tr>
<tr><td>F</td><td>2. _____</td><td>Who was in this story?
(Jim and Sue; two children;
mother)</td></tr>
<tr><td>F</td><td>3. _____</td><td>What did the children see in the
snow?
(birds)</td></tr>
<tr><td>F</td><td>4. _____</td><td>What did the birds want?
(food)</td></tr>
<tr><td>F</td><td>5. _____</td><td>Why couldn't the birds find any
food?
(the snow was deep)</td></tr>
<tr><td>F</td><td>6. _____</td><td>Where did the children get bread
for the birds?
(from their mother)</td></tr>
<tr><td>F</td><td>7. _____</td><td>Where did Jim put the bread?
(on the snow)</td></tr>
<tr><td>I</td><td>8. _____</td><td>What season of the year is it?
(winter)</td></tr>
<tr><td>E</td><td>9. _____</td><td>How do you think the children
felt about the hungry birds? Why?
(any logical response)</td></tr>
<tr><td>V</td><td>10. _____</td><td>What does "fat" mean?
(big; large)</td></tr>
</table>

Retelling Notes

[ ] Questions
    Missed

Comprehension Scoring Guide	
Questions Missed	Level
0–1	Independent
1½–2	Ind./Inst.
2½	Instructional
3–4½	Inst./Frust.
5 +	Frustration

Retelling
Excellent
Satisfactory
Unsatisfactory

Student Copy is on page 232.

C 7141 (Grade 1) Activating Background: Read the title to yourself; then tell me what you think will happen.

Background: Low ├─────┼─────┤ High

Fun with Leaves

	MISCUES						
	Substitution	Insertion	Omission	Reversal	Repetition	Self-Correction of Unacceptable Miscue	Meaning Change (Significant Miscue)
Bill had many leaves in his yard. He							
raked them into a big pile. Pat helped.							
Then Bill got a very good idea.							
He ran and jumped in that pile of leaves.							
"Wow! What fun!"							
"Let me jump," said Pat. He							
jumped in the leaves.							
Soon both boys were jumping.							
They threw leaves up into the air.							
Mother looked out and said, "I see							
two boys having fun. Come in for							
something to eat."							
"See our big pile!" said Bill.							
"Where?" asked Mother.							
The boys looked around. The pile was							
not big now. The leaves were all over the							
yard.							
TOTAL							

Word Recognition Scoring Guide		
Total Miscues	Level	Significant Miscues
0–1	Independent	0–1
2–4	Ind./Inst.	2
5	Instructional	3
6–9	Inst./Frust.	4
10 +	Frustration	5 +

Total Miscues ☐   Significant Miscues ☐

$\frac{}{6000}$ WPM

C 7141 (Grade 1)
Comprehension Questions

<table>
<tr><td>T</td><td>1. _____</td><td>What is the story about?
(boys raking and playing or
jumping in leaves)</td></tr>
<tr><td>F</td><td>2. _____</td><td>Who was in this story?
(Bill and Pat; two boys; Mother)</td></tr>
<tr><td>F</td><td>3. _____</td><td>What was in the yard?
(leaves)</td></tr>
<tr><td>F</td><td>4. _____</td><td>What did the boys do with the
leaves?
(raked them; jumped or dived in
them; threw them about)</td></tr>
<tr><td>F</td><td>5. _____</td><td>What did Pat do?
(he jumped into the pile too; he
helped to rake the leaves)</td></tr>
<tr><td>F</td><td>6. _____</td><td>What did Mother want the boys
to do?
(come in to eat)</td></tr>
<tr><td>F</td><td>7. _____</td><td>What happened to the pile of
leaves?
(it was all over the yard; the boys
messed it up)</td></tr>
<tr><td>I</td><td>8. _____</td><td>What season do you think it was?
Why?
(fall; any logical response)</td></tr>
<tr><td>E</td><td>9. _____</td><td>How do you think Mother felt
about what the boys were doing?
(any logical response)</td></tr>
<tr><td>V</td><td>10. _____</td><td>What is "jumping"?
(to go up and down)</td></tr>
</table>

Retelling Notes

☐ Questions Missed

Comprehension Scoring Guide	
Questions Missed	Level
0–1	Independent
1½–2	Ind./Inst.
2½	Instructional
3–4½	Inst./Frust.
5 +	Frustration

Retelling
Excellent
Satisfactory
Unsatisfactory

Student Copy is on page 233.

C 8224 (Grade 2) Activating Background: Read the title to yourself; then tell me what you think will happen.

Background: Low ├────┼────┤ High

Zoo Work

	MISCUES							
	Substitution	Insertion	Omission	Reversal	Repetition	Self-Correction of Unacceptable Miscue	Meaning Change (Significant Miscue)
Bob works at the zoo. He takes care							
of all kinds of animals. The animals are							
brought to the zoo from all over the world.							
Bob gives hay to the elephants. He feeds							
raw meat to the lions and fresh fish to the							
seals. He knows just what to give every							
animal. Each day Bob washes the cages in							
the zoo. When an animal gets sick, Bob							
takes it to the zoo doctor. He will make it							
well. Bob keeps the zoo keys. When the							
people go home, Bob locks the gates to the							
zoo. Then he can go home.							
TOTAL							

Word Recognition Scoring Guide		
Total Miscues	Level	Significant Miscues
0–1	Independent	0–1
2–4	Ind./Inst.	2
5	Instructional	3
6–9	Inst./Frust.	4
10 +	Frustration	5 +

Total Miscues [ ]   Significant Miscues [ ]

_____ WPM

)6000

Comprehension Questions

			Retelling Notes

T   1. _____ What is this story about?
(Bob and the zoo; Bob's work at the zoo)

F   2. _____ What does Bob do?
(works at the zoo; takes care of animals; washes cages)

F   3. _____ Where do the animals come from?
(all over the world)

F   4. _____ What did Bob feed the lions and what did he feed the seals?
(meat to the lions and fish to the seals)

F   5. _____ How often does Bob wash the cages?
(each day; every day)

F   6. _____ Who takes care of sick animals?
(zoo doctor)

F   7. _____ What does Bob do when the people go home?
(locks the gates and goes home)

I   8. _____ How does Bob know what to feed the animals?
(any logical response)

E   9. _____ Why do you think Bob locks the gates to the zoo?
(any logical response)

V 10. _____ What is "raw" meat?
(meat that is not cooked)

[ ] Questions Missed

Comprehension Scoring Guide	
Questions Missed	Level
0–1	Independent
1½–2	Ind./Inst.
2½	Instructional
3–4½	Inst./Frust.
5 +	Frustration

Retelling
Excellent
Satisfactory
Unsatisfactory

Reading/Listening Comprehension/Study Skills Exercises

Analogies

Analyzing Details

Author's Purpose

Author's Purpose

Author's Purpose: To Entertain

Author's Purpose: To Inform

Author's Purpose: To Persuade

Categorizing

Cause And Effect

Character Description

Character Mood

Character Traits

Character's Mood

Character's Motives/Feelings

Character's P.O.V.

Charts

Classifying Sentences

Classifying Words And Phrases

Compare And Contrast

Comprehension Casino

Connotation/Denotation

Description

Details In A Paragraph

Details In A Sentence

Diagrams

Dialogue

Distinguish Between Fact And Opinion

Distinguish Between Fantasy/Reality

Distinguish Between Fiction And Non-Fiction

Drawing Conclusions

Drawing Conclusions

Evaluate Evidence And Sources Of Information

Evaluation/Making Judgments

Exaggeration

Expository Writing

Figurative Language

Fix-It

Flashback

Foreshadowing

Form Generalizations

Graphic Aids

Hyperbole/Exaggeration

Idioms

Idioms

Illustrations

Imagery

Imagery

Main Idea

Main Idea & Supporting Details

Making Generalizations

Making Inferences

Making Inferences

Maps

Metaphors

Mood

Multiple Meaning Words

Naming A Paragraph

Organizing Information By Topics

Paraphrasing

Personification

Persuasion

Persuasive Writing

Point Of View

Prediction

Problem And Solution

Propaganda

Puns

Reality And Fantasy

Repetition/Rhythm/Rhyme

Sequence

Similes

Skimming/Scanning

Summarization

Supporting Details

Symbolism

Titling A Paragraph

Unfamiliar Words

Student Copy is on page 234.

C 3183 (Grade 3) Activating Background: Read the title to yourself; then tell me what you think will happen.

Background: Low ├──────┼──────┤ High

The Pet Shop

	MISCUES						
	Substitution	Insertion	Omission	Reversal	Repetition	Self-Correction of Unacceptable Miscue	Meaning Change (Significant Miscue)
Maria really wanted a little dog. One							
day she went with her parents to the pet							
shop. They looked at the fish, turtles,							
parrots, and many kinds of dogs. Maria							
and her parents saw one nice puppy that							
acted very lively. It looked like a small,							
bouncing, black ball of fur. The puppy was							
a fluffy black poodle. It jumped around in							
its cage. When Maria petted the puppy, it							
sat up and begged. Maria and her parents							
laughed because the poodle looked so cute.							
They decided to buy the poodle. After all,							
who could resist such a nice dog?							
TOTAL							

Word Recognition Scoring Guide		
Total Miscues	Level	Significant Miscues
0–1	Independent	0–1
2–4	Ind./Inst.	2
5	Instructional	3
6–9	Inst./Frust.	4
10 +	Frustration	5 +

Total Miscues ☐

Significant Miscues ☐

_____ WPM

)6000

T   1. _____ What is this story about?
              (Maria and her parents buying a
              poodle; a trip to the pet shop)

F   2. _____ Where did Maria and her parents go?
              (to the pet shop)

F   3. _____ What did Maria and her parents see?
              (fish; turtles; parrots; dogs
              [any 2])

F   4. _____ What did the poodle look like?
              (small; furry; black; fluffy;
              bouncing ball of fur; cute [any 2])

F   5. _____ What did the poodle do when Maria
              petted it?
              (it sat up and begged)

F   6. _____ Why did Maria and her parents
              laugh?
              (the poodle looked so cute)

F   7. _____ What happened to the poodle?
              (Maria and her parents bought it)

I   8. _____ Why do you think Maria wanted a
              dog?
              (any logical response; she liked
              dogs; she didn't have anyone to play
              with)

E   9. _____ What do you think they will do with
              the dog once they get it home?
              (any logical response)

V   10. _____ What does "bouncing" mean?
               (to spring back; to go up and down)

[ ] Questions
    Missed

Comprehension Scoring Guide	
Questions Missed	Level
0–1	Independent
1½–2	Ind./Inst.
2½	Instructional
3–4½	Inst./Frust.
5 +	Frustration

Retelling
Excellent
Satisfactory
Unsatisfactory

Student Copy is on page 235.

C 5414 (Grade 4) Activating Background: Read the title to yourself; then tell me what you think will happen.

Background: Low ├────┼────┤ High

The Soccer Game

	MISCUES						
	Substitution	Insertion	Omission	Reversal	Repetition	Self-Correction of Unacceptable Miscue	Meaning Change (Significant Miscue)
There were only two minutes to go							
in the big soccer game between the							
Jets and the Bombers. The score was							
tied. The ball was in the Jets' area							
dangerously close to their goal. Rosa, a							
Jets halfback, ran for the ball. She got							
to the ball and delivered a great kick.							
The ball went sailing over the midline							
into Bomber territory.							
With a yell, Kim got the ball and							
dribbled hard for the Bomber goal.							
There was no time for a mistake. The							
shot must be true. Kim faked right.							
Then Kim kicked left and scored as the							
game ended.							
TOTAL							

Word Recognition Scoring Guide		
Total Miscues	Level	Significant Miscues
0–1	Independent	0–1
2–4	Ind./Inst.	2
5	Instructional	3
6–9	Inst./Frust.	4
10 +	Frustration	5 +

Total Miscues ☐   Significant Miscues ☐

WPM
)6000

261

Comprehension Questions

T 1. _____ What is this story about?
(a soccer game)

F 2. _____ How much time was left in the
game?
(2 minutes)

F 3. _____ What was the score near the end
of the game?
(it was tied)

F 4. _____ What was the name of the team
Rosa was on?
(Jets)

F 5. _____ What position did Rosa play?
(halfback)

F 6. _____ When Rosa kicked the ball,
where did it go?
(over the midline; into Bomber
territory)

F 7. _____ Who scored the final goal of the
game?
(Kim)

I 8. _____ Which team lost the game?
(the Bombers)

E 9. _____ If you were the coach, what
would you tell your players to do
with two minutes to go in the
game?
(any logical response; try your
hardest; try to get in a goal)

V 10. _____ What does "sailing" mean in this
story?
(in the air; flying; soaring; to
glide through the air)

[ ] Questions
Missed

Retelling Notes

Comprehension Scoring Guide	
Questions Missed	Level
0–1	Independent
1½–2	Ind./Inst.
2½	Instructional
3–4½	Inst./Frust.
5 +	Frustration

Retelling
Excellent
Satisfactory
Unsatisfactory

Student Copy is on page 236.

C 8595 (Grade 5) Activating Background: Read the title to yourself; then tell me what you think will happen.

Background: Low ├─────┼─────┤ High

Pioneer House Building

	MISCUES						
	Substitution	Insertion	Omission	Reversal	Repetition	Self-Correction of Unacceptable Miscue	Meaning Change (Significant Miscue)
When the first pioneers came to							
America, there were no special people							
to build houses, so they did the work							
together. All the people in the area							
would come and help. Some people							
would cut trees. Other people would take							
this wood and start forming the frame							
of the house. The older children							
helped by carting bits of wood or							
cutting the limbs. Younger children							
played. The work was difficult and							
long and gave the people enormous							
appetites. Large quantities of food							
were prepared and set outside on long							
wooden tables. Then everyone gathered							
around the table and feasted.							
TOTAL							

Word Recognition Scoring Guide		
Total Miscues	Level	Significant Miscues
0–1	Independent	0–1
2–4	Ind./Inst.	2
5	Instructional	3
6–9	Inst./Frust.	4
10 +	Frustration	5 +

Total Miscues ☐   Significant Miscues ☐

_____ WPM

)6000

C 8595 (Grade 5)
Comprehension Questions

T 1. _____ What is this passage about?
              (work the pioneers did to build a
              house)

F 2. _____ Why did the pioneers have to
              build their own houses?
              (there were no special people to
              do it)

F 3. _____ Who came and helped?
              (all the people in the area)

F 4. _____ What did the younger children do?
              (play)

F 5. _____ What did the older children do?
              (carted bits of wood; cut the limbs)

F 6. _____ What other jobs did people do?
              (cut trees; form frames; prepare
              food)

F 7. _____ Where was the food placed and
              eaten?
              (on tables outside)

I 8. _____ What do you think was the
              hardest job? Why?
              (any logical response)

E 9. _____ Which job would you pick?
              Why?
              (any logical response)

V 10. _____ What does "enormous" mean?
              (large; big)

Retelling Notes

[ ] Questions
      Missed

Comprehension Scoring Guide	
Questions Missed	Level
0–1	Independent
1½–2	Ind./Inst.
2½	Instructional
3–4½	Inst./Frust.
5 +	Frustration

Retelling
Excellent
Satisfactory
Unsatisfactory

Student Copy is on page 237.

C 6867 (Grade 6) Activating Background: Read the title to yourself; then tell me what you think will happen.

Background: Low ├─────┼─────┤ High

Museum Visit

	MISCUES						
	Substitution	Insertion	Omission	Reversal	Repetition	Self-Correction of Unacceptable Miscue	Meaning Change (Significant Miscue)
On our field trip we visited the new							
museum. We saw different exhibits about							
science and the world around us. The							
telephone exhibit was definitely the most							
interesting. Phones from the early days							
were made of wood and metal. People							
had to ring the operator to make a call.							
The exhibit displayed many other types of							
phones. Some had televisions so that you							
could see the person you were talking to.							
There were also wireless phones for people							
and cars that transmit calls with radio							
signals. We saw movies that showed us							
how telephones help us in our everyday							
lives.							
TOTAL							

Word Recognition Scoring Guide		
Total Miscues	Level	Significant Miscues
0–1	Independent	0–1
2–4	Ind./Inst.	2
5	Instructional	3
6–9	Inst./Frust.	4
10 +	Frustration	5 +

Total Miscues ☐   Significant Miscues ☐

_____ WPM
)6000

265

C 6867 (Grade 6)
Comprehension Questions

T   1. _____ What is this passage about?
(a field trip to the museum; a telephone exhibit)

F   2. _____ What were some of the exhibits?
(science; telephone; world around us [any 2])

F   3. _____ Which exhibit was the most interesting?
(telephone)

F   4. _____ What materials were used to make the early phones?
(wood and metal)

F   5. _____ What did you have to do to make a phone call with early phones?
(call the operator)

F   6. _____ What other types of phones were mentioned?
(phones with televisions; car phones [must include both])

F   7. _____ How do wireless phones in cars transmit messages?
(with radio signals)

I   8. _____ Do you think our phones are better than the early phones? Why?
(any logical response)

E   9. _____ Do you think telephones have made our lives better? Why?
(any logical response)

V 10. _____ What is an "exhibit"?
(any logical response; a display of objects)

Retelling Notes

☐ Questions Missed

Comprehension Scoring Guide	
Questions Missed	Level
0–1	Independent
1½–2	Ind./Inst.
2½	Instructional
3–4½	Inst./Frust.
5 +	Frustration

Retelling
Excellent
Satisfactory
Unsatisfactory

266

Student Copy is on page 238.

C 3717 (Grade 7) Activating Background: Read the title to yourself; then tell me what you think will happen.

Background: Low ├──────┼──────┤ High

Capture and Freedom

	MISCUES						
	Substitution	Insertion	Omission	Reversal	Repetition	Self-Correction of Unacceptable Miscue	Meaning Change (Significant Miscue)
One of the most beloved tales is of the							
princess and a knight. The princess,							
shackled to a rock, caught the eye of the							
wandering knight. He galloped over and,							
with a single stroke of his sword, freed							
her from the iron chain. Taking her hand,							
he led her away from the dreadful							
confinement of the rock. While relaxing in							
a sunny meadow, he comforted her with							
reassuring words. The princess told him							
that she had been seized by pirates. These							
pirates had brought her to this savage							
island as a peace offering to the terrible							
monsters of the sea.							
TOTAL							

Word Recognition Scoring Guide		
Total Miscues	Level	Significant Miscues
0–1	Independent	0–1
2–4	Ind./Inst.	2
5	Instructional	3
6–9	Inst./Frust.	4
10 +	Frustration	5 +

Total Miscues □   Significant Miscues □

_____ WPM
)6000

C 3717 (Grade 7)
Comprehension Questions

T   1. _____   What is this story about?
              (a princess and her knight)

F   2. _____   How was the princess held
              captive?
              (she was shackled to a rock)

F   3. _____   Who saw the princess?
              (a knight)

F   4. _____   How did the knight free the
              princess?
              (with his sword; he cut the chain)

F   5. _____   What did the knight do after
              freeing the princess?
              (comforted her with reassuring
              words; led her away)

F   6. _____   Who took the princess to this
              island?
              (the pirates)

F   7. _____   Why was the princess taken to
              this island?
              (as a peace offering to the
              monsters)

I   8. _____   Why do you think the pirates
              used her as a peace offering?
              (any logical response; she was
              beautiful, powerful, etc.)

E   9. _____   What qualities do you think a
              knight should have?
              (any logical response; bravery;
              courage)

V   10. _____   What does "savage" mean?
              (wild; rugged)

Retelling Notes

☐ Questions Missed

Comprehension Scoring Guide	
Questions Missed	Level
0–1	Independent
1½–2	Ind./Inst.
2½	Instructional
3–4½	Inst./Frust.
5 +	Frustration

Retelling
Excellent
Satisfactory
Unsatisfactory

Student Copy is on page 239.

C 8183 (Grade 8) Activating Background: Read the title to yourself; then tell me what you think will happen.

Background: Low ├──────┼──────┤ High

Mount Kilarma

	MISCUES						
	Substitution	Insertion	Omission	Reversal	Repetition	Self-Correction of Unacceptable Miscue	Meaning Change (Significant Miscue)
The large mountain loomed ominously							
in the foreground. Many had tried to							
defeat this magnificent creation of nature,							
but to date no one had. There it was, the							
lonely unconquered giant, Mount Kilarma.							
In sheer size, there was nothing imposing							
about the 15,000 foot height of Mount							
Kilarma. The dangers rested in the skirt							
of glaciers around the steep sides of the							
mountain and in the fiercely changing							
winds that tore at the summit. The small							
band of mountaineers stared at the huge							
mass of ice. Could they reach the							
mountain's peak and do what no one had							
ever accomplished?							
TOTAL							

Word Recognition Scoring Guide		
Total Miscues	Level	Significant Miscues
0–1	Independent	0–1
2–4	Ind./Inst.	2
5	Instructional	3
6–9	Inst./Frust.	4
10 +	Frustration	5 +

Total Miscues ☐   Significant Miscues ☐

WPM

)6000

269

C 8183 (Grade 8)
Comprehension Questions

T 1. _____ What is this passage about?
(the mountain; Mount Kilarma)

F 2. _____ How tall is Mount Kilarma?
(15,000 feet)

F 3. _____ What are the dangers of Mount
Kilarma?
(the glaciers and changing winds
at the summit)

F 4. _____ How many people had reached
the mountain's peak?
(no one)

F 5. _____ What covered the mountain?
(ice; glaciers)

F 6. _____ On what parts of the mountain
were the glaciers?
(the steep sides)

F 7. _____ What tore at the summit?
(winds)

I 8. _____ Why do you think these people
would risk their lives to climb the
mountain?
(any logical response; no one had
ever scaled the mountain)

E 9. _____ What do you believe the mountaineers were thinking as they
stared at Mount Kilarma?
(any logical response; whether
they would be successful in the
climb)

V 10. _____ What does "ominously" mean?
(threatening; menacing)

Retelling Notes

[ ] Questions
Missed

Comprehension Scoring Guide	
Questions Missed	Level
0–1	Independent
1½–2	Ind./Inst.
2½	Instructional
3–4½	Inst./Frust.
5 +	Frustration

Retelling
Excellent
Satisfactory
Unsatisfactory

FORM D

Silent Reading

Form D is intended for silent reading. The student silently reads the graded passages from the student copy. The teacher records the student's responses to the comprehension questions and the oral rereading in the performance booklet.

Form D may also be used for oral reading.

Form D
Graded Passages
(Student Copy)

Pete's Red Ball

"I can not find my ball," said Pete. "My ball is a big ball. It is red."

"Here is a ball," Rosa said. "The ball is blue. It is little. It is not red."

"I see a ball," said Pete. "It is red. It is big. It is my ball."

Jill's Egg

A white house was in the woods. Jill lived there. The sun made Jill happy. The air smelled clean. She took a walk.

Jill found something along the road in the grass. It was round and white.

"Oh!" said Jill. "What a nice egg. I'll take it home."

Mother was home.

She said, "Jill, you must keep the egg warm."

Jill filled a box with rags. She set the egg in it. She put it near the stove.

The next day Jill heard a sound she did not know.

"Cheep." A baby bird was born. Jill had a new pet.

At the Zoo

Dan wanted to go to the zoo. He asked his mother. She said, "Yes." Dan had fun at the zoo. There were many animals he liked. One animal looked like it had two tails. It was an elephant. One had a nice back to ride on. It was a big turtle. Dan looked at many things. He saw many furry animals. He laughed at them.

It got dark. "Where is my mother?" he asked. Dan looked and looked for his mother. He was lost! He sat down and cried. Then Dan looked up. He saw his mother running to him!

A Spider Friend

A spider sat down by a boy. The boy was afraid of it. He should not have been scared. The spider would not hurt him. Most spiders are friendly. Spiders belong to a group of animals that have eight legs. Spiders are not insects.

In the fall the mother spider lays about 500 eggs. Only the strong baby spiders live. When spring comes they leave their nest. They eat flies, bugs, and ants. They also eat insects that harm our crops. Some large spiders eat mice and birds. You should be able to find a spider web where you live.

D 8224

Cricket Song

It is a summer night. I try to sleep, but a sound keeps waking me. It is a cricket. This bug does not sing with its mouth. The rough wings of the male cricket make sounds. It rubs its wings against each other.

I try to find the bug, but it is hard. The sound does not come from one spot. It would also be hard to see the cricket because it can be as small as the nail on my thumb. Some people think the cricket brings luck. Maybe they know how to fall asleep to the cricket song.

Oldest Living Things

There are over three hundred thousand different kinds of plants. The oxygen in the air we breathe comes from plants. Some plants grow bigger and live longer than animals. Plants grow in many sizes and shapes. Some are smaller than the period at the end of this sentence. These plants can only be seen with a microscope. Other plants, like the giant pine, tower high in the sky. Most plants have stems and leaves. Plants can live in a variety of places. Some even seem to grow out of rocks. Others live in water, old bread, and even old shoes!

Flight

Older airplanes were moved through
the air by the use of propellers. Now, most
planes are driven by large jet engines.
Some fly faster than sound. The first thing
you may notice about a plane is the wings
that stick out on either side of its long
body. Today jet planes land and take off
from major airports every few seconds.
People can travel several hundred miles
in less than an hour. It can take travelers
longer to retrieve their luggage than to fly
to their destination. Planes have been
much improved since the Wright brothers
first flew in 1903.

Sunflowers

One of the most amazing flowers found in the Midwest is the sunflower. Legend states that the flower got its name from its strange habit of "turning" its head in order to face the sun. The sunflower is a very strong plant. It ranges in height from three to fifteen feet. The head of the sunflower is similar to that of a daisy. Both have an outer circle of wide petals and an inner circle of small brown flowers. Seeds later form from these small flowers. These seeds produce some of the most unique patterns found in the plant world.

Indian Celebrations

Indians worshipped the power in natural things, such as the stars, moon, and the sun. At various times during the year, they would hold celebrations in honor of this power that they named the Great Spirit. On these occasions, they would have ceremonies of dancing and feasting. The Indians would decorate their bodies and faces and dress themselves in their best clothes. A medicine man would lead them in the celebration that continued for several days. While gathered about the council fire, the Indians prayed that the Great Spirit would reveal its wish for them by sending a natural sign.

Our Environment

Besides using plants and animals for food, people use the hides of animals for shoes, the wood from trees to build houses, the fiber from the cotton plant to make skirts and shirts, and the wool from sheep to make suits and coats. Even the synthetic fibers that people use are made from matter found in the environment.

People and the environment are interdependent, but that is not the whole story. Modern people can do much more; they can use science and technology to change their environment. Because of their advanced brains, people can investigate and use their precious environment.

Performance Booklet
(Teacher Copy)

 Note: This Performance Booklet is on the CD-ROM that accompanies the Basic Reading Inventory.

BASIC READING INVENTORY PERFORMANCE BOOKLET
Jerry L. Johns, Ph.D.

D Silent Reading

Student _____ Grade _____ Sex   M   F   Date of Test _____

School _____ Examiner _____ Date of Birth _____

Address _____ Current Book/Level _____ Age _____

SUMMARY OF STUDENT'S READING PERFORMANCE

Grade	Word Recognition						Comprehension			
	Isolation (Word Lists)				Context (Passages)		Oral Reading Form ___		Silent Reading Form D	
	Sight	Analysis	Total	Level	Miscues	Level	Questions Missed	Level	Questions Missed	Level
PP										
P										
1										
2										
3										
4										
5										
6										
7										
8										
9										
10										
11										
12										

ESTIMATE OF READING LEVELS

Independent _____   Instructional _____   Frustration _____

LISTENING LEVEL

Grade	Form ___ Questions Missed	Level
PP		
P		
1		
2		
3		
4		
5		
6		
7		
8		

ESTIMATED LEVEL: _____

GENERAL OBSERVATIONS

INFORMAL MISCUE ANALYSIS SUMMARY

Types of Miscues	Frequency of Occurrence			General Impact of Miscues on Meaning		
	Seldom	Sometimes	Frequently	No Change	Little Change	Much Change
Substitutions						
Insertions						
Omissions						
Reversals						
Repetitions						

QUALITATIVE ANALYSIS OF BASIC READING INVENTORY INSIGHTS

General Directions: Note the degree to which the student shows behavior or evidence in the following areas. Space is provided for additional items.

	Seldom / Weak / Poor				Always / Strong / Excellent

COMPREHENSION

Seeks to construct meaning
Makes predictions
Activates background knowledge
Possesses appropriate concepts
    and vocabulary
Monitors reading
Varies reading rate as needed
Understands topic and major ideas
Remembers facts or details
Makes and supports appropriate
    inferences
Evaluates ideas from passages
Understands vocabulary used
Provides appropriate definitions
    of words
Engagement with passages
_____
_____

WORD IDENTIFICATION

Possesses numerous strategies
Uses strategies flexibly
Uses graphophonic information
Uses semantic information
Uses syntactic information
Knows basic sight words
    automatically
Possesses sight vocabulary
_____
_____

ORAL AND SILENT READING

Reads fluently
Reads with expression
Attends to punctuation
Keeps place while reading
Appropriate rate
Reads silently without vocalization
_____
_____

ATTITUDE AND CONFIDENCE

Enjoys reading
Demonstrates willingness to risk
Possesses positive self-concept
Chooses to read
Regards himself/herself as a reader
Exhibits persistence
_____
_____

Student Copy is on page 274.

D-D (Pre-Primer) Activating Background: Look at the picture and read the title to yourself. Then tell me what you think will happen.

Background: Low |———|———| High

Pete's Red Ball

	MISCUES							
	Substitution	Insertion	Omission	Reversal	Repetition	Self-Correction of Unacceptable Miscue	Meaning Change (Significant Miscue)	
"I can not find my ball," said Pete.								
"My ball is a big ball. **It is red**."								
"Here is a ball," Rosa said. "The ball is								
blue. It is little. It is not red."								
"I see a ball," said Pete. "It is red. It								
is big. It is my ball."								
TOTAL								

Oral Rereading: Find and read out loud the sentence that tells what color Pete's ball is.

Word Recognition Scoring Guide		
Total Miscues	Level	Significant Miscues
0	Independent	0
1–2	Ind./Inst.	1
3	Instructional	2
4	Inst./Frust.	3
5 +	Frustration	4 +

Total Miscues ☐   Significant Miscues ☐

_____ WPM
)3000

D-D (Pre-Primer)
Comprehension Questions

T   1. _____ What happened to Pete?
               (he lost his ball)

F   2. _____ What did the ball Rosa found
               look like?
               (blue and little)

E   3. _____ What kind of game do you think
               Pete might play with his ball?
               (any logical response)

I   4. _____ How did Pete know that the ball
               Rosa found wasn't his?
               (any logical response; it was little
               and blue; it wasn't red)

V   5. _____ What is a "ball"?
               (something you play with; it is
               round; any logical response)

Retelling Notes

☐ Questions
   Missed

Comprehension Scoring Guide	
Questions Missed	Level
0	Independent
1	Ind./Inst.
1½	Instructional
2	Inst./Frust.
2½ +	Frustration

Retelling
Excellent
Satisfactory
Unsatisfactory

Student Copy is on page 275.

D (Primer) Activating Background: Read the title to yourself; then tell me what you think will happen.

Background: Low ├─────┼─────┤ High

Jill's Egg

	MISCUES						
	Substitution	Insertion	Omission	Reversal	Repetition	Self-Correction of Unacceptable Miscue	Meaning Change (Significant Miscue)
A white house was in the woods. Jill							
lived there. The sun made Jill happy. The							
air smelled clean. She took a walk.							
Jill found something along the road							
in the grass. It was round and white.							
"Oh!" said Jill. "What a nice egg.							
I'll take it home."							
Mother was home.							
She said, **"Jill, you must keep the**							
egg warm."							
Jill filled a box with rags. She set the							
egg in it. She put it near the stove.							
The next day Jill heard a sound							
she did not know.							
"Cheep." A baby bird was born. Jill							
had a new pet.							
TOTAL							

Oral Rereading: Find and read out loud the sentence that tells what mother told Jill to do with the egg.

Word Recognition Scoring Guide		
Total Miscues	Level	Significant Miscues
0–1	Independent	0–1
2–4	Ind./Inst.	2
5	Instructional	3
6–9	Inst./Frust.	4
10 +	Frustration	5 +

Total Miscues ☐   Significant Miscues ☐

_____ WPM

)6000

D (Primer)
Comprehension Questions

		Retelling Notes

T   1. _____   What is this story about?
(a girl named Jill who found an
egg that hatched)

F   2. _____   Where did Jill live?
(in the woods; in a white house)

F   3. _____   What made Jill happy?
(the sun)

F   4. _____   What happened to Jill?
(she took a walk; she found an egg)

F   5. _____   Where did Jill find the egg?
(along the road in the grass)

F   6. _____   What happened to the egg?
(it hatched; a baby chick was born)

F   7. _____   What did Jill do to make the egg
hatch?
(put it near the stove in a box)

I   8. _____   How do you think the egg got in
the grass along the road?
(any logical response)

E   9. _____   What other things might Jill have
found on her walk?
(any logical response; tracks,
leaves, rocks, and so on.)

V   10. _____   What is a "pet"?
(an animal to love, play with, and
so on.)

[ ] Questions
Missed

Comprehension Scoring Guide	
Questions Missed	Level
0–1	Independent
1½–2	Ind./Inst.
2½	Instructional
3–4½	Inst./Frust.
5 +	Frustration

Retelling
Excellent
Satisfactory
Unsatisfactory

291

Student Copy is on page 276.

D 7141 (Grade 1) Activating Background: Read the title to yourself; then tell me what you think will happen.

Background: Low ├────┼────┤ High

At the Zoo

	Substitution	Insertion	Omission	Reversal	Repetition	Self-Correction of Unacceptable Miscue	Meaning Change (Significant Miscue)
	MISCUES						
Dan wanted to go to the zoo. He							
asked his mother. She said, "Yes."							
Dan had fun at the zoo. There were many							
animals he liked. One animal looked like it							
had two tails. It was an elephant. One had							
a nice back to ride on. It was a big turtle.							
Dan looked at many things. He saw many							
furry animals. He laughed at them.							
It got dark. "Where is my mother?"							
he asked. Dan looked and looked for his							
mother. He was lost! **He sat down and**							
cried. Then Dan looked up. He saw							
his mother running to him!							
TOTAL							

Oral Rereading: Find and read out loud the sentence that tells what Dan did when he was lost.

Word Recognition Scoring Guide		
Total Miscues	Level	Significant Miscues
0–1	Independent	0–1
2–4	Ind./Inst.	2
5	Instructional	3
6–9	Inst./Frust.	4
10 +	Frustration	5 +

Total Miscues ☐   Significant Miscues ☐

_____ WPM
)6000

D 7141 (Grade 1)
Comprehension Questions

T   1. _____   What is this story about?
                (a boy's trip to the zoo)

F   2. _____   Who went with Dan?
                (his mother)

F   3. _____   What did Dan think he could do
                with the turtle?
                (ride it)

F   4. _____   What other types of animals did
                Dan see at the zoo?
                (furry animals; elephant)

F   5. _____   How did Dan think the elephant
                looked?
                (like it had two tails)

F   6. _____   Why did Dan cry?
                (he was lost; he was scared)

F   7. _____   What did Dan see when he
                looked up?
                (his mother running to him)

I   8. _____   What do you think the furry
                animals were?
                (any logical response; monkeys;
                bears)

E   9. _____   What did you think the furry
                animals did?
                (any logical response)

V   10. _____   What does "furry" mean?
                (covered with fur; soft)

Retelling Notes

☐ Questions
   Missed

Comprehension Scoring Guide	
Questions Missed	Level
0–1	Independent
1½–2	Ind./Inst.
2½	Instructional
3–4½	Inst./Frust.
5 +	Frustration

Retelling
Excellent
Satisfactory
Unsatisfactory

293

Student Copy is on page 277.

D 8224 (Grade 2) Activating Background: Read the title to yourself; then tell me what you think will happen.

Background: Low |——————+——————| High

A Spider Friend

| | MISCUES | | | | | | |
	Substitution	Insertion	Omission	Reversal	Repetition	Self-Correction of Unacceptable Miscue	Meaning Change (Significant Miscue)
A spider sat down by a boy. The							
boy was afraid of it. He should not have							
been scared. The spider would not hurt							
him. Most spiders are friendly. Spiders							
belong to a group of animals that have							
eight legs. Spiders are not insects.							
In the fall the mother spider lays							
about 500 eggs. Only the strong baby							
spiders live. **When spring comes they**							
leave their nest. They eat flies, bugs, and							
ants. They also eat insects that harm our							
crops. Some large spiders eat mice and							
birds. You should be able to find a							
spider web where you live.							
TOTAL							

Oral Rereading: Find and read out loud the sentence that tells what spiders do in the spring.

Word Recognition Scoring Guide		
Total Miscues	Level	Significant Miscues
0–1	Independent	0–1
2–4	Ind./Inst.	2
5	Instructional	3
6–9	Inst./Frust.	4
10 +	Frustration	5 +

Total Miscues [ ]   Significant Miscues [ ]

WPM

)6000

D 8224 (Grade 2)
Comprehension Questions

T 1. _____ What is this story about?
(spiders)

F 2. _____ What did the spider do first in this story?
(sat by a little boy)

F 3. _____ How many legs does a spider have?
(eight)

F 4. _____ When do mother spiders lay their eggs?
(in the fall)

F 5. _____ How many eggs does a mother spider lay?
(500)

F 6. _____ When do baby spiders leave their nest?
(in the spring)

F 7. _____ What do large spiders eat?
(mice and birds [either 1])

I 8. _____ What happens to weak baby spiders?
(any logical response; they die)

E 9. _____ Why do you think some people are afraid of spiders?
(any logical response)

V 10. _____ What are "crops"?
(any logical response; what farmers grow)

☐ Questions
Missed

Comprehension Scoring Guide	
Questions Missed	Level
0–1	Independent
1½–2	Ind./Inst.
2½	Instructional
3–4½	Inst./Frust.
5 +	Frustration

Retelling
Excellent
Satisfactory
Unsatisfactory

Retelling Notes

Student Copy is on page 278.

D 3183 (Grade 3) Activating Background: Read the title to yourself; then tell me what you think will happen.

Background: Low |—————|—————| High

Cricket Song

	MISCUES				Repetition	Self-Correction of Unacceptable Miscue	Meaning Change (Significant Miscue)
	Substitution	Insertion	Omission	Reversal			
It is a summer night. I try to sleep, but							
a sound keeps waking me. It is a cricket.							
This bug does not sing with its mouth. The							
rough wings of the male cricket make							
sounds. It rubs its wings against each							
other.							
I try to find the bug, but it is hard. The							
sound does not come from one spot. **It**							
would also be hard to see the cricket							
because it can be as small as the nail on my							
thumb. Some people think the cricket							
brings luck. Maybe they know how to fall							
asleep to the cricket song.							
TOTAL							

Oral Rereading: Find and read out loud the sentence that tells why the cricket is hard to see.

Word Recognition Scoring Guide		
Total Miscues	Level	Significant Miscues
0–1	Independent	0–1
2–4	Ind./Inst.	2
5	Instructional	3
6–9	Inst./Frust.	4
10 +	Frustration	5 +

Total Miscues ☐   Significant Miscues ☐

WPM
)6000

D 3183 (Grade 3)
Comprehension Questions

T   1. _____ What is this story about?
(how a cricket makes a song; a cricket)

F   2. _____ When does this story take place?
(night; summer)

F   3. _____ Why can't the person in the story sleep?
(a sound keeps him or her awake; the cricket song)

F   4. _____ How does the cricket make its sound?
(it rubs its wings together)

F   5. _____ What type of cricket makes this sound?
(male)

F   6. _____ Why was the cricket difficult to find?
(the sound didn't seem to come from one spot; the cricket is very small [any 1])

F   7. _____ What do some people think the cricket brings?
(luck)

I   8. _____ Why might only the male make this sound?
(any logical response; females don't have rough wings)

E   9. _____ How do you think you would feel if a cricket kept you awake? Why?
(any logical response; tired; angry)

V 10. _____ What does "nail" mean in this story?
(what's on your finger; part of finger that protects the tip)

Retelling Notes

☐ Questions Missed

Comprehension Scoring Guide	
Questions Missed	Level
0–1	Independent
1½–2	Ind./Inst.
2½	Instructional
3–4½	Inst./Frust.
5 +	Frustration

Retelling
Excellent
Satisfactory
Unsatisfactory

Student Copy is on page 279.

D 5414 (Grade 4) Activating Background: Read the title to yourself; then tell me what you think the passage will be about.

Background: Low |———|———| High

Oldest Living Things

	MISCUES						
	Substitution	Insertion	Omission	Reversal	Repetition	Self-Correction of Unacceptable Miscue	Meaning Change (Significant Miscue)
There are over three hundred							
thousand different kinds of plants. The							
oxygen in the air we breathe comes from							
plants. Some plants grow bigger and live							
longer than animals. Plants grow in many							
sizes and shapes. Some are smaller than							
the period at the end of this sentence.							
These plants can only be seen with a							
microscope. Other plants, like the giant							
pine, tower high in the sky. Most plants							
have stems and leaves. Plants can live in							
a variety of places. Some even seem to							
grow out of rocks. Others live in water,							
old bread, and even old shoes!							
TOTAL							

Oral Rereading: Find and read out loud the sentence that tells how to see very small plants.

Word Recognition Scoring Guide		
Total Miscues	Level	Significant Miscues
0–1	Independent	0–1
2–4	Ind./Inst.	2
5	Instructional	3
6–9	Inst./Frust.	4
10 +	Frustration	5 +

Total Miscues ☐   Significant Miscues ☐

———— WPM
)6000

D 5414 (Grade 4)
Comprehension Questions

T   1. _____   What is this passage about?
(plants)

F   2. _____   How many plants are there?
(over 300,000)

F   3. _____   Why are plants important to people?
(they provide oxygen)

F   4. _____   How small can plants be?
(smaller than a period at the end of a sentence; so small you need a microscope)

F   5. _____   What do most plants have?
(stems and leaves)

F   6. _____   According to the passage, where can plants live?
(water; bread; shoes [any 2] or a variety of places)

F   7. _____   What is used to see small plants?
(a microscope)

I   8. _____   Name some plants that would probably live longer than most animals.
(any logical response; trees)

E   9. _____   What do you think would happen if all the plants died? Why?
(any logical response; there would be no life on earth)

V   10. _____   What is a "microscope"?
(a thing that makes small things seem larger)

☐ Questions Missed

Comprehension Scoring Guide	
Questions Missed	Level
0–1	Independent
1½–2	Ind./Inst.
2½	Instructional
3–4½	Inst./Frust.
5 +	Frustration

Retelling
Excellent
Satisfactory
Unsatisfactory

Retelling Notes

Student Copy is on page 280.

D 8595 (Grade 5) Activating Background: Read the title to yourself; then tell me what you think the passage will be about.

Background: Low ├────┼────┤ High

Flight

	MISCUES						
	Substitution	Insertion	Omission	Reversal	Repetition	Self-Correction of Unacceptable Miscue	Meaning Change (Significant Miscue)
Older airplanes were moved through							
the air by the use of propellers. Now, most							
planes are driven by large jet engines.							
Some fly faster than sound. **The first thing**							
you may notice about a plane is the wings							
that stick out on either side of its long							
body. Today jet planes land and take off							
from major airports every few seconds.							
People can travel several hundred miles							
in less than an hour. It can take travelers							
longer to retrieve their luggage than to fly							
to their destination. Planes have been							
much improved since the Wright brothers							
first flew in 1903.							
TOTAL							

Oral Rereading: Find and read out loud the sentence that tells what you might first notice about a plane.

Word Recognition Scoring Guide		
Total Miscues	Level	Significant Miscues
0–1	Independent	0–1
2–4	Ind./Inst.	2
5	Instructional	3
6–9	Inst./Frust.	4
10 +	Frustration	5 +

Total Miscues ☐   Significant Miscues ☐

_____ WPM
)6000

D 8595 (Grade 5)
Comprehension Questions

T   1. _____ What is this passage about?
                (airplanes; the development of planes
                through the years)

F   2. _____ What kind of engines do most airplanes
                have today?
                (jet engines)

F   3. _____ How fast can some planes fly?
                (faster than sound)

F   4. _____ How were older planes moved through
                the air?
                (propellers)

F   5. _____ In what year did the Wright brothers
                fly?
                (1903)

F   6. _____ According to this passage, how long
                does it take for people to fly several
                hundred miles?
                (less than an hour)

F   7. _____ According to the passage, how often do
                airplanes take off and land from major
                airports?
                (every few seconds)

I   8. _____ How do you think the Wright brothers
                felt after the first flight? Why?
                (any logical response)

E   9. _____ Do you think jet airplanes have
                changed our lives for the better? Why?
                (any logical response)

V   10. _____ What is a "destination"?
                (a place you are trying to get to)

<table>
<tr><td>Questions
Missed</td></tr>
</table>

Comprehension Scoring Guide	
Questions Missed	Level
0–1	Independent
1½–2	Ind./Inst.
2½	Instructional
3–4½	Inst./Frust.
5 +	Frustration

Retelling
Excellent
Satisfactory
Unsatisfactory

Retelling Notes

Student Copy is on page 281.

D 6867 (Grade 6) Activating Background: Read the title to yourself; then tell me what you think the passage will be about.

Background: Low ├────┼────┤ High

Sunflowers

	MISCUES						
	Substitution	Insertion	Omission	Reversal	Repetition	Self-Correction of Unacceptable Miscue	Meaning Change (Significant Miscue)
One of the most amazing flowers							
found in the Midwest is the sunflower.							
Legend states that the flower got its name							
from its strange habit of "turning" its head							
in order to face the sun. The sunflower is							
a very strong plant. It ranges in height							
from three to fifteen feet. The head of the							
sunflower is similar to that of a daisy. Both							
have an outer circle of wide petals and							
an inner circle of small brown flowers.							
Seeds later form from these small flowers.							
These seeds produce some of the most							
unique patterns found in the plant world.							
TOTAL							

Oral Rereading: Find and read out loud the sentence that tells what happens to the brown flowers.

Word Recognition Scoring Guide		
Total Miscues	Level	Significant Miscues
0–1	Independent	0–1
2–4	Ind./Inst.	2
5	Instructional	3
6–9	Inst./Frust.	4
10 +	Frustration	5 +

Total Miscues ☐

Significant Miscues ☐

WPM
)6000

302

D 6867 (Grade 6)
Comprehension Questions

T   1. _____   What is this paragraph about?
(sunflowers)

F   2. _____   How did the sunflower get its name?
(turning its head to face the sun)

F   3. _____   How tall is the sunflower?
(three to fifteen feet)

F   4. _____   What is on the outside of the
sunflower?
(wide petals)

F   5. _____   What color is the inner circle of
the sunflower?
(brown)

F   6. _____   What is the head of the sunflower
similar to?
(daisy)

F   7. _____   What comes from the small
flowers in the middle?
(seeds)

I   8. _____   Would some sunflowers be taller
than you are? Why?
(any logical response)

E   9. _____   Why do you think a sunflower
would be considered a strong
plant?
(any logical response)

V   10. _____   What does "unique" mean?
(different; any logical response)

Retelling Notes

☐ Questions Missed

Comprehension Scoring Guide	
Questions Missed	Level
0–1	Independent
1½–2	Ind./Inst.
2½	Instructional
3–4½	Inst./Frust.
5 +	Frustration

Retelling
Excellent
Satisfactory
Unsatisfactory

303

Student Copy is on page 282.

D 3717 (Grade 7) Activating Background: Read the title to yourself; then tell me what you think the passage will be about.

Background: Low ├────┼────┤ High

Indian Celebrations

	MISCUES						
	Substitution	Insertion	Omission	Reversal	Repetition	Self-Correction of Unacceptable Miscue	Meaning Change (Significant Miscue)
Indians worshipped the power in							
natural things, such as the stars, moon,							
and the sun. At various times during the							
year, they would hold celebrations in honor							
of this power that they named the Great							
Spirit. On these occasions, they would have							
ceremonies of dancing and feasting. The							
Indians would decorate their bodies and							
faces and dress themselves in their best							
clothes. **A medicine man would lead them**							
in the celebration that continued for							
several days. While gathered about the							
council fire, the Indians prayed that the							
Great Spirit would reveal its wish for them							
by sending a natural sign.							
TOTAL							

Oral Rereading: Find and read out loud the sentence that tells who led the celebration.

Word Recognition Scoring Guide		
Total Miscues	Level	Significant Miscues
0–1	Independent	0–1
2–4	Ind./Inst.	2
5	Instructional	3
6–9	Inst./Frust.	4
10 +	Frustration	5 +

Total Miscues ☐   Significant Miscues ☐

WPM
)6000

D 3717 (Grade 7)
Comprehension Questions

<table>
<tr><td>T</td><td>1. ____</td><td>What is this passage about?
(Indian worship; how Indians celebrated)</td></tr>
<tr><td>F</td><td>2. ____</td><td>What did the Indians worship?
(the power in natural things; sun, moon, stars)</td></tr>
<tr><td>F</td><td>3. ____</td><td>Why did the Indians hold celebrations?
(to honor the Great Spirit)</td></tr>
<tr><td>F</td><td>4. ____</td><td>How did the Indians decorate themselves for the celebrations?
(painted their faces and bodies; wore their best clothes)</td></tr>
<tr><td>F</td><td>5. ____</td><td>What did the medicine man do during the celebration?
(led them)</td></tr>
<tr><td>F</td><td>6. ____</td><td>What were the Indians doing at their celebrations?
(dancing, feasting, decorating themselves, and praying [any 2])</td></tr>
<tr><td>F</td><td>7. ____</td><td>What did the Indians pray for?
(a sign from the Great Spirit)</td></tr>
<tr><td>I</td><td>8. ____</td><td>What sign do you think the Indians wanted from the Great Spirit?
(any logical response)</td></tr>
<tr><td>E</td><td>9. ____</td><td>Why do you think the Indians worshipped things of nature?
(any logical response)</td></tr>
<tr><td>V</td><td>10. ____</td><td>What is meant by "reveal"?
(show; make known)</td></tr>
</table>

Retelling Notes

☐ Questions Missed

Comprehension Scoring Guide	
Questions Missed	Level
0–1	Independent
1½–2	Ind./Inst.
2½	Instructional
3–4½	Inst./Frust.
5 +	Frustration

Retelling
Excellent
Satisfactory
Unsatisfactory

Student Copy is on page 283.

D 8183 (Grade 8) Activating Background: Read the title to yourself; then tell me what you think the passage will be about.

Background: Low ├────┼────┤ High

Our Environment

	MISCUES						
	Substitution	Insertion	Omission	Reversal	Repetition	Self-Correction of Unacceptable Miscue	Meaning Change (Significant Miscue)
Besides using plants and animals for							
food, people use the hides of animals for							
shoes, the wood from trees to build houses,							
the fiber from the cotton plant to make							
skirts and shirts, and the wool from sheep							
to make suits and coats. Even the synthetic							
fibers that people use are made from							
matter found in the environment.							
People and the environment are							
interdependent, but that is not the whole							
story. **Modern people can do much more;**							
they can use science and technology to							
change their environment. Because of							
their advanced brains, people can							
investigate and use their precious							
environment.							
TOTAL							

Oral Rereading: Find and read out loud the sentence that tells what two things people use to change their environment.

Word Recognition Scoring Guide		
Total Miscues	Level	Significant Miscues
0–1	Independent	0–1
2–4	Ind./Inst.	2
5	Instructional	3
6–9	Inst./Frust.	4
10 +	Frustration	5 +

Total Miscues ☐   Significant Miscues ☐

WPM

)6000

D 8183 (Grade 8)
Comprehension Questions

T	1. _____	What is this passage about? (people's interdependence with their environment; how people use their environment)
F	2. _____	What do modern people use to change the environment? (science and technology)
F	3. _____	Why are people able to investigate their environment? (they have a brain)
F	4. _____	What are synthetic fibers made from? (matter found in the environment)
F	5. _____	What are some of the things in the environment which people use? (plants; animals; wood; cotton; wool [any 2])
F	6. _____	What does the passage say people use to make skirts and shirts? (fiber from the cotton plant)
F	7. _____	According to the passage, what are the hides of animals used for? (shoes)
I	8. _____	What are some of the ways in which people have changed the environment? (any logical response)
E	9. _____	Do you think it's a good thing for people to change their environment? Why? (any logical response)
V	10. _____	What does "synthetic" mean? (made from several things put together)

Retelling Notes

☐ Questions Missed

Comprehension Scoring Guide	
Questions Missed	Level
0–1	Independent
1½–2	Ind./Inst.
2½	Instructional
3–4½	Inst./Frust.
5 +	Frustration

Retelling
Excellent
Satisfactory
Unsatisfactory

FORM LN

Narrative

*Form LN contains ten longer **narrative** passages that range in difficulty from grade three through grade twelve. These passages may be used for oral or silent reading to help verify, supplement, or expand knowledge and insights about the student's reading.*

Form LN
Graded Passages
(Student Copy)

A Day in the Woods

Sue was visiting her grandparents' farm for a week. She decided to have a picnic in the woods. She packed a lunch with a peanut-butter and jelly sandwich, an apple, two cookies, and grape juice to drink. Sue had put her lunch in her back pack and started out the door when she remembered Jane. She ran back into the house and got Jane, her favorite doll.

Sue had a good time in the woods. She walked on small paths that the animals had made. After walking all morning, she was very hungry. At noon she found a fallen tree and sat on it to eat her lunch.

After lunch Sue found an animal trail that led to a quiet spring. She looked into the water and saw small fish swimming. She must remember to tell her grandparents about the little fish in the spring.

Sue realized that it was time to start back to her grandparents' house, but she didn't know which way to go. Just then she heard rustling in the bushes right behind her. She was frightened and started to run. The noise followed her as she ran. It kept getting closer. All of a sudden something jumped at her! It was Rusty, her grandparents' dog. Sue was so happy to see him she gave him a big hug.

Sue and Rusty got back to the farm just as the sun was setting. Sue's grandparents were worried. Sue promised never to go so deep in the woods again.

Danny and the Dragon

"Mother, there's a dragon after me! It won't go away!"

The next day when Danny went out, there it was. It roared and blew fire at Danny. It was so big and Danny was so small. "Leave me alone!"

Danny ran down the path to the river and hid behind a rock to see if the dragon was still coming. It was. He had to get rid of that dragon. He went home through the woods. He needed a plan to trick the dragon.

In bed that night, Danny made his plan. He had to trick the dragon into the river. He knew the dragon couldn't swim.

While it was still dark, Danny climbed out his window. He got a rope and tiptoed away from his house. Then he ran to the big rock by the river. Danny laid the rope across the path. He tied one end of the rope to a tree. He laid the other end on the ground behind the big rock. Danny ran home through the woods. There was the dragon lying by the door to his house. Danny climbed quietly in his window to wait.

In the morning Danny went out. Roaring, the dragon blew fire and leaped at him. Danny dodged it and ran toward the river. He flew down the path, dove behind the rock, and grabbed the rope.

Down the path came the dragon. Then it tripped on the rope and crashed into the river. The river carried it far, far away.

Jerry, looking at the sky, promised himself, "I'm going to fly some day."

Jerry, a ten-year-old boy from a small town in Iowa, had dreamed of flying since he was a little boy. He wasn't just going to fly in an airplane. He was going to fly like a hawk.

He spent many hours watching hawks fly. They made it look so easy. With their powerful wings they built up speed, then they would glide. It was beautiful and breath-taking watching them ride the air currents. "I am going to fly."

As he climbed to the top of the cliff, his imagination was far ahead of him telling him how exciting it would be. At the top he paused only for a moment, then he dove off the cliff into the air. "This is wonderful! This is better than I had ever imagined!" He soared, he dipped, and rose again, riding the air currents. Flying was better than he had imagined.

When Jerry awoke, his parents were standing by the hospital bed. "The doctor said you will be fine. You will have to miss two more weeks of school because of your tonsil operation."

After Jerry's parents left, he thought a moment, "I really felt like I was flying. I could feel the cool air blowing through my hair. I saw the landscape below me." Was it a dream or not? If it was a dream, where did he get the hawk feather he was holding?

Action at Brantwood

As Kay got off the passenger train at Brantwood, she was rudely shoved. Turning quickly, she saw a young man elbowing his way through the bustling crowd toward an older woman. As Kay proceeded across the train platform, she saw the older woman trip and tumble to the pavement. The fallen woman's handbag flew open and its contents spilled all over the ground. Her suitcase also snapped open and its contents, too, were strewn over the snow.

Kay rushed up to help the stunned woman. She was brushed aside by the man who had collided with her earlier. The man assumed charge of the woman's belongings in a most possessive manner. He was short, slender, blonde, and had a rosy complexion. Kay picked up the woman's handbag from the snow, but the young man snatched it from her almost as if he suspected her of trying to steal it.

"Just a minute, please!" exclaimed Kay. "I'm just trying to help this lady. May I ask why you are trying to take charge of her things?"

"I am her son!" retorted the young man unpleasantly as he went on hastily collecting the things which had burst from the suitcase. Kay concentrated her attention on the woman and tried to help her up. "Where are my purse and my suitcase!" she cried anxiously.

"Your son has them," Kay said reassuringly. "Don't worry about them. He'll bring you everything as soon as he has it all collected."

"My son!" the lady exclaimed sharply. "I have no son!"

Adapted from *The Double Disguise* by Frances K. Judd.

A sharp sound startled him. Somewhere, off in the blackness, someone had fired a gun three times.

Rainsford sprang up and moved quickly to the rail, mystified. He strained his eyes in the direction from which the reports had come, but it was like trying to see through a blanket. He leaped up onto the rail and balanced himself there to get a greater elevation; his pipe, striking a rope, was knocked from his mouth. He lunged for it. A short, hoarse cry came from his lips as he realized he had reached too far and had fallen overboard. The cry was pinched off as the blood-warm waters of the Caribbean Sea closed over his head.

He struggled up to the surface and tried to cry for help, but the wash from the speeding yacht slapped him in the face. The salty water in his open mouth gagged and strangled him. Desperately he struck out with strong strokes after the receding lights of the yacht, but he stopped before he had covered fifty feet. He calmed down and assessed his situation. It was not the first time he had been in a tough situation. There was a chance that his cries could be heard by someone aboard the yacht. But the chance was slim and grew much slimmer as the yacht continued on. He shouted with all his might. The lights of the yacht became faint, looking like ever-vanishing fireflies. Then they were blotted out entirely by the black night.

Adapted from *"The Most Dangerous Game"* by Richard Connell. Copyright, 1924, by Richard Connell. Copyright renewed, 1952, by Louise Fox Connell. Special adaptation permission of reprint by Brandt & Brandt Literary Agents, Inc.

The Angel of the Candy Counter

The Angel of the candy counter had found me out at last and was demanding extreme payment for all the Snickers, Mounds, suckers, and Hershey bars. I had two huge cavities that were rotten to the gums. The pain was well past the help of crushed aspirins or oil of cloves. Only one thing could help me now, so I prayed earnestly that I'd be allowed to sit under the house and have the entire building collapse on my jaw.

Since there was no dentist in Stamps, nor doctor either, for that matter, Momma had dealt with other toothaches. She would try yanking them out with a string tied to the tooth and the other end looped over her fist, as well as pain killers and prayer. In this case the medicine proved ineffective. There wasn't enough enamel left to hook a string on, and the prayers were being ignored because some demon was blocking their way.

I lived some days and nights in blinding pain, not so much toying with, as seriously considering, the idea of jumping in the well. So Momma decided I had to be taken to a dentist. The nearest dentist was in Mason, twenty miles away, and I was sure that I'd be dead long before we reached half the distance. Momma said we'd go to Dr. Lincoln, and he'd take care of me. She said we'd have to take the bus. I didn't know of anyone who'd been to see him, but Momma said we had to go.

Adapted from *I Know Why the Caged Bird Sings* by Maya Angelou. Reprinted by permission of Random House, Inc.

The Most Beautiful

Of the gods of ancient Greece, Apollo was the most beautiful. His hair was brilliant gold; his eyes were stormy blue. He wore a flowing tunic of golden panther skin, carried a quiver of golden arrows, and used a golden bow. His chariot was beaten gold; his horse was white with a platinum mane and flame-colored eyes. Apollo was always the god of the sun, but later he became patron of music, poetry, mathematics, and medicine. As an adult, Apollo was known for his unparalleled wisdom, but in his youth he was known for his barbarous exploits. Several times he was almost expelled from the company of the gods by Zeus whom he angered with his youthful folly.

One objectionable folly was Apollo's treatment of a satyr named Marsyas. Marsyas was an excellent musician; Apollo considered this his talent and would allow no rivalry. Hearing Marsyas praised continually, Apollo invited him to a musical contest. The winner was to choose a penalty to which the loser would have to submit, and the Muses were their judges. Marsyas played his melodious flute, and Apollo played his lyre. They played so exquisitely that the Muses could not choose between them, so Apollo suggested that they play their instruments upside down and sing simultaneously. Apollo turned his lyre upside down, played, and chanted a beautiful poem. Because Marsyas could not play his flute upside down and sing at the same time, the despondent satyr was declared the loser. Consequently, Apollo collected the prize.

Adapted from *The Greek Gods* by Bernard Evslin, Dorothy Evslin, and Ned Hoopes. Reprinted by permission of Scholastic Book Services.

LN 4959

Elizabeth Meets Darcy

Elizabeth watched for the first appearance of Pemberley Woods with some perturbation; and when at length they turned in at the lodge, her spirits were in a high flutter.

The park was very large and contained great variety of ground. They entered it in one of its lowest points, and drove for some time through a beautiful wood, stretching over a wide extent.

Elizabeth's mind was too full for conversation, but she saw and admired every remarkable spot and point of view. They gradually ascended for half a mile, and then found themselves at the top of a considerable eminence, where the wood ceased, and the eye was instantly caught by Pemberley House, situated on the opposite side of a valley, into which the road with some abruptness wound. It was a large, handsome, stone building, standing well on rising ground, and backed by a ridge of high woody hills. She had never seen a place for which nature had done more, or where natural beauty had been so little counteracted by an awkward taste. They were all of them warm in their admiration, and at the moment she felt that to be mistress of Pemberley might be something!

They descended the hill, crossed the bridge, and drove to the door; and, while examining the nearer aspect of the house, all her apprehensions of meeting its owner returned. As she walked across the lawn, Elizabeth turned back to look again, and the owner himself suddenly came forward from the road.

Adapted from *Pride and Prejudice* by Jane Austen.

Bookworm or Earthworm

To read or to weed is the problem that confronts me whenever I have a few extra minutes. Reading satisfies the wanderlust in me. It affords the opportunity to abandon the monotonous paths of everyday life and to trip excitedly along the mysterious trails in the enchanting land of books. Lost in the magic of the printed page, I can cast off my customary clothing and array myself in the raiment of a victorious knight or a football star. No longer shackled by the chains of time and space, I shiver with Washington's valiant men in the biting cold of Valley Forge and I kneel in reverent awe at Bethlehem's crib. Is it any wonder that I am unable to resist the beckoning call of a good book?

My interest in weeding is probably the result of my interest in reading. This occupation puts me on a par with those noble characters that I have admired in books. Few tasks are more intriguing to me than that of rescuing struggling plants from the greedy claws of choking weeds. I like the feel of the cold and damp earth as I eject the intruding roots. With the confident swagger of a conquering hero, I march triumphantly through our flower garden, leaving grateful shrubs in my wake. Even the squirming worms wriggle their gratitude for my noble deed. Yes, recreation time is always debating time for me. The topic of this secret controversy ever remains the same: to read or to weed?

Adapted with permission from *Voyages in English* by Reverend Paul E. Campbell and Sister Mary Donatus Macnickle. Copyrighted by Loyola University Press.

American in Paris

On a brilliant day in May, in the year 1868, a gentleman was reclining at his ease on the great circular divan which occupied the center of the Salon Carré, in the Museum of the Louvre. He had taken serene possession of the softest spot of this commodious ottoman. With his head thrown back and his legs outstretched, he was staring at Murillo's beautiful moon-borne Madonna in profound enjoyment of his posture. He had removed his hat and flung down beside him a little red guidebook and an opera glass. The day was warm; he was heated with walking, and he repeatedly passed his handkerchief over his forehead with a somewhat wearied gesture. His exertions on this particular day had been of an unwonted sort, and he had often performed great physical feats which left him less jaded than his tranquil stroll through the Louvre. He had looked at all the pictures to which an asterisk was affixed in those formidable pages of fine print in his Bädeker guidebook; his attention had been strained and his eyes dazzled, and he had sat down with an aesthetic headache. His physiognomy would have sufficiently indicated that he was a shrewd and capable fellow. In truth, he had often sat up all night over a bristling bundle of accounts and heard the cock crow without a yawn. But Raphael and Titian and Rubens were a new kind of arithmetic, and they made him, for the first time in his life, wonder.

Adapted from The American *by Henry James.*

Performance Booklet
(Teacher Copy)

 Note: This Performance Booklet is on the CD-ROM that accompanies the Basic Reading Inventory.

BASIC READING INVENTORY PERFORMANCE BOOKLET
Jerry L. Johns, Ph.D.

Student _____ Grade _____ Sex M F   Date of Test _____

School _____ Examiner _____ Date of Birth _____

Address _____ Current Book/Level _____ Age _____

SUMMARY OF STUDENT'S READING PERFORMANCE

Grade	FORM LN: NARRATIVE				FORM LE: EXPOSITORY			
	Word Recognition		Comprehension		Word Recognition		Comprehension	
	Miscues	Level	Questions Missed	Level	Miscues	Level	Questions Missed	Level
3								
4								
5								
6								
7								
8								
9								
10								
11								
12								

ESTIMATE OF READING LEVELS

Independent _____   Instructional _____   Frustration _____

LISTENING LEVEL

Grade	Form _____	
	Questions Missed	Level
3		
4		
5		
6		
7		
8		
9		
10		
11		
12		

ESTIMATED LEVEL: _____

GENERAL OBSERVATIONS

INFORMAL MISCUE ANALYSIS SUMMARY

Types of Miscues	Frequency of Occurrence			General Impact of Miscues on Meaning		
	Seldom	Sometimes	Frequently	No Change	Little Change	Much Change
Substitutions						
Insertions						
Omissions						
Reversals						
Repetitions						

QUALITATIVE ANALYSIS OF BASIC READING INVENTORY INSIGHTS

General Directions: Note the degree to which the student shows behavior or evidence in the following areas. Space is provided for additional items.

	Seldom / Weak / Poor				Always / Strong / Excellent

COMPREHENSION

Seeks to construct meaning
Makes predictions
Activates background knowledge
Possesses appropriate concepts
   and vocabulary
Monitors reading
Varies reading rate as needed
Understands topic and major ideas
Remembers facts or details
Makes and supports appropriate
   inferences
Evaluates ideas from passages
Understands vocabulary used
Provides appropriate definitions
   of words
Engagement with passages

WORD IDENTIFICATION

Possesses numerous strategies
Uses strategies flexibly
Uses graphophonic information
Uses semantic information
Uses syntactic information
Knows basic sight words
   automatically
Possesses sight vocabulary

ORAL AND SILENT READING

Reads fluently
Reads with expression
Attends to punctuation
Keeps place while reading
Appropriate rate
Reads silently without vocalization

ATTITUDE AND CONFIDENCE

Enjoys reading
Demonstrates willingness to risk
Possesses positive self-concept
Chooses to read
Regards himself/herself as a reader
Exhibits persistence

A Day in the Woods

Sue was visiting her grandparents' farm for a week. She decided to have a picnic in the woods. She packed a lunch with a peanut-butter and jelly sandwich, an apple, two cookies, and grape juice to drink. Sue had put her lunch in her back pack and started out the door when she remembered Jane. She ran back into the house and got Jane, her favorite doll.

Sue had a good time in the woods. She walked on small paths that the animals had made. After walking all morning, she was very hungry. At noon she found a fallen tree and sat on it to eat her lunch.

After lunch Sue found an animal trail that led to a quiet spring. She looked into the water and saw small fish swimming. She must remember to tell her grandparents about the little fish in the spring.

Sue realized that it was time to start back to her grandparents' house, but she didn't know which way to go. Just then she heard rustling in the bushes right behind her. She was frightened and started to run. The noise followed her as she ran. It kept getting closer. All of a sudden something jumped at her! It was Rusty, her grandparents' dog. Sue was so happy to see him she gave him a big hug.

Sue and Rusty got back to the farm just as the sun was setting. Sue's grandparents were worried. Sue promised never to go so deep in the woods again.

Total Miscues ☐   Significant Miscues ☐ $\overline{)15000}$ WPM

Word Recognition Scoring Guide		
Total Miscues	Level	Significant Miscues
0–3	Independent	0–2
4–12	Ind./Inst.	3–6
13	Instructional	7
14–24	Inst./Frust.	8–12
25+	Frustration	13+

General Observations

Student Copy is on page 312.

LN 3183 (Grade 3) Activating Background: Read the title to yourself; then tell me what you think will happen.

Background: Low ├───────┼───────┤ High

A Day in the Woods

T   1. _____   What is this story about?
(a girl going for a walk in the woods and getting lost)

F   2. _____   What did Sue take with her?
(her doll, Jane; her lunch; her backpack [any 2])

F   3. _____   What did Sue bring to eat for her lunch?
(peanut-butter and jelly sandwich; an apple; two cookies; and grape juice [any 2])

F.   4. _____   Where did Sue eat her lunch?
(in the woods; on a fallen tree)

F   5. _____   What did Sue find in the woods?
(a fallen tree; animal trails; water; a spring; fish; Rusty [any 2])

F   6. _____   How did Sue know where to go?
(she followed animal trails or paths)

F   7. _____   Why did Sue start running when she was in the woods?
(she heard rustling in the bushes)

I   8. _____   What do you think Sue thought was following her in the woods?
(any logical response; a wild animal)

E   9. _____   Why do you think Sue promised never to go so deep in the woods again?
(any logical response; because she had been so frightened; so she wouldn't get lost)

V   10. _____   Explain what "spring" means in this sentence: Sue saw fish swimming in a spring.
(a small stream of water coming from the earth; a little river; a little pond)

Questions Missed ☐

Comprehension Scoring Guide	
Questions Missed	Level
0–1	Independent
1½–2	Ind./Inst.
2½	Instructional
3–4½	Inst./Frust.
5 +	Frustration

Retelling
Excellent
Satisfactory
Unsatisfactory

General Observations

327

Danny and the Dragon

"Mother, there's a dragon after me! It won't go away!"

The next day when Danny went out, there it was. It roared and blew fire at Danny. It was so big and Danny was so small. "Leave me alone!"

Danny ran down the path to the river and hid behind a rock to see if the dragon was still coming. It was. He had to get rid of that dragon. He went home through the woods. He needed a plan to trick the dragon.

In bed that night, Danny made his plan. He had to trick the dragon into the river. He knew the dragon couldn't swim.

While it was still dark, Danny climbed out his window. He got a rope and tiptoed away from his house. Then he ran to the big rock by the river. Danny laid the rope across the path. He tied one end of the rope to a tree. He laid the other end on the ground behind the big rock. Danny ran home through the woods. There was the dragon lying by the door to his house. Danny climbed quietly in his window to wait.

In the morning Danny went out. Roaring, the dragon blew fire and leaped at him. Danny dodged it and ran toward the river. He flew down the path, dove behind the rock, and grabbed the rope.

Down the path came the dragon. Then it tripped on the rope and crashed into the river. The river carried it far, far away.

Total Miscues ☐   Significant Miscues ☐   )‾15000 WPM

Word Recognition Scoring Guide		
Total Miscues	Level	Significant Miscues
0–3	Independent	0–2
4–12	Ind./Inst.	3–6
13	Instructional	7
14–24	Inst./Frust.	8–12
25+	Frustration	13+

General Observations

LN 5414

Student Copy is on page 313.

LN 5414 (Grade 4) Activating Background: Read the title to yourself; then tell me what you think will happen.

Background: Low ├─────┼─────┤ High

Danny and the Dragon

T   1. _____   What is this story about?
(how Danny gets rid of the dragon)

F   2. _____   When did Danny make his plan?
(during the night)

F   3. _____   What was Danny's plan?
(to trick the dragon)

F   4. _____   How did Danny get out of his house that night?
(he climbed out his window)

F   5. _____   What did Danny do with the rope?
(laid it across the path and tied it to a tree)

F   6. _____   Where was the dragon lying?
(by the door to his house)

F   7. _____   What did the dragon do to Danny?
(roared; blew fire; chased him; wouldn't leave him alone [any 2])

I   8. _____   What do you think happened to the dragon when it was in the river? Why?
(any logical response; it drowned because it could not swim)

E   9. _____   What might be another plan you could use to get rid of the dragon?
(any logical response)

V 10. _____   Explain what "tiptoed" means in this sentence: He tiptoed away from his house.
(sneak; walk on tiptoes very quietly)

Questions
Missed ☐

Comprehension Scoring Guide	
Questions Missed	Level
0–1	Independent
1½–2	Ind./Inst.
2½	Instructional
3–4½	Inst./Frust.
5 +	Frustration

Retelling
Excellent
Satisfactory
Unsatisfactory

General Observations

I Want to Fly

Jerry, looking at the sky, promised himself, "I'm going to fly some day."

Jerry, a ten-year-old boy from a small town in Iowa, had dreamed of flying since he was a little boy. He wasn't just going to fly in an airplane. He was going to fly like a hawk.

He spent many hours watching hawks fly. They made it look so easy. With their powerful wings they built up speed, then they would glide. It was beautiful and breath-taking watching them ride the air currents. "I am going to fly."

As he climbed to the top of the cliff, his imagination was far ahead of him telling him how exciting it would be. At the top he paused only for a moment, then he dove off the cliff into the air. "This is wonderful! This is better than I had ever imagined!" He soared, he dipped, and rose again, riding the air currents. Flying was better than he had imagined.

When Jerry awoke, his parents were standing by the hospital bed. "The doctor said you will be fine. You will have to miss two more weeks of school because of your tonsil operation."

After Jerry's parents left, he thought a moment, "I really felt like I was flying. I could feel the cool air blowing through my hair. I saw the landscape below me." Was it a dream or not? If it was a dream, where did he get the hawk feather he was holding?

Total Miscues ☐　Significant Miscues ☐　$\overline{)15000}$ WPM

Word Recognition Scoring Guide		
Total Miscues	Level	Significant Miscues
0–3	Independent	0–2
4–12	Ind./Inst.	3–6
13	Instructional	7
14–24	Inst./Frust.	8–12
25+	Frustration	13+

General Observations

Student Copy is on page 314.

LN 8595 (Grade 5) Activating Background: Read the title to yourself; then tell me what you think will happen.

Background: Low ├────────┼────────┤ High

I Want to Fly

T 1. _____ What is this story about?
(Jerry wants to fly like a hawk)

F 2. _____ How old is Jerry?
(ten years old)

F 3. _____ Where did Jerry live?
(in a small town; in Iowa)

F 4. _____ What did Jerry spend hours watching?
(hawks flying)

F 5. _____ Why was Jerry in the hospital?
(he had a tonsil operation)

F 6. _____ Who came to visit Jerry?
(his parents)

F 7. _____ How much school will Jerry miss?
(two more weeks)

I 8. _____ Do you think Jerry really flew? Why?
(any logical response; no, he was dreaming; he imagined it; people can't fly)

E 9. _____ Where do you think the hawk feather came from?
(any logical response; he found it and brought it with him; his mom and dad brought it to him; it blew in his window)

V 10. _____ Explain what "landscape" means in this sentence: Jerry saw the landscape below him.
(a stretch of scenery)

Questions Missed ☐

Comprehension Scoring Guide	
Questions Missed	Level
0–1	Independent
1½–2	Ind./Inst.
2½	Instructional
3–4½	Inst./Frust.
5 +	Frustration

Retelling
Excellent
Satisfactory
Unsatisfactory

General Observations

Action at Brantwood

As Kay got off the passenger train at Brantwood, she was rudely shoved. Turning quickly, she saw a young man elbowing his way through the bustling crowd toward an older woman. As Kay proceeded across the train platform, she saw the older woman trip and tumble to the pavement. The fallen woman's handbag flew open and its contents spilled all over the ground. Her suitcase also snapped open and its contents, too, were strewn over the snow.

Kay rushed up to help the stunned woman. She was brushed aside by the man who had collided with her earlier. The man assumed charge of the woman's belongings in a most possessive manner. He was short, slender, blonde, and had a rosy complexion. Kay picked up the woman's handbag from the snow, but the young man snatched it from her almost as if he suspected her of trying to steal it.

"Just a minute, please!" exclaimed Kay. "I'm just trying to help this lady. May I ask why you are trying to take charge of her things?"

"I am her son!" retorted the young man unpleasantly as he went on hastily collecting the things which had burst from the suitcase. Kay concentrated her attention on the woman and tried to help her up. "Where are my purse and my suitcase!" she cried anxiously.

"Your son has them," Kay said reassuringly. "Don't worry about them. He'll bring you everything as soon as he has it all collected."

"My son!" the lady exclaimed sharply. "I have no son!"

Total Miscues ☐	Significant Miscues ☐	)15000 WPM

Word Recognition Scoring Guide		
Total Miscues	Level	Significant Miscues
0–3	Independent	0–2
4–12	Ind./Inst.	3–6
13	Instructional	7
14–24	Inst./Frust.	8–12
25+	Frustration	13+

General Observations

Adapted from *The Double Disguise* by Frances K. Judd.

LN 6867

Student Copy is on page 315.

LN 6867 (Grade 6) Activating Background: Read the title to yourself; then tell me what you think will happen.

Background: Low ├───────┼───────┤ High

Action at Brantwood

T   1. ____   What is this story about?
(a man's attempt to steal an older woman's things; Kay's attempt to help an older woman who falls at the train station)

F   2. ____   Where does this story take place?
(Brantwood; a train station)

F   3. ____   What happened when Kay got off the train?
(she was shoved; an older woman tripped and fell)

F   4. ____   Describe the young man?
(short; slender; blonde; rosy complexion [any 2])

F   5. ____   What happened when the older woman fell down?
(her handbag flew open; her suitcase snapped open in the snow)

F   6. ____   What did the young man do when Kay tried to help?
(he brushed Kay aside; he snatched the handbag from her)

F   7. ____   Why did the young man think he had a right to pick up the older lady's possessions?
(he said he was her son)

I   8. ____   How do you think Kay felt about the young man before and after talking to the older woman? Why?
(any logical response; first she was understanding; then angry; irritated)

E   9. ____   Which character would you believe, the young man or the older woman? Why?
(any logical response)

V 10. ____   Explain what "stunned" means in this sentence: Kay rushed up to help the stunned woman.
(didn't know what was going on; shocked; startled)

Questions
Missed   ☐

Comprehension Scoring Guide	
Questions Missed	Level
0–1	Independent
1½–2	Ind./Inst.
2½	Instructional
3–4½	Inst./Frust.
5 +	Frustration

Retelling
Excellent
Satisfactory
Unsatisfactory

General Observations

Man Overboard

A sharp sound startled him. Somewhere, off in the blackness, someone had fired a gun three times.

Rainsford sprang up and moved quickly to the rail, mystified. He strained his eyes in the direction from which the reports had come, but it was like trying to see through a blanket. He leaped up onto the rail and balanced himself there to get a greater elevation; his pipe, striking a rope, was knocked from his mouth. He lunged for it. A short, hoarse cry came from his lips as he realized he had reached too far and had fallen overboard. The cry was pinched off as the blood-warm waters of the Caribbean Sea closed over his head.

He struggled up to the surface and tried to cry for help, but the wash from the speeding yacht slapped him in the face. The salty water in his open mouth gagged and strangled him. Desperately he struck out with strong strokes after the receding lights of the yacht, but he stopped before he had covered fifty feet. He calmed down and assessed his situation. It was not the first time he had been in a tough situation. There was a chance that his cries could be heard by someone aboard the yacht. But the chance was slim and grew much slimmer as the yacht continued on. He shouted with all his might. The lights of the yacht became faint, looking like ever-vanishing fireflies. Then they were blotted out entirely by the black night.

Total Miscues ☐ Significant Miscues ☐ $\overline{)15000}$ WPM

Word Recognition Scoring Guide		
Total Miscues	Level	Significant Miscues
0–3	Independent	0–2
4–12	Ind./Inst.	3–6
13	Instructional	7
14–24	Inst./Frust.	8–12
25+	Frustration	13+

General Observations

LN 3717

Student Copy is on page 316.

LN 3717 (Grade 7) Activating Background: Read the title to yourself; then tell me what you think will happen.

Background: Low ├──────┼──────┤ High

Man Overboard

T 1. _____ What is this story about?
(a man in a dangerous situation; a man who falls overboard)

F 2. _____ What sounds did Rainsford hear?
(gunshots; someone fired a gun three times)

F 3. _____ Why was Rainsford standing on the rail?
(to have better elevation; to have a better view)

F 4. _____ What caused Rainsford to fall overboard?
(he reached too far forward trying to catch his pipe)

F 5. _____ How did the water feel when he fell overboard?
(blood-warm)

F 6. _____ Why did Rainsford have difficulty crying for help?
(the water kept getting in his mouth)

F 7. _____ About how far did he swim before he stopped?
(fifty feet)

I 8. _____ Why do you think that the people aboard the yacht didn't hear Rainsford?
(any logical response; noisy motor; music on the yacht; the noise of the sea)

E 9. _____ What would you do if you were in the same situation as Rainsford?
(any logical response)

V 10. _____ Explain what "mystified" means in this sentence: He moved quickly to the rail, mystified.
(confused; curious; perplexed; bewildered)

Questions Missed □

Comprehension Scoring Guide	
Questions Missed	Level
0–1	Independent
1½–2	Ind./Inst.
2½	Instructional
3–4½	Inst./Frust.
5 +	Frustration

Retelling
Excellent
Satisfactory
Unsatisfactory

General Observations

335

The Angel of the Candy Counter

The Angel of the candy counter had found me out at last and was demanding extreme payment for all the Snickers, Mounds, suckers, and Hershey bars. I had two huge cavities that were rotten to the gums. The pain was well past the help of crushed aspirins or oil of cloves. Only one thing could help me now, so I prayed earnestly that I'd be allowed to sit under the house and have the entire building collapse on my jaw.

Since there was no dentist in Stamps, nor doctor either, for that matter, Momma had dealt with other toothaches. She would try yanking them out with a string tied to the tooth and the other end looped over her fist, as well as pain killers and prayer. In this case the medicine proved ineffective. There wasn't enough enamel left to hook a string on, and the prayers were being ignored because some demon was blocking their way.

I lived some days and nights in blinding pain, not so much toying with, as seriously considering, the idea of jumping in the well. So Momma decided I had to be taken to a dentist. The nearest dentist was in Mason, twenty miles away, and I was sure that I'd be dead long before we reached half the distance. Momma said we'd go to Dr. Lincoln, and he'd take care of me. She said we'd have to take the bus. I didn't know of anyone who'd been to see him, but Momma said we had to go.

Total Miscues ☐   Significant Miscues ☐   )15000 WPM

Word Recognition Scoring Guide		
Total Miscues	Level	Significant Miscues
0–3	Independent	0–2
4–12	Ind./Inst.	3–6
13	Instructional	7
14–24	Inst./Frust.	8–12
25+	Frustration	13+

General Observations

Adapted from *I Know Why the Caged Bird Sings* by Maya Angelou. Reprinted by permission of Random House, Inc.

LN 8183

Student Copy is on page 317.

LN 8183 (Grade 8) Activating Background: Read the title to yourself; then tell me what you think will happen.

Background: Low ├──────┼──────┤ High

The Angel of the Candy Counter

T 1. _____ What is this story about?
(someone who has a toothache and has to go to the dentist)

F 2. _____ What remedies had already been tried to ease the pain?
(crushed aspirins; oil of clove; prayer [any 1])

F 3. _____ Why didn't Momma pull the teeth that were hurting?
(they were too rotten; there wasn't enough enamel to hook a string on)

F 4. _____ Why weren't the prayers being answered?
(a demon or devil was blocking their way)

F 5. _____ In what town did the narrator live?
(Stamps)

F 6. _____ How far was the nearest dentist from home?
(20 miles)

F 7. _____ What is the name of the dentist?
(Dr. Lincoln)

I 8. _____ What did this person think was responsible for the pain?
(candy)

E 9. _____ Why do you think Stamps had no dentist or doctor?
(any logical response; small town; poor town; the story takes place many years ago)

V 10. _____ Explain what "earnestly" means in this sentence: I prayed earnestly that the house would fall on my jaw.
(seriously; with determination)

Questions
Missed ☐

Comprehension Scoring Guide	
Questions Missed	Level
0–1	Independent
1½–2	Ind./Inst.
2½	Instructional
3–4½	Inst./Frust.
5 +	Frustration

Retelling
Excellent
Satisfactory
Unsatisfactory

General Observations

The Most Beautiful

Of the gods of ancient Greece, Apollo was the most beautiful. His hair was brilliant gold; his eyes were stormy blue. He wore a flowing tunic of golden panther skin, carried a quiver of golden arrows, and used a golden bow. His chariot was beaten gold; his horse was white with a platinum mane and flame-colored eyes. Apollo was always the god of the sun, but later he became patron of music, poetry, mathematics, and medicine. As an adult, Apollo was known for his unparalleled wisdom, but in his youth he was known for his barbarous exploits. Several times he was almost expelled from the company of the gods by Zeus whom he angered with his youthful folly.

One objectionable folly was Apollo's treatment of a satyr named Marsyas. Marsyas was an excellent musician; Apollo considered this his talent and would allow no rivalry. Hearing Marsyas praised continually, Apollo invited him to a musical contest. The winner was to choose a penalty to which the loser would have to submit, and the Muses were their judges. Marsyas played his melodious flute, and Apollo played his lyre. They played so exquisitely that the Muses could not choose between them, so Apollo suggested that they play their instruments upside down and sing simultaneously. Apollo turned his lyre upside down, played, and chanted a beautiful poem. Because Marsyas could not play his flute upside down and sing at the same time, the despondent satyr was declared the loser. Consequently, Apollo collected the prize.

Total Miscues ☐   Significant Miscues ☐   )15000 WPM

Word Recognition Scoring Guide		
Total Miscues	Level	Significant Miscues
0–3	Independent	0–2
4–12	Ind./Inst.	3–6
13	Instructional	7
14–24	Inst./Frust.	8–12
25+	Frustration	13+

General Observations

Adapted from *The Greek Gods* by Bernard Evslin, Dorothy Evslin, and Ned Hoopes. Reprinted by permission of Scholastic Book Services.

Student Copy is on page 318.

LN 4959 (Grade 9) Activating Background: Read the title to yourself; then tell me what you think will happen.

Background: Low ├──────┼──────┤ High

The Most Beautiful

T   1. ____   What is this story about?
(the god Apollo's rivalry with Marsyas; Apollo)

F   2. ____   What was the reason Apollo challenged Marsyas to a contest?
(to see who was the best musician)

F   3. ____   Describe what happened at the contest.
(Marsyas was to play his flute and Apollo his lyre and the Muses were to judge which was best)

F   4. ____   What was Apollo god of?
(sun; music; poetry; mathematics; medicine [any 3])

F   5. ____   How would you describe Apollo?
(beautiful with golden hair and blue eyes; strong; wise [any 2])

F   6. ____   What instrument did Apollo play?
(lyre)

F   7. ____   Who won the contest?
(Apollo)

I   8. ____   What lessons could be learned from this myth?
(any logical response)

E   9. ____   What is your opinion of Apollo's trick? Why? (if necessary, restate trick: to play their instruments upside down and sing at the same time)
(any logical response)

V   10. ____   Explain what "simultaneously" means in this sentence: Apollo suggested that they play their instruments upside down and sing simultaneously.
(at the same time)

Questions
Missed   ☐

Comprehension Scoring Guide	
Questions Missed	Level
0–1	Independent
1½–2	Ind./Inst.
2½	Instructional
3–4½	Inst./Frust.
5 +	Frustration

Retelling
Excellent
Satisfactory
Unsatisfactory

General Observations

Elizabeth Meets Darcy

Elizabeth watched for the first appearance of Pemberley Woods with some perturbation; and when at length they turned in at the lodge, her spirits were in a high flutter.

The park was very large and contained great variety of ground. They entered it in one of its lowest points, and drove for some time through a beautiful wood, stretching over a wide extent.

Elizabeth's mind was too full for conversation, but she saw and admired every remarkable spot and point of view. They gradually ascended for half a mile, and then found themselves at the top of a considerable eminence, where the wood ceased, and the eye was instantly caught by Pemberley House, situated on the opposite side of a valley, into which the road with some abruptness wound. It was a large, handsome, stone building, standing well on rising ground, and backed by a ridge of high woody hills. She had never seen a place for which nature had done more, or where natural beauty had been so little counteracted by an awkward taste. They were all of them warm in their admiration, and at the moment she felt that to be mistress of Pemberley might be something!

They descended the hill, crossed the bridge, and drove to the door; and, while examining the nearer aspect of the house, all her apprehensions of meeting its owner returned. As she walked across the lawn, Elizabeth turned back to look again, and the owner himself suddenly came forward from the road.

Total Miscues ☐   Significant Miscues ☐ $\overline{)15000}$ WPM

Word Recognition Scoring Guide		
Total Miscues	Level	Significant Miscues
0–3	Independent	0–2
4–12	Ind./Inst.	3–6
13	Instructional	7
14–24	Inst./Frust.	8–12
25+	Frustration	13+

General Observations

Adapted from *Pride and Prejudice* by Jane Austen.

Student Copy is on page 319.

LN 1047 (Grade 10) Activating Background: Read the title to yourself; then tell me what you think will happen.

Background: Low ├───────┼───────┤ High

Elizabeth Meets Darcy

T   1. _____   What is this story about?
(Elizabeth going to Pemberley Woods)

F   2. _____   What did Pemberley House look like?
(large; handsome; a stone building [any 1])

F   3. _____   Describe Pemberley Woods.
(large; a forest; hilly; valley; woody [any 2])

F   4. _____   How did the group feel about what they were seeing?
(warm in their admiration; excited; happy)

F   5. _____   What did they see when the woods ceased?
(Pemberley House)

F   6. _____   When did Elizabeth see the owner of Pemberley Woods?
(when she came up to the outside of the house; as she walked across the lawn)

F   7. _____   How did Elizabeth get to Pemberley Woods?
(drove)

I   8. _____   What does it mean when the story says that "Elizabeth's mind was too full for conversation"?
(any logical response; Elizabeth's mind was preoccupied with worry)

E   9. _____   Under what circumstances might someone be nervous about meeting the owner of a large mansion?
(any logical response)

V   10. _____   Explain what "ascended" means in this sentence: They gradually ascended for half a mile.
(went up)

Questions
Missed   ▢

Comprehension Scoring Guide	
Questions Missed	Level
0–1	Independent
1½–2	Ind./Inst.
2½	Instructional
3–4½	Inst./Frust.
5 +	Frustration

Retelling
Excellent
Satisfactory
Unsatisfactory

General Observations

Bookworm or Earthworm

To read or to weed is the problem that confronts me whenever I have a few extra minutes. Reading satisfies the wanderlust in me. It affords the opportunity to abandon the monotonous paths of everyday life and to trip excitedly along the mysterious trails in the enchanting land of books. Lost in the magic of the printed page, I can cast off my customary clothing and array myself in the raiment of a victorious knight or a football star. No longer shackled by the chains of time and space, I shiver with Washington's valiant men in the biting cold of Valley Forge and I kneel in reverent awe at Bethlehem's crib. Is it any wonder that I am unable to resist the beckoning call of a good book?

My interest in weeding is probably the result of my interest in reading. This occupation puts me on a par with those noble characters that I have admired in books. Few tasks are more intriguing to me than that of rescuing struggling plants from the greedy claws of choking weeds. I like the feel of the cold and damp earth as I eject the intruding roots. With the confident swagger of a conquering hero, I march triumphantly through our flower garden, leaving grateful shrubs in my wake. Even the squirming worms wriggle their gratitude for my noble deed. Yes, recreation time is always debating time for me. The topic of this secret controversy ever remains the same: to read or to weed?

Total Miscues [ ]   Significant Miscues [ ] $\overline{)15000}$ WPM

Word Recognition Scoring Guide		
Total Miscues	Level	Significant Miscues
0–3	Independent	0–2
4–12	Ind./Inst.	3–6
13	Instructional	7
14–24	Inst./Frust.	8–12
25 +	Frustration	13 +

General Observations

Adapted with permission from *Voyages in English* by Reverend Paul E. Campbell and Sister Mary Donatus Macnickle. Copyrighted by Loyola University Press.

LN 1187

Student Copy is on page 320.

LN 1187 (Grade 11) Activating Background: Read the title to yourself; then tell me what you think will happen.

Background: Low ├──────┼──────┤ High

Bookworm or Earthworm

T 1. _____ What is this story about?
(whether the author should read or weed)

F 2. _____ The author makes mention of casting off customary clothing and dressing in the raiment of what?
(a victorious knight or football star [either 1])

F 3. _____ How did the author develop an interest in weeding?
(from an interest in reading)

F 4. _____ Where does the author weed?
(in the flower garden)

F 5. _____ What historical person was mentioned in the story?
(George Washington)

F 6. _____ What do the worms do to show their gratitude for the weeding of the garden?
(they wriggle)

F 7. _____ What task, or job, is intriguing to the author?
(rescuing struggling plants from the greedy claws of choking weeds; simply weeding)

I 8. _____ What does the author probably mean by "reverent awe at Bethlehem's crib?"
(any logical response; the birth of Jesus)

E 9. _____ Reading satisfies the author's wanderlust. What satisfies wanderlust for you? Why?
(any logical response)

V 10. _____ Explain what "swagger" means in this phrase: With the confident swagger of a conquering hero.
(stride; strut)

Questions
Missed   ☐

Comprehension Scoring Guide	
Questions Missed	Level
0–1	Independent
1½–2	Ind./Inst.
2½	Instructional
3–4½	Inst./Frust.
5 +	Frustration

Retelling
Excellent
Satisfactory
Unsatisfactory

General Observations

American in Paris

On a brilliant day in May, in the year 1868, a gentleman was reclining at his ease on the great circular divan which occupied the center of the Salon Carré, in the Museum of the Louvre. He had taken serene possession of the softest spot of this commodious ottoman. With his head thrown back and his legs outstretched, he was staring at Murillo's beautiful moon-borne Madonna in profound enjoyment of his posture. He had removed his hat and flung down beside him a little red guidebook and an opera glass. The day was warm; he was heated with walking, and he repeatedly passed his handkerchief over his forehead with a somewhat wearied gesture. His exertions on this particular day had been of an unwonted sort, and he had often performed great physical feats which left him less jaded than his tranquil stroll through the Louvre. He had looked at all the pictures to which an asterisk was affixed in those formidable pages of fine print in his Bädeker guidebook; his attention had been strained and his eyes dazzled, and he had sat down with an aesthetic headache. His physiognomy would have sufficiently indicated that he was a shrewd and capable fellow. In truth, he had often sat up all night over a bristling bundle of accounts and heard the cock crow without a yawn. But Raphael and Titian and Rubens were a new kind of arithmetic, and they made him, for the first time in his life, wonder.

Total Miscues ☐   Significant Miscues ☐   )15000 WPM

Word Recognition Scoring Guide		
Total Miscues	Level	Significant Miscues
0–3	Independent	0–2
4–12	Ind./Inst.	3–6
13	Instructional	7
14–24	Inst./Frust.	8–12
25 +	Frustration	13 +

General Observations

Note: Do not count the mispronunciation of proper nouns as significant miscues.

Adapted from *The American* by Henry James.

Student Copy is on page 321.

LN 1296 (Grade 12) Activating Background: Read the title to yourself; then tell me what you think will happen.

Background: Low |——————|—————————| High

American in Paris

T   1. _____ What is this story about?
(an American gentleman in the Louvre Museum)

F   2. _____ What is the gentleman holding in his hand?
(a handkerchief)

F   3. _____ What did the gentleman remove as he took his position on the ottoman?
(his hat)

F   4. _____ When does this story take place?
(1868; over one hundred years ago)

F   5. _____ What is he staring at?
(Murillo's Madonna; a painting)

F   6. _____ Describe the weather.
(warm)

F   7. _____ What kind of a book has he been reading?
(a red guidebook; Bädeker guidebook)

I   8. _____ What do you think the man's job was? Why?
(any logical response; accounting; some type of business)

E   9. _____ Why might Raphael, Titian, and Rubens make the gentleman wonder?
(any logical response)

V   10. _____ Explain what "physiognomy" means in this sentence: His physiognomy would have sufficiently indicated that he was a shrewd and capable fellow.
(outward appearance)

Questions
Missed   ☐

Comprehension Scoring Guide	
Questions Missed	Level
0–1	Independent
1½–2	Ind./Inst.
2½	Instgructional
3–4½	Inst./Frust.
5 +	Frustration

Retelling
Excellent
Satisfactory
Unsatisfactory

General Observations

FORM LE

Expository

*Form LE contains ten longer **expository** passages that range in difficulty from grade three through grade twelve. These passages may be used for oral or silent reading to help verify, supplement, or expand knowledge and insights about the student's reading.*

Form LE
Graded Passages
(Student Copy)

Hawks

Most hawks hunt for prey alone. In New Mexico, there is a type of hawk called Harris' hawks. Harris' hawks work together as a team to catch their prey. This idea was interesting to a wildlife scientist. He decided to study these hawks.

The first thing he had to do was catch one hawk in a group. He then put a radio transmitter on the bird's leg. This helped him keep track of where the bird went. He did this with one hawk from each group.

The scientist went to a high place to watch the hawks. This took a lot of time and hard work. He discovered that most of the time the hawks caught rabbits. These were large rabbits that would be hard for one hawk to catch. The hawks worked together as a team so that they could catch their prey. Then they all shared the meal.

The scientist watched as the hawks would stalk their prey. First, they would fly across a large area. Sometimes the hawks would sit in trees to watch the ground. When the hawks saw a rabbit, they would start following it. When the rabbit slowed down in an open place, the hawks would dive at it. The hawks would wait until the rabbit became tired to make their final dive.

These hawks are very good at working as a team. This helps them to find food and stay alive. They have learned that it is very important to help each other.

Early Travel

It was early winter when Martha and Johnny Stine began their journey. They were traveling from Kansas to Colorado. When it was night, they would set up camp wherever they could. This type of trip was not easy. The year was 1891, which was before cars or airplanes. Good roads were not available. Martha and Johnny traveled in a covered wagon pulled by horses.

As time passed, the weather became colder. One night when they stopped to sleep, it was six degrees below zero. The next night they were caught in a blizzard. Martha and Johnny stopped at a house to ask for directions. They were asked if they wanted to spend the night there because of the blizzard. Johnny didn't want to stay, although Martha did. They continued on their journey in the blinding blizzard until they could no longer see. The roads were covered with snow. The team of horses couldn't be forced to continue through the ice and snow any longer. Then they saw the shadow of a small cabin. When they reached the cabin, it was locked. They pulled up beside the cabin in order to get shelter from the wind and snow. Weary, they fell into a restless sleep. Martha felt very depressed. They were lost in a blizzard and tired from traveling.

Four days later they arrived at their destination. Martha was so happy she cried. It had been four long weeks since they had started. Martha was happy to see the trip end.

Orville and Wilbur Wright invented and built the first successful airplane. Orville flew it in December of 1903. These famous brothers had an interesting childhood.

In 1879, Wilbur was twelve and Orville was eight. Their father brought them a toy made of paper, bamboo sticks, and cork after a trip to Ohio. It was called a helicopter. They turned a stick that twisted a rubber band, fastened it, and then tossed the helicopter into the air. Orville and Wilbur reached to catch it before it fell. The toy helicopter flew several feet across the room. The boys played with it until it broke.

Orville had many plans for making money. He learned to make and fly kites, and he made money by selling them to his friends. By the time he was fourteen, he had a printing press and business. Wilbur became interested in the business. In a short time, they published a weekly news-paper.

Bicycles became popular in the 1890s. These early bikes were very dangerous and difficult to ride. The front wheel was five feet high. The back wheel was eighteen inches high. A new bicycle was then built with two wheels of equal size, similar to today's bikes. The brothers rented a shop. They began repairing and selling bicycles. Now they had two businesses.

One day, Wilbur saw a photograph of a glider with a man hanging beneath the wings. He showed it to Orville. That may have been the beginning of their serious talk of flying.

Teacher

Many people know that Helen Keller was deaf and blind. Not as many people know about Anne Sullivan. She taught Helen Keller to read and write and was her companion for fifty years.

Anne Sullivan was born in 1866—more than 125 years ago. She was nearly blind herself. At the age of ten, she was sent to a poor house away from her family. When Anne was fourteen, she was admitted to an institute for the blind in the city of Boston. She had several eye operations and was able to learn to read.

When she was twenty-one, Anne was hired to teach Helen Keller, a seven year old who was deaf and blind. Anne studied how she might teach Helen Keller. In March of 1887, Anne went to Alabama to begin her new job. She even took a doll for Helen.

Teaching Helen was not easy. Anne tried to spell out words on Helen's hand through touch. Once Helen understood, she was able to learn many words. When Helen wanted to know Anne's name, she spelled teacher in Helen's hand. From that day on, Helen called Anne teacher. Anne was also called a miracle worker.

Anne was Helen's teacher and friend for about fifty years. Near the end of Anne's life, her eyesight became very poor again. She went blind. Fortunately, Anne knew all of the letters in braille——an alphabet that makes it possible for blind people to read. When Anne died, she was called truly great.

LE 6867

Homes of American Indians

Native American Indians built a variety of dwellings to suit their lifestyles and the environment they lived in.

In Northern forests, Algonquin families lived in wigwams. They needed a house that was easy to construct because they moved seasonally. The wigwam had a frame of long, slender poles that were lashed together at the top. This frame was then covered with woven rush mats and large sheets of bark.

The Iroquois Indians would build a village of rectangular longhouses. Each house was at least sixty feet long and ten to twelve families lived in it. The longhouse had a strong wooden frame covered with overlapping slabs of bark. Each family had its own room facing another one across the center hallway.

The Mandan Indians made their large, round homes of earth. Each Mandan lodge was about sixty feet across. The floor was scraped flat and wet down. Then they laid burned, dry grass over it until the floor was as hard as baked clay. Thick, wooden poles and willow rods supported a heavy covering of sod for the roof.

The Sioux and Cheyenne Indians had the most portable type of home, the teepee, which could be set up in less than one hour. The slightly tilted frame of long poles had a covering of buffalo hides, leaving a smoke hole in the top.

No matter where they lived, the Indians of North America devised original and adaptable houses that perfectly fit their environment and the type of lives they lived.

Friend of Lions

At the break of dawn, he rises from the bed that is placed just outside the door to his hut. Dressed only in shorts and sandals, he sets out on his daily prowl of Kenya's Kora Game Preserve in Eastern Africa. He is looking for lions.

George Adamson is not a hunter; on the contrary, his days are spent trying to preserve what few wild lions remain on this part of the African continent. The Kenyan government closed Adamson's lion rehabilitation program after several people at his camp were assaulted by the cats he considers the perfection of ageless beauty and grace. Now he searches for the lions he returned from captivity and for their offspring. They come to him when he calls. He feeds them like pets, and he protects them from poachers.

In the late 1950s, when he was a government game warden, Adamson shot a man-eating lioness who had a cub. The story of how he and his wife Joy raised the cub, Elsa, is told in the book and the movie titled *Born Free*. This story brought the cause of wildlife conservation to the attention of people in many countries around the world. It also raised $600,000 that has been used for a variety of wildlife conservation projects.

Since Joy's death in 1980, Adamson has wandered the lonely landscape of this vast preserve. His long, flowing, golden hair and white beard make him appear like one of the creatures he loves so much—the lion.

Destruction

Pompeii, an ancient city in Southern Italy, was settled in the 8th century B.C. It was overtaken by the Romans in 310 B.C. and became part of the Roman Empire. During its first five hundred years, Pompeii grew from a small farming village to an important trading center. Then in 62 A.D. an earthquake hit the city, leaving it demolished. The residents of the city began rebuilding, but while they were in the middle of rebuilding the city temple, a more permanent disaster struck. Mount Vesuvius, a volcano which had been considered extinct, erupted in 79 A.D. covering Pompeii with smoldering lava.

Eye-witnesses watched Mount Vesuvius erupt as brilliant flames towered in the sky and black smoke covered the sun. Volcanic ash and lava covered the city until virtually no buildings were left standing. As the volcanic eruption hit Pompeii, the universe seemed to revolt against the city sending lightning, earthquakes, and tidal waves. This horror continued for three days, killing all who had survived the volcano. When the dust settled, 15 feet of smoking debris covered what had once been Pompeii.

Pompeii was buried under ashes, stone, and cinders for almost 2,000 years. After the volcano, looters took what they could find from the city, and Pompeii was forgotten until the nineteenth century when the site was rediscovered and excavation began. For more than 100 years the task of excavating and restoring Pompeii has continued. Much has been learned about the manners and customs of the ancient Romans. Today, visitors can walk through Pompeii and view a city almost 3,000 years old.

Beating the Bonk

Bonk describes the symptoms that occur when your body's carbohydrate stores are used up as a result of sustained exercise. As you exercise, most of the fuel being burned is consumed by your muscles. Both fats and carbohydrates can be used for this process. Fat, stored in fatty tissue, is reduced to free fatty acids which are transported by the blood to the muscles. In contrast, carbohydrates are stored within the muscles as glycogen. During exercise, individual molecules of glycogen are removed and used as energy.

Your vital organs also need a continuous supply of fuel. Whether at rest or during exercise, your brain and nervous system depend on blood glucose. The reason why they need glycogen is because the cells of your nervous system don't store glycogen and can't use fat. To meet energy requirements, your blood glucose levels must stay at the same level. This job is largely done by your liver, which contains large amounts of glycogen that can be converted to glucose.

With the muscles and organs vying for glucose, lengthy exercise can drain the liver. When blood glucose levels become too low to meet the fuel requirement of your central nervous system, you begin to feel tired, irritated, and unhappy. In a word, you bonk.

Fortunately, you can remedy the bonk. When your blood glucose levels fall, you can replenish them by eating or drinking something rich in carbohydrates. Carbohydrates are quickly digested into glycogen, which is transported to the liver, muscles, and other organs.

Adapted from *Nutrition for Cyclists*. Reprinted by permission of Rodale Press.

Earthquakes

Earthquakes can be devastating natural disasters. The infamous San Francisco earthquake of 1906 caused over $200-million worth of damage, destroyed almost 30,000 buildings, and killed about 450 persons. In Japan, the cities of Tokyo and Yokohama were leveled by the earthquake of 1923 in which more than 140,000 persons were killed by falling buildings and fires, and over a million people were left homeless—all in 30 seconds.

Hundreds of earthquakes occur every year throughout the world. Fortunately, few are as destructive as those described above. The development of an accurate system for predicting earthquakes would lessen the loss of life and property, but at present scientists can only study these phenomena. The study of earthquakes is called seismology. Seismographs, instruments sensitive to ground movement, are used to chart each motion, and the Richter Scale is commonly used to grade each earthquake's strength on a 1-to-10 scale.

It is now known that earthquakes are created by sudden shifts that occur along faults deep in the earth's crust. According to the Theory of Continental Drift, the earth's crust consists of about twenty rigid sections, or plates, that are in continuous movement. This movement grinds and presses rocks at the edge of the plates. If the pressure becomes too great, the rocks shift, and the resulting movement sends energy, or seismic waves, to the surface of the earth. Most major earthquakes occur along the edge of the plates, and the most damaging impact occurs at the first surface-point reached by the seismic waves.

Beards

The history of beards has been a topic of increasing interest in today's society. Early man first cherished a beard for religious reasons; primitive races were convinced there was a sacred connection between all parts of a man's body, including his hair, and his personality. Hence, hair had to be carefully guarded from possible foes—this accounts for ancient man's custom of burning hair clippings to prevent them from being used by his enemies for nefarious purposes.

Thus, the earliest beard was faith-conditioned and therefore meticulously cared for. Ancient Egyptians used tongs, curling irons, dyes, and even gold dust to give it a golden sheen.

In those days, shaving was considered perverted. It was a practice reserved for the defeated enemy and the dangerously sick; lepers were shaved to warn others of their infection. Sometimes those in mourning also shaved as a symbol of vital sacrifice to the dead.

The whims of individual rulers also played a part in determining the fate of beards. Queen Elizabeth I, who disliked beards, taxed anyone sprouting a beard of more than two weeks' growth—the amount of assessment depended upon the man's social standing. In France, the beard became fashionable when it was the personal preference of the current king. Francis I grew a beard to hide an ugly scar on his chin, and his male subjects emulated the fashion. During the eighteenth century, the Spaniards considered the beard to be in poor taste because their king was unable to grow one.

Adapted with permission from *How Did It Begin?* by R. Brasch.

Performance Booklet
(Teacher Copy)

 Note: This Performance Booklet is on the CD-ROM that accompanies the Basic Reading Inventory.

Eighth Edition

BASIC READING INVENTORY PERFORMANCE BOOKLET

Jerry L. Johns, Ph.D.

LE Expository

Student _____   Grade _____ Sex M F   Date of Test _____

School _____   Examiner _____   Date of Birth _____

Address _____   Current Book/Level _____   Age _____

SUMMARY OF STUDENT'S READING PERFORMANCE

Grade	FORM LN: NARRATIVE				FORM LE: EXPOSITORY			
	Word Recognition		Comprehension		Word Recognition		Comprehension	
	Miscues	Level	Questions Missed	Level	Miscues	Level	Questions Missed	Level
3								
4								
5								
6								
7								
8								
9								
10								
11								
12								

ESTIMATE OF READING LEVELS

Independent _____   Instructional _____   Frustration _____

LISTENING LEVEL

Form _____

Grade	Questions Missed	Level
3		
4		
5		
6		
7		
8		
9		
10		
11		
12		

ESTIMATED LEVEL: _____

GENERAL OBSERVATIONS

INFORMAL MISCUE ANALYSIS SUMMARY

Types of Miscues	Frequency of Occurrence			General Impact of Miscues on Meaning		
	Seldom	Sometimes	Frequently	No Change	Little Change	Much Change
Substitutions						
Insertions						
Omissions						
Reversals						
Repetitions						

QUALITATIVE ANALYSIS OF BASIC READING INVENTORY INSIGHTS

General Directions: Note the degree to which the student shows behavior or evidence in the following areas. Space is provided for additional items.

	Seldom / Weak / Poor				Always / Strong / Excellent

COMPREHENSION

Seeks to construct meaning
Makes predictions
Activates background knowledge
Possesses appropriate concepts
   and vocabulary
Monitors reading
Varies reading rate as needed
Understands topic and major ideas
Remembers facts or details
Makes and supports appropriate
   inferences
Evaluates ideas from passages
Understands vocabulary used
Provides appropriate definitions
   of words
Engagement with passages

WORD IDENTIFICATION

Possesses numerous strategies
Uses strategies flexibly
Uses graphophonic information
Uses semantic information
Uses syntactic information
Knows basic sight words
   automatically
Possesses sight vocabulary

ORAL AND SILENT READING

Reads fluently
Reads with expression
Attends to punctuation
Keeps place while reading
Appropriate rate
Reads silently without vocalization

ATTITUDE AND CONFIDENCE

Enjoys reading
Demonstrates willingness to risk
Possesses positive self-concept
Chooses to read
Regards himself/herself as a reader
Exhibits persistence

Hawks

Most hawks hunt for prey alone. In New Mexico, there is a type of hawk called Harris' hawks. Harris' hawks work together as a team to catch their prey. This idea was interesting to a wildlife scientist. He decided to study these hawks.

The first thing he had to do was catch one hawk in a group. He then put a radio transmitter on the bird's leg. This helped him keep track of where the bird went. He did this with one hawk from each group.

The scientist went to a high place to watch the hawks. This took a lot of time and hard work. He discovered that most of the time the hawks caught rabbits. These were large rabbits that would be hard for one hawk to catch. The hawks worked together as a team so that they could catch their prey. Then they all shared the meal.

The scientist watched as the hawks would stalk their prey. First, they would fly across a large area. Sometimes the hawks would sit in trees to watch the ground. When the hawks saw a rabbit, they would start following it. When the rabbit slowed down in an open place, the hawks would dive at it. The hawks would wait until the rabbit became tired to make their final dive.

These hawks are very good at working as a team. This helps them to find food and stay alive. They have learned that it is very important to help each other.

Total Miscues ☐   Significant Miscues ☐ $\overline{)15000}$ WPM

Word Recognition Scoring Guide		
Total Miscues	Level	Significant Miscues
0–3	Independent	0–2
4–12	Ind./Inst.	3–6
13	Instructional	7
14–24	Inst./Frust.	8–12
25 +	Frustration	13 +

General Observations

Student Copy is on page 350.

LE 3183 (Grade 3) Activating Background: Read the title to yourself; then tell me what you think the passage will be about.

Background: Low ├────┼────┤ High

Hawks

T   1. _____   What is this passage about?
(what hawks do; what they eat; hawks that work together as a team to catch their prey)

F   2. _____   What is this type of hawk called?
(Harris' hawk)

F   3. _____   Where do these hawks live?
(New Mexico)

F   4. _____   Why do Harris' hawks work together as a team?
(to catch their prey; they are too small to work alone)

F   5. _____   What did the scientist do with the bird after he caught it?
(he put a radio transmitter on the bird's leg)

F   6. _____   Where did the scientist go to watch the hawks?
(to a high place)

F   7. _____   What type of animal did the hawk usually catch?
(rabbits)

I   8. _____   Why do you think the hawks would wait until the rabbit was in an open place before they would start diving at it?
(any logical response; because they could see it better; trees and bushes weren't in the way)

E   9. _____   If you were a scientist, what would you like to spend time studying? Why?
(any logical response)

V   10. _____   Explain what "prey" means in this sentence: Most hawks hunt for prey alone.
(animals hunted or seized for food, especially by another animal)

Questions Missed [ ]

Comprehension Scoring Guide	
Questions Missed	Level
0–1	Independent
1½–2	Ind./Inst.
2½	Instructional
3–4½	Inst./Frust.
5 +	Frustration

Retelling
Excellent
Satisfactory
Unsatisfactory

General Observations

Early Travel

It was early winter when Martha and Johnny Stine began their journey. They were traveling from Kansas to Colorado. When it was night, they would set up camp wherever they could. This type of trip was not easy. The year was 1891, which was before cars or airplanes. Good roads were not available. Martha and Johnny traveled in a covered wagon pulled by horses.

As time passed, the weather became colder. One night when they stopped to sleep, it was six degrees below zero. The next night they were caught in a blizzard. Martha and Johnny stopped at a house to ask for directions. They were asked if they wanted to spend the night there because of the blizzard. Johnny didn't want to stay, although Martha did. They continued on their journey in the blinding blizzard until they could no longer see. The roads were covered with snow. The team of horses couldn't be forced to continue through the ice and snow any longer. Then they saw the shadow of a small cabin. When they reached the cabin, it was locked. They pulled up beside the cabin in order to get shelter from the wind and snow. Weary, they fell into a restless sleep. Martha felt very depressed. They were lost in a blizzard and tired from traveling.

Four days later they arrived at their destination. Martha was so happy she cried. It had been four long weeks since they had started. Martha was happy to see the trip end.

Total Miscues ☐   Significant Miscues ☐   )15000 WPM

Word Recognition Scoring Guide		
Total Miscues	Level	Significant Miscues
0–3	Independent	0–2
4–12	Ind./Inst.	3–6
13	Instructional	7
14–24	Inst./Frust.	8–12
25+	Frustration	13+

General Observations

Student Copy is on page 351.

LE 5414 (Grade 4) Activating Background: Read the title to yourself; then tell me what you think the passage will be about.

Background: Low ├────────┼────────┤ High

Early Travel

T   1. ____   What is this passage about?
(Martha and Johnny Stine's trip by covered wagon in the winter)

F   2. ____   What state were the Stine's coming from and what state were they going to?
(they were traveling from Kansas to Colorado)

F   3. ____   What year did this story take place?
(1891)

F   4. ____   Who wanted to stay at the house where they stopped and asked for directions?
(Martha)

F   5. ____   What did they discover about the cabin when they found it in a blizzard?
(it was locked)

F   6. ____   What was the temperature when they stopped to sleep one night?
(6 degrees below zero; below zero)

F   7. ____   How long did it take the Stine's from when they started their trip until they reached their destination?
(4 weeks)

I   8. ____   When they stopped at a house in the blizzard to ask for directions, they were asked if they wanted to spend the night there. Why do you think Johnny didn't want to stay?
(any logical response; he wanted to continue on; he was afraid of the strangers)

E   9. ____   If you were taking this trip with Martha and Johnny, what would you take with you? Why?
(any logical response; warm clothes; sleeping bag; food)

V   10. ____   Explain what "depressed" means in this sentence: Martha felt depressed when they were lost.
(sad; gloomy; low-spirited)

Questions Missed ☐

Comprehension Scoring Guide	
Questions Missed	Level
0–1	Independent
1½–2	Ind./Inst.
2½	Instructional
3–4½	Inst./Frust.
5 +	Frustration

Retelling
Excellent
Satisfactory
Unsatisfactory

General Observations

Two Famous Brothers

Orville and Wilbur Wright invented and built the first successful airplane. Orville flew it in December of 1903. These famous brothers had an interesting childhood.

In 1879, Wilbur was twelve and Orville was eight. Their father brought them a toy made of paper, bamboo sticks, and cork after a trip to Ohio. It was called a helicopter. They turned a stick that twisted a rubber band, fastened it, and then tossed the helicopter into the air. Orville and Wilbur reached to catch it before it fell. The toy helicopter flew several feet across the room. The boys played with it until it broke.

Orville had many plans for making money. He learned to make and fly kites, and he made money by selling them to his friends. By the time he was fourteen, he had a printing press and business. Wilbur became interested in the business. In a short time, they published a weekly newspaper.

Bicycles became popular in the 1890's. These early bikes were very dangerous and difficult to ride. The front wheel was five feet high. The back wheel was eighteen inches high. A new bicycle was then built with two wheels of equal size, similar to today's bikes. The brothers rented a shop. They began repairing and selling bicycles. Now they had two businesses.

One day, Wilbur saw a photograph of a glider with a man hanging beneath the wings. He showed it to Orville. That may have been the beginning of their serious talk of flying.

Total Miscues ☐   Significant Miscues ☐   )15000 WPM

Word Recognition Scoring Guide		
Total Miscues	Level	Significant Miscues
0–3	Independent	0–2
4–12	Ind./Inst.	3–6
13	Instructional	7
14–24	Inst./Frust.	8–12
25+	Frustration	13+

General Observations

Student Copy is on page 352.

LE 8595 (Grade 5) Activating Background: Read the title to yourself; then tell me what you think the passage will be about.

Background: Low ├────────┤ High

Two Famous Brothers

T 1. _____ What is this passage about?
(Wilbur and Orville Wright; their childhood; two brothers)

F 2. _____ What are the names of the two famous brothers?
(Orville; Wilbur)

F 3. _____ What are the Wright brothers famous for?
(building and flying the first successful airplane)

F 4. _____ Who gave the brothers the toy helicopter?
(their father)

F 5. _____ What was the toy helicopter made of?
(paper; bamboo sticks; cork; a rubber band [any 2])

F 6. _____ Name one of the brothers' businesses.
(making and selling kites; publishing a newspaper; repairing and selling bicycles)

F 7. _____ What made early bikes dangerous and difficult to ride?
(the wheels were different sizes)

I 8. _____ Why do you think the newer bikes were better than the early bikes?
(any logical response; the wheels were of equal size)

E 9. _____ Why do you think Orville and Wilbur had more than one business?
(any logical response; they wanted to make money; they were interested in many things)

V 10. _____ Explain what "glider" means in this sentence: Wilbur saw a photograph of a glider.
(like an airplane; an airplane without a motor)

Questions
Missed ▢

Comprehension Scoring Guide	
Questions Missed	Level
0–1	Independent
1½–2	Ind./Inst.
2½	Instructional
3–4½	Inst./Frust.
5 +	Frustration

Retelling
Excellent
Satisfactory
Unsatisfactory

General Observations

Teacher

Many people know that Helen Keller was deaf and blind. Not as many people know about Anne Sullivan. She taught Helen Keller to read and write and was her companion for fifty years.

Anne Sullivan was born in 1866—more than 125 years ago. She was nearly blind herself. At the age of ten, she was sent to a poor house away from her family. When Anne was fourteen, she was admitted to an institute for the blind in the city of Boston. She had several eye operations and was able to learn to read.

When she was twenty-one, Anne was hired to teach Helen Keller, a seven year old who was deaf and blind. Anne studied how she might teach Helen Keller. In March of 1887, Anne went to Alabama to begin her new job. She even took a doll for Helen.

Teaching Helen was not easy. Anne tried to spell out words on Helen's hand through touch. Once Helen understood, she was able to learn many words. When Helen wanted to know Anne's name, she spelled teacher in Helen's hand. From that day on, Helen called Anne teacher. Anne was also called a miracle worker.

Anne was Helen's teacher and friend for about fifty years. Near the end of Anne's life, her eyesight became very poor again. She went blind. Fortunately, Anne knew all of the letters in braille—an alphabet that makes it possible for blind people to read. When Anne died, she was called truly great.

Total Miscues ☐   Significant Miscues ☐ $\frac{\text{WPM}}{)15000}$

Word Recognition Scoring Guide		
Total Miscues	Level	Significant Miscues
0–3	Independent	0–2
4–12	Ind./Inst.	3–6
13	Instructional	7
14–24	Inst./Frust.	8–12
25 +	Frustration	13 +

General Observations

LE 6867

Student Copy is on page 353.

LE 6867 (Grade 6) Activating Background: Read the title to yourself; then tell me what you think the passage will be about.

Background: Low ├─────┼─────┤ High

Teacher

T   1. ____ What is this passage about?
(Anne Sullivan; Helen Keller's teacher)

F   2. ____ How did Anne Sullivan gain her sight?
(she had many operations)

F   3. ____ What name did Helen call Anne?
(teacher)

F   4. ____ How old was Anne when she began teaching Helen?
(twenty-one)

F   5. ____ How long werc Anne and Helen together?
(fifty years)

F   6. ____ How did Anne teach Helen to spell words?
(Anne would spell out words on Helen's hand through touch)

F   7. ____ What did Anne take Helen when she first went to begin to teach her?
(a doll)

I   8. ____ Why do you think Anne decided to be a teacher for the blind?
(any logical response; she had once been blind, and knew how wonderful it was to learn to read)

E   9. ____ How do you think Helen Keller learned braille?
(any logical response; she taught herself)

V   10. ____ Explain what "braille" means in this sentence: Helen Keller taught Anne Sullivan braille.
(an alphabet composed of a series of raised bumps that allows blind people to read)

Questions Missed ☐

Comprehension Scoring Guide	
Questions Missed	Level
0–1	Independent
1½–2	Ind./Inst.
2½	Instructional
3–4½	Inst./Frust.
5 +	Frustration

Retelling
Excellent
Satisfactory
Unsatisfactory

General Observations

Homes of American Indians

Native American Indians built a variety of dwellings to suit their lifestyles and the environment they lived in.

In Northern forests, Algonquin families lived in wigwams. They needed a house that was easy to construct because they moved seasonally. The wigwam had a frame of long, slender poles that were lashed together at the top. This frame was then covered with woven rush mats and large sheets of bark.

The Iroquois Indians would build a village of rectangular longhouses. Each house was at least sixty feet long and ten to twelve families lived in it. The longhouse had a strong wooden frame covered with overlapping slabs of bark. Each family had its own room facing another one across the center hallway.

The Mandan Indians made their large, round homes of earth. Each Mandan lodge was about sixty feet across. The floor was scraped flat and wet down. Then they laid burned, dry grass over it until the floor was as hard as baked clay. Thick, wooden poles and willow rods supported a heavy covering of sod for the roof.

The Sioux and Cheyenne Indians had the most portable type of home, the teepee, which could be set up in less than one hour. The slightly tilted frame of long poles had a covering of buffalo hides, leaving a smoke hole in the top.

No matter where they lived, the Indians of North America devised original and adaptable houses that perfectly fit their environment and the type of lives they lived.

Total Miscues ☐   Significant Miscues ☐ $\overline{)15000}$ WPM

Word Recognition Scoring Guide		
Total Miscues	Level	Significant Miscues
0–3	Independent	0–2
4–12	Ind./Inst.	3–6
13	Instructional	7
14–24	Inst./Frust.	8–12
25+	Frustration	13+

General Observations

LE 3717

Student Copy is on page 354.

LE 3717 (Grade 7) Activating Background: Read the title to yourself; then tell me what you think the passage will be about.

Background: Low ├───────┼───────┤ High

Homes of American Indians

T   1. _____ What is this passage about?
(different types of American Indian homes)

F   2. _____ Why did some Indians need portable homes?
(they moved seasonally)

F   3. _____ How many Iroquois families lived in one longhouse?
(10 to 12 families)

F   4. _____ In what kind of home did Algonquin families live?
(wigwam)

F   5. _____ What did the Mandan Indians use to make their large, round homes?
(earth; soil; sod)

F   6. _____ How long did it take to set up a teepee?
(less than one hour)

F   7. _____ Which Indians had the most portable homes?
(Sioux; Cheyenne [either 1])

I   8. _____ Why did the American Indians need to rely on materials they found to build their homes?
(any logical response; there wasn't any way to transport materials over long distances; there were no stores; they were the only materials available)

E   9. _____ Why did some of the Indians need to move seasonally?
(any logical response; weather conditions; food supply; supply of materials)

V 10. _____ Explain what "adaptable" means in this sentence: The Indians built adaptable homes.
(suit the environment where they live; adjust to different conditions)

Questions Missed ☐

Comprehension Scoring Guide	
Questions Missed	Level
0–1	Independent
1½–2	Ind./Inst.
2½	Instructional
3–4½	Inst./Frust.
5 +	Frustration

Retelling
Excellent
Satisfactory
Unsatisfactory

General Observations

Friend of Lions

At the break of dawn, he rises from the bed that is placed just outside the door to his hut. Dressed only in shorts and sandals, he sets out on his daily prowl of Kenya's Kora Game Preserve in Eastern Africa. He is looking for lions.

George Adamson is not a hunter; on the contrary, his days are spent trying to preserve what few wild lions remain on this part of the African continent. The Kenyan government closed Adamson's lion rehabilitation program after several people at his camp were assaulted by the cats he considers the perfection of ageless beauty and grace. Now he searches for the lions he returned from captivity and for their offspring. They come to him when he calls. He feeds them like pets, and he protects them from poachers.

In the late 1950s, when he was a government game warden, Adamson shot a man-eating lioness who had a cub. The story of how he and his wife Joy raised the cub, Elsa, is told in the book and the movie titled *Born Free*. This story brought the cause of wildlife conservation to the attention of people in many countries around the world. It also raised $600,000 that has been used for a variety of wildlife conservation projects.

Since Joy's death in 1980, Adamson has wandered the lonely landscape of this vast preserve. His long, flowing, golden hair and white beard make him appear like one of the creatures he loves so much—the lion.

Total Miscues ☐   Significant Miscues ☐ $\overline{)15000}$ WPM

Word Recognition Scoring Guide		
Total Miscues	Level	Significant Miscues
0–3	Independent	0–2
4–12	Ind./Inst.	3–6
13	Instructional	7
14–24	Inst./Frust.	8–12
25+	Frustration	13+

General Observations

Student Copy is on page 355.

LE 8183 (Grade 8) Activating Background: Read the title to yourself; then tell me what you think the passage will be about.

Background: Low ├────────┼────────┤ High

Friend of Lions

T   1. _____ What is this passage about?
(a man who loves and protects lions)

F   2. _____ In what country does George Adamson live?
(Kenya)

F   3. _____ On what continent is Kenya located?
(Africa)

F   4. _____ What is the title of the book and the movie that tells the story of how the Adamsons raised a motherless lion cub?
(*Born Free*)

F   5. _____ In what way are the lions, to Adamson, just like household cats are to us?
(they will come to him when he calls; he feeds them like pets)

F   6. _____ How did *Born Free* aid the cause of wildlife conservation?
(it brought wildlife conservation to the attention of the world; it raised money for wildlife conservation projects)

F   7. _____ What was Adamson's job title at the time when he shot a man-eating lioness?
(he was a government game warden)

I   8. _____ Why do you think Adamson and his wife decided to raise Elsa, the motherless lion cub?
(any logical response; because they shot her mother; she was unable to survive without their help)

E   9. _____ Why do you think the authorities allow Adamson to live out in the wild, completely unprotected?
(any logical response; the lions are used to him; he is a friend of the lions)

V 10. _____ Explain what "poachers" means in this sentence: George Adamson protects lions from poachers.
(take fish or game illegally)

Questions
Missed ☐

Comprehension Scoring Guide	
Questions Missed	Level
0–1	Independent
1½–2	Ind./Inst.
2½	Instructional
3–4½	Inst./Frust.
5 +	Frustration

Retelling
Excellent
Satisfactory
Unsatisfactory

General Observations

Destruction

Pompeii, an ancient city in Southern Italy, was settled in the 8th century B.C. It was overtaken by the Romans in 310 B.C. and became part of the Roman Empire. During its first five hundred years, Pompeii grew from a small farming village to an important trading center. Then in 62 A.D. an earthquake hit the city, leaving it demolished. The residents of the city began rebuilding, but while they were in the middle of rebuilding the city temple, a more permanent disaster struck. Mount Vesuvius, a volcano which had been considered extinct, erupted in 79 A.D. covering Pompeii with smoldering lava.

Eye-witnesses watched Mount Vesuvius erupt as brilliant flames towered in the sky and black smoke covered the sun. Volcanic ash and lava covered the city until virtually no buildings were left standing. As the volcanic eruption hit Pompeii, the universe seemed to revolt against the city sending lightning, earthquakes, and tidal waves. This horror continued for three days, killing all who had survived the volcano. When the dust settled, 15 feet of smoking debris covered what had once been Pompeii.

Pompeii was buried under ashes, stone, and cinders for almost 2,000 years. After the volcano, looters took what they could find from the city, and Pompeii was forgotten until the nineteenth century when the site was rediscovered and excavation began. For more than 100 years the task of excavating and restoring Pompeii has continued. Much has been learned about the manners and customs of the ancient Romans. Today, visitors can walk through Pompeii and view a city almost 3,000 years old.

Total Miscues ☐ Significant Miscues ☐ $\overline{)15000}$ WPM

Word Recognition Scoring Guide		
Total Miscues	Level	Significant Miscues
0–3	Independent	0–2
4–12	Ind./Inst.	3–6
13	Instructional	7
14–24	Inst./Frust.	8–12
25 +	Frustration	13 +

General Observations

Student Copy is on page 356.

LE 4959 (Grade 9) Activating Background: Read the title to yourself; then tell me what you think the passage will be about.

Background: Low ├──────┼──────┤ High

Destruction

T   1. _____   What is this passage about?
(an ancient city, Pompeii, destroyed by a volcano and other natural forces)

F   2. _____   Where is Pompeii located?
(Italy; in Southern Italy)

F   3. _____   How was Pompeii first destroyed?
(by an earthquake)

F   4. _____   What was the name of the volcano that erupted?
(Mount Vesuvius)

F   5. _____   During the volcanic eruption, what other natural disasters happened at the same time?
(lightning; earthquakes; tidal waves [any 2])

F   6. _____   When was Pompeii rediscovered?
(in the nineteenth century; 200 years ago)

F   7. _____   How old is Pompeii today?
(almost 3,000 years old)

I   8. _____   What do you suppose the looters may have taken?
(any logical response)

E   9. _____   If a disaster destroyed where you live, what would be your thoughts, feelings, and actions?
(any logical response)

V   10. _____   Explain what "virtually" means in this sentence: Volcanic ash and lava covered the city until virtually no buildings were left standing.
(almost; finally; eventually)

Questions
Missed ☐

Comprehension Scoring Guide	
Questions Missed	Level
0–1	Independent
1½–2	Ind./Inst.
2½	Instructional
3–4½	Inst./Frust.
5 +	Frustration

Retelling
Excellent
Satisfactory
Unsatisfactory

General Observations

Beating the Bonk

Bonk describes the symptoms that occur when your body's carbohydrate stores are used up as a result of sustained exercise. As you exercise, most of the fuel being burned is consumed by your muscles. Both fats and carbohydrates can be used for this process. Fat, stored in fatty tissue, is reduced to free fatty acids which are transported by the blood to the muscles. In contrast, carbohydrates are stored within the muscles as glycogen. During exercise, individual molecules of glycogen are removed and used as energy.

Your vital organs also need a continuous supply of fuel. Whether at rest or during exercise, your brain and nervous system depend on blood glucose. The reason why they need glycogen is because the cells of your nervous system don't store glycogen and can't use fat. To meet energy requirements, your blood glucose levels must stay at the same level. This job is largely done by your liver, which contains large amounts of glycogen that can be converted to glucose.

With the muscles and organs vying for glucose, lengthy exercise can drain the liver. When blood glucose levels become too low to meet the fuel requirement of your central nervous system, you begin to feel tired, irritated, and unhappy. In a word, you bonk.

Fortunately, you can remedy the bonk. When your blood glucose levels fall, you can replenish them by eating or drinking something rich in carbohydrates. Carbohydrates are quickly digested into glycogen, which is transported to the liver, muscles, and other organs.

Total Miscues ☐   Significant Miscues ☐ $\dfrac{\text{WPM}}{)15000}$

Word Recognition Scoring Guide		
Total Miscues	Level	Significant Miscues
0–3	Independent	0–2
4–12	Ind./Inst.	3–6
13	Instructional	7
14–24	Inst./Frust.	8–12
25 +	Frustration	13 +

General Observations

LE 1047

378

Student Copy is on page 357.

LE 1047 (Grade 10) Activating Background: Read the title to yourself; then tell me what you think the passage will be about.

Background: Low ├────────┼────────┤ High

Beating the Bonk

T   1. _____   What is this passage about?
(what happens when you bonk and how to avoid it; what fuel the body uses; how a diet rich in carbohydrates can cure the bonk)

F   2. _____   What does it mean to bonk?
(to use up carbohydrates by exercise; to feel tired, irritated, unhappy; lose glycogen)

F   3. _____   What is used by your muscles for food?
(fats and carbohydrates [either 1])

F   4. _____   What is glycogen?
(the substance that is stored in muscles from carbohydrates; storage form of glucose; what gives you energy)

F   5. _____   Why does your body need glycogen?
(to meet energy requirements for your brain, muscles, and nervous system; so you can be active; so you won't bonk)

F   6. _____   According to the passage, what are the symptoms of low blood glucose levels?
(you feel tired, irritable, unhappy [any 2])

F   7. _____   How can you overcome bonking?
(by eating or drinking something rich in carbohydrates)

I   8. _____   Why do you think athletes should try to avoid bonking?
(any logical response; it slows performance)

E   9. _____   Based on this passage, if you were an athletic coach what advice about diet would you share?
(any logical response; a diet rich in carbohydrates)

V   10. _____   Explain what "vying" means in this phrase: With your muscles and organs vying for glucose. . . .
(wanting or needing; competing)

Questions Missed ☐

Comprehension Scoring Guide	
Questions Missed	Level
0–1	Independent
1½–2	Ind./Inst.
2½	Instructional
3–4½	Inst./Frust.
5 +	Frustration

Retelling
Excellent
Satisfactory
Unsatisfactory

General Observations

Earthquakes

Earthquakes can be devastating natural disasters. The infamous San Francisco earthquake of 1906 caused over $200-million worth of damage, destroyed almost 30,000 buildings, and killed about 450 persons. In Japan, the cities of Tokyo and Yokohama were leveled by the earthquake of 1923 in which more than 140,000 persons were killed by falling buildings and fires, and over a million people were left homeless—all in 30 seconds.

Hundreds of earthquakes occur every year throughout the world. Fortunately, few are as destructive as those described above. The development of an accurate system for predicting earthquakes would lessen the loss of life and property, but at present scientists can only study these phenomena. The study of earthquakes is called seismology. Seismographs, instruments sensitive to ground movement, are used to chart each motion, and the Richter Scale is commonly used to grade each earthquake's strength on a 1-to-10 scale.

It is now known that earthquakes are created by sudden shifts that occur along faults deep in the earth's crust. According to the Theory of Continental Drift, the earth's crust consists of about twenty rigid sections, or plates, that are in continuous movement. This movement grinds and presses rocks at the edge of the plates. If the pressure becomes too great, the rocks shift, and the resulting movement sends energy, or seismic waves, to the surface of the earth. Most major earthquakes occur along the edge of the plates, and the most damaging impact occurs at the first surface-point reached by the seismic waves.

Total Miscues ☐ Significant Miscues ☐ $\overline{)15000}$ WPM

Word Recognition Scoring Guide		
Total Miscues	Level	Significant Miscues
0–3	Independent	0–2
4–12	Ind./Inst.	3–6
13	Instructional	7
14–24	Inst./Frust.	8–12
25 +	Frustration	13 +

General Observations

LE 1187

Student Copy is on page 358.

LE 1187 (Grade 11) Activating Background: Read the title to yourself; then tell me what you think the passage will be about.

Background: Low ├────────┤ High

Earthquakes

T   1. _____   What is this passage about?
(earthquakes; scientific study of earthquakes; how earthquakes occur)

F   2. _____   This article named three cities where earthquakes have caused extensive damage. Name two.
(Tokyo; Yokohama; San Francisco [any 2])

F   3. _____   How many earthquakes occur throughout the world each year?
(hundreds)

F   4. _____   According to the article, what problems do earthquakes cause for people?
(people are killed; fires erupt; buildings fall [any 2])

F   5. _____   What is a seismograph?
(an instrument sensitive to ground movement)

F   6. _____   What is the purpose of a Richter Scale?
(to grade an earthquake's strength)

F   7. _____   How do earthquakes occur?
(a sudden shifting of rocks in the earth's crust sends seismic waves, or energy, to the surface of the earth; any reasonable explanation)

I   8. _____   What probably explains why so many people were killed in Japan's 1923 earthquake?
(any logical response; the earthquake occurred in two cities with large populations)

E   9. _____   What services would probably become most important to people who survive a major earthquake? Why?
(any logical response)

V   10. _____   Explain what "infamous" means in this sentence: The infamous San Francisco earthquake of 1906 caused over $200-million worth of damage.
(notorious; famously bad)

Questions Missed ☐

Comprehension Scoring Guide	
Questions Missed	Level
0–1	Independent
1½–2	Ind./Inst.
2½	Instructional
3–4½	Inst./Frust.
5 +	Frustration

Retelling
Excellent
Satisfactory
Unsatisfactory

General Observations

Beards

The history of beards has been a topic of increasing interest in today's society. Early man first cherished a beard for religious reasons; primitive races were convinced there was a sacred connection between all parts of a man's body, including his hair, and his personality. Hence, hair had to be carefully guarded from possible foes—this accounts for ancient man's custom of burning hair clippings to prevent them from being used by his enemies for nefarious purposes.

Thus, the earliest beard was faith-conditioned and therefore meticulously cared for. Ancient Egyptians used tongs, curling irons, dyes, and even gold dust to give it a golden sheen.

In those days, shaving was considered perverted. It was a practice reserved for the defeated enemy and the dangerously sick; lepers were shaved to warn others of their infection. Sometimes those in mourning also shaved as a symbol of vital sacrifice to the dead.

The whims of individual rulers also played a part in determining the fate of beards. Queen Elizabeth I, who disliked beards, taxed anyone sprouting a beard of more than two weeks' growth—the amount of assessment depended upon the man's social standing. In France, the beard became fashionable when it was the personal preference of the current king. Francis I grew a beard to hide an ugly scar on his chin, and his male subjects emulated the fashion. During the eighteenth century, the Spaniards considered the beard to be in poor taste because their king was unable to grow one.

Total Miscues ☐   Significant Miscues ☐ $\overline{)15000}$ WPM

Word Recognition Scoring Guide		
Total Miscues	Level	Significant Miscues
0–3	Independent	0–2
4–12	Ind./Inst.	3–6
13	Instructional	7
14–24	Inst./Frust.	8–12
25 +	Frustration	13 +

General Observations

Adapted with permission from *How Did It Begin?* by R. Brasch.

LE 1296

Student Copy is on page 359.

LE 1296 (Grade 12) Activating Background: Read the title to yourself; then tell me what you think the passage will be about.

Background: Low ├──────┼──────┤ High

Beards

T   1. _____   What is this passage about?
(history of beards)

F   2. _____   Name two of the major reasons men grew beards.
(any answer encompassing both religion and politics)

F   3. _____   Why did primitive man wear a beard?
(religious reasons; hair was sacred; there was a connection between all parts of man's body)

F   4. _____   Why did King Francis I grow a beard?
(to cover a scar on his chin)

F   5. _____   Why were lepers shaved?
(to warn others of their infectious disease)

F   6. _____   What did the ancient Egyptians use on their beards?
(tongs; curling irons; dyes; gold dust [any 2])

F   7. _____   Why did the Spaniards consider the beard to be in poor taste?
(their king was unable to grow one)

I   8. _____   Would men probably have beards during the reign of Queen Elizabeth I? Why?
(any logical response; no, she taxed anyone with a beard)

E   9. _____   What are some of the reasons that could account for the present popularity or unpopularity of beards?
(any logical response)

V   10. _____   Explain what "nefarious" means in this phrase: Man's custom of burning hair clippings to prevent them from being used by his enemies for nefarious purposes.
(evil; villainous; wicked; criminal)

Questions Missed ☐

Comprehension Scoring Guide	
Questions Missed	Level
0–1	Independent
1½–2	Ind./Inst.
2½	Instructional
3–4½	Inst./Frust.
5 +	Frustration

Retelling
Excellent
Satisfactory
Unsatisfactory

General Observations

PART THREE

Appendices, References, and Index

Appendix   A

Early Literacy Assessments

INTRODUCTION

Some students may experience difficulty with the easiest word lists and passages in the Basic Reading Inventory. The informal measures in Appendix A will be helpful to assess emergent reading behavior. For each measure, there are directions for the teacher and materials for the student.

A separate Record Booklet is provided for noting the student's responses and making other comments that may be helpful for instruction. Additional early literacy assessments and helpful teaching strategies are available in Johns, Lenski, and Elish-Piper (1999).

Use the measures in Appendix A to gather insights about student behaviors that indicate the degree of movement toward what might be called conventional reading. Although there are numerals that can be attached to some of the measures, their major purpose is to provide a means to gather qualitative judgments related to the student's current abilities.

For example:

"Literacy Knowledge" helps determine the degree to which the student understands directionality in reading and concepts about letters, words, and punctuation.

"Wordless Picture Reading" provides the student with an opportunity to dictate a story based on pictures and then read it. During the reading, speech-to-print pointing can be assessed. Follow-up questions help determine the student's ability to locate several words and a specific sentence.

Tasks like "Phoneme Awareness" and "Phoneme Segmentation" have been identified as being among the best predictors of early reading acquisition (Yopp, 1995). Phonological awareness also seems to underlie the learning of letter-sound relationships and subsequent growth in reading.

These assessments are intended to be used with emergent readers. Some of these students may be just beginning their schooling; others may be struggling readers throughout the grades. Select the assessments that will help you gain greater insights into students' emerging reading abilities so quality instruction can be provided.

Alphabet Knowledge

Overview: Alphabet Knowledge contains upper-case and lower-case letters of the alphabet in non-sequential order to help assess letter-identification ability.

Materials Needed: The pages in the manual containing upper-case letters, lower-case letters, two 3" X 5" cards, and the Record Booklet.

PROCEDURE

1. Duplicate the appropriate page of the Record Booklet.

2. Place the alphabet page before the student and ask him or her to identify any known letters. Say, **"Here are some letters. I want to see how many you know."** Encourage the student to say "pass" or "skip it" if a particular letter is not known.

3. Use the 3" X 5" cards to block off everything but the lines being read. If necessary, point to each letter with a finger.

4. As the student responds, use the Record Booklet to note correct (+) and incorrect responses. When responses are incorrect, record the actual response or D.K. (student doesn't know) above the stimulus letter. If the student self-corrects, write OK; self-corrections can be made at any time.

Letter	Meaning of Recording
+ O	Identified correctly
D.K. H	Don't know
C S	Said C for S
B ok E	Said B for E but self-corrected

SCORING AND INTERPRETATION

Count the correct number of responses for the upper-case letters and the lower-case letters. Note the scores in the box on the record sheet and on the front of the Record Booklet. Based on the number of correct responses, make a judgment of the student's alphabet knowledge, and record an X on the continuum located on the summary page of the Record Booklet. Unknown letters or incorrect responses may help form the basis for instructional interventions.

For teaching strategies, consult Section 3.7 in Johns, Lenski, and Elish-Piper (1999).

O H S E G P

X V I M J D K

B T R Z F N

Y Q W C U A L

b x e c j m g

l u r t q h y

s d o a k w a

i p v f n z g

Writing

Overview: The student will demonstrate his or her ability to write words, letters, and sentences.

Materials Needed: A pencil or pen, paper (lined and unlined), and the Record Booklet.

PROCEDURE

1. Give the student lined and unlined paper and a pencil or pen. If possible, have choices of paper and writing instruments.

2. Say, **"I'd like you to write some letters, words, and sentences."** Be patient and encouraging. You might want to ask the student to begin by writing his or her first name. If there is some success, try the last name.

3. After the student has finished, invite him or her to share what was written. Make mental notes or use the Record Booklet.

4. For the student who says "I can't write," you might ask him or her to print an X. Continue with a *few* other letters and perhaps names and numbers that the student may know. You might also suggest general categories of words: pets, colors, foods, things you can do.

SCORING AND INTERPRETATION

Informally evaluate the student's writing using the areas on the Writing page in the Record Booklet. Record an X on the continuum located on the front page of the Record Booklet that represents your overall judgment.

For teaching strategies, consult Section 3.8 in Johns, Lenski, and Elish-Piper (1999).

Literacy Knowledge

Overview: This assessment contains questions you ask while sharing written material with the student. These questions will help you assess the student's knowledge of print directionality, letters, words, punctuation, and the like.

Materials Needed: Reading material you select (a book, magazine, pamphlet, newspaper, etc.), two 3" X 5" cards, and the Record Booklet. You may also want to use the book *New Shoes*.

PROCEDURE

1. Duplicate the appropriate section of the Record Booklet.

2. Use *New Shoes* or secure some type of reading material that may be of interest to the student. The student will *not* have to read; rather he or she will be given an opportunity to demonstrate understanding of how print works and basic knowledge of words, letters, and punctuation. Be sure the items on the test are appropriate for the type of reading material you have selected.

3. Say, **"I'd like you to show me some of the things you know about reading. You won't have to read."**

4. Begin with the first item in the Record Booklet and proceed through the test.

5. Stop if the student seems frustrated.

6. Note any relevant observations in the Record Booklet.

SCORING AND INTERPRETATION

1. Circle plus (+) for correct responses and minus (–) for incorrect responses.

2. Count the number of pluses, and record the total in the box on the record sheet and on the front of the Record Booklet. The maximum score is 20.

Informally judge the student's knowledge of literacy concepts on the Literacy Knowledge page in the Record Booklet, and record an X on the continuum located on the front of the Record Booklet. Areas of concern can be strengthened by the instructional program you design for the student.

For teaching strategies, consult Section 3.5 in Johns, Lenski, and Elish-Piper (1999).

Note:

Remove and bind the following
New Shoes booklet for use with the
Literacy Knowledge assessment.

Wordless Picture Reading

Overview: Wordless picture reading will help assess the student's ability to tell a story using pictures.

Materials Needed: One of the pages in the manual containing a wordless picture story, the Record Booklet, and a tape recorder.

PROCEDURE

1. Show the student the entire page containing the wordless picture story.

2. Invite the student to look at each frame in order. Point to each frame in order as you say, **"I think you can use these pictures to tell me a story. Think about the story the pictures tell."** Give the student time to study the pictures.

3. Then ask the student to look at the pictures again and when ready, begin telling the story with the first picture (point to it). Say, **"Tell me your story from the pictures. Begin here. I'll write it for you."**

4. As the student tells the story, write the student's dictation on a copy of the record sheet of the wordless picture story or on a separate piece of paper. This is similar to what teachers do in a language experience activity. You may also want to tape record the student's story for later in-depth analysis.

5. After the student has finished dictating, have him or her read it aloud while pointing to the words. If the reading is similar to the text, mentally note miscues. If the text is "read" quite differently from the text, you may wish to write what the student says.

6. Following the student's reading, ask the student to point to several words in the text and to find where a particular sentence begins and ends.

SCORING AND INTERPRETATION

Make qualitative judgments regarding the student's ability to follow directions and the level of language used in telling the story. Look for evidence that the story connects to the pictures and the degree to which the student has a sense of story and any evidence that the student uses book language. Then record Xs that reflect your judgments on the continuums located on the front of the Record Booklet.

For teaching strategies, consult Section 3.4 in Johns, Lenski, and Elish-Piper (1999).

Wordless Picture Reading • Student Copy

Caption Reading

Overview: This story will help assess the student's ability to read a brief story with helpful picture clues.

Materials Needed: The page in the manual containing the story and the Record Booklet.

PROCEDURE

1. Show the student the page containing the pictures and captions.

2. Invite the student to look at frames of the story (pictures and text) in order as numbered.

3. Then ask the student to read the story aloud. Say, **"I want you to read the story to me."** As the student reads, mentally note any miscues or record them on the appropriate page of the Record Booklet.

4. If the student has difficulty reading the story, have the student listen while you read it aloud. Say, **"You listen to me read the story. Then I will want you to read it to me."** After your reading, invite the student to read.

5. Encourage the student to talk about the story with you.

SCORING AND INTERPRETATION

Informally note the miscues the student made, the degree of fluency, and other behaviors on the Caption Reading page in the Record Booklet. Record your qualitative judgment of the reading with an X on the continuum located on the front page of the Record Booklet. If the student was able to read the story, you can informally analyze fluency, miscues, and overall engagement with the task.

If you read the story first, evaluate the degree to which the student was able to memorize and repeat text. Be alert for how the student uses language as you talk about the story.

For teaching strategies, consult Section 3.4 in Johns, Lenski, and Elish-Piper (1999).

1 The cat sits.	**2** The cat walks.
3 The cat eats.	**4** The cat sleeps.

Auditory Discrimination

Overview: This test will help evaluate the student's ability to distinguish between words that differ in one phoneme (sound).

Materials Needed: The page in the Record Booklet containing the auditory discrimination test and the Record Booklet.

PROCEDURE

1. Practice the words on the list, saying them clearly in a normal voice.

2. Do not rush the student during the assessment. Place a ✓ in the appropriate column, total correct responses, and record the score in the box.

3. If the student misses a pair or asks for one to be repeated, move on to the next item and return to any such items at the conclusion of the test.

4. Facing the student, say:

   "Listen to the words I am about to say: fair-far.

   Do they sound exactly the same or are they different? (For young children, the examiner may prefer the words 'alike' and 'not alike' in place of the words 'same' and 'different.')

   Yes, they are different.

   Listen to these two words: cap-cap.

   Are they the same or different?

   Now I am going to read you pairs of words. I want you to tell me if they are the same or different. Do you understand what you are to do? Please turn your back to me and listen very carefully."

5. Say all the words distinctly but in a normal voice.

6. Be alert for students who do not understand the concepts "same" and "different."

SCORING AND INTERPRETATION

Note the number of correct responses, enter the total in the box, and enter this score on the front of the Record Booklet. Based on the score, make a judgment of the student's auditory discrimination ability, and record an X on the continuum located on the summary page of the Record Booklet.

For teaching strategies, consult Section 3.6 in Johns, Lenski, and Elish-Piper (1999).

Phoneme Awareness (Spelling)*

Overview: This brief spelling test will help assess the student's ability to associate letters with the sounds in words.

Materials Needed: A pencil, the Record Booklet page for the student to write on, and the Record Booklet.

PROCEDURE

1. Say, **"I'm going to ask you to spell some words. Before you spell them, let's do a couple together."** Begin by modeling the spelling of *mat* by asking the student to think about what letter comes first, what next, and so on. You could say:

    "Let's begin with the word *m a t.*"

    "What letter comes first in *m a t*?" If the student says *m*, write the *m* on the record sheet. If the student says an incorrect letter, say, **"No, it is an *m.*"**

    Ask the student to say the word *mat* and ask, **"What else do you hear?"** If the student says *t*, write it on the record sheet with a space for the vowel. If necessary, correct the student by using a comment similar to that already mentioned.

    Ask, **"What else do you hear?"** If the student says *e*, say, **"No, it is an *a.*"** Write the word and show it to the student.

2. Repeat the above process with *lip*. If the student is able to say the correct beginning letters for *mat* and *lip*, begin the test without any additional prompting.

3. Give the student the pencil and begin to dictate the 12 words in sentences. You may help once on the first letter for the words *back* and *feet*. No help should be given on the remaining words. The student can say the word out loud as it is being written. If the student asks how to form a letter and asks for it specifically, you may show the student how the letter is made.

4. Observe the spelling and ask the student to identify any letters that are unreadable.

5. If the student is unable to provide the correct initial consonant on *both* the sample words *and* the first two test words, stop the test.

6. The twelve words and sentences are:

1. back	I came back to school.		7. side	I'm at the side door.
2. feet	My feet are small.		8. chin	I hurt my chin.
3. step	I took a big step.		9. dress	You can dress yourself.
4. junk	I have junk in my desk.		10. peeked	I peeked in the box.
5. picking	I am picking up paper.		11. lamp	Turn off the lamp.
6. mail	Please mail the letter.		12. road	The road is bumpy.

SCORING AND INTERPRETATION

Count the number of correct responses and place the score in the box on the record sheet and on the front of the Record Booklet. Then make an overall judgment of the student's spelling. You may want to make separate judgments for word—"B" beginnings, "M" middles, "E" ends. Be sure your focus is on sounds, not letters. For *junk*, both *j* and *g* would be considered correct. Record B, M, and E on the continuum located on the summary page of the record booklet and use an X to represent your overall assessment.

For teaching strategies, consult Section 3.9 in Johns, Lenski, and Elish-Piper (1999).

*Based on the work of Darrell Morris.

415

Phoneme Segmentation

Overview: Phonemic awareness refers to the student's knowledge of phonemes or sounds in speech. This ability is strongly related to success in reading and spelling acquisition.

Note: This assessment was designed for use with English speaking kindergartners. It may also be used with older students experiencing difficulty in literacy acquisition.

Materials Needed: The page in the Record Booklet containing the test and the Record Booklet.

PROCEDURE

1. Duplicate the appropriate section of the Record Booklet.

2. With the student, say **"Today we're going to play a word game. I'm going to say a word and I want you to break the word apart. You are going to tell me each sound in the word in order. For example, if I say 'old,' you should say '/o/-/l/-/d/.'"** (Administrator: *Be sure to say the sounds, not the letters, in the word.*)

3. Then say: **"Let's try a few together."** The practice items are *ride, go*, and *man*. If necessary, help the student by segmenting the word for the student. Encourage the student to repeat the segmented sounds. You could move a marker for each sound or drop a penny into a cup for each sound to highlight the segmentation.

4. During the test, feedback is provided to the student. You could nod or say "Right" or "That's right." If the student is incorrect, correct him or her. You should also provide the appropriate response.

5. Proceed through all 22 items. Circle those items that the student correctly segments. Incorrect responses may be recorded on the blank line following the item.

SCORING AND INTERPRETATION

The student's score is the number of items he or she correctly segments into all constituent phonemes. No partial credit is given. For example, *she* (item 5) contains two phonemes /sh/-/e/; *grew* (item 7) contains three phonemes /g/-/r/-/ew/; and *three* (item 15) contains three phonemes /th/-/r/-/ee/. If the student notes letter names instead of sounds, the response is coded as incorrect, and the type of error is noted in the Record Booklet. Such notes are helpful in understanding the student. Some students may partially segment, simply repeat the stimulus item, provide nonsense responses, or give letter names. Total the number of correct responses and place the score in the box on the record sheet and on the front page of the Record Booklet. Then make an overall judgment of the student's phoneme segmentation abilities. For further information on this test, see Hallie Kay Yopp, "A Test for Assessing Phonemic Awareness in Young Children," *The Reading Teacher,* 49 (September 1995), 20–29. A wide range of scores is likely. Yopp (1995) reported that two samples of kindergartners achieved mean scores of 11.78 and 11.39.

For teaching strategies, consult Section 3.6 Johns, Lenski, and Elish-Piper (1999). Additional teaching strategies can be found in Johns and Lenski (2001), Opitz (2000), and Yopp and Yopp (2000).

Basic Word Knowledge

Overview: This test contains twenty words to help assess the student's ability to identify the most basic words in English.

Materials Needed: A 4" X 6" card, the appropriate pages in the manual, and the Record Booklet.

PROCEDURE

1. Duplicate the appropriate section of the Record Booklet.

2. Place the page containing the words before the student with the words covered. Say, **"I want to see if you know some words. Let's begin with this one."**

3. Move the card below each word and ask the student to say the word. If the student says the number, cover it up and point to the word. Then proceed to the next word.

4. Encourage the student to say "pass" or "skip it" for any unknown words; say, **"Just do the best you can."** Stop if no response is given to the first four words.

5. As the student reads, note correct responses with a plus (+) in the appropriate place of the Record Booklet. Record any incorrect responses by using the following:

Word	Meaning of Recording
+ men	Pronounced correctly
car can	Word mispronounced
D.K. girl	Don't know
h — him	Partial pronunciation

6. Proceed until you observe anxiety, frustration, or reluctance on the part of the student.

SCORING AND INTERPRETATION

Count the number of words pronounced correctly, and record the score in the box on the record sheet and on the front of the Record Booklet. Based on the correct responses, make a judgment of the student's word knowledge, and record an X on the continuum located on the front of the Record Booklet. An informal analysis of incorrect responses should help you develop tentative instructional interventions for word identification. The words in the list account for over 25 percent of the running words in printed English.

For teaching strategies, consult Section 3.11 in Johns, Lenski, and Elish-Piper (1999).

1. the
2. of
3. and
4. to
5. a
6. in
7. is
8. that
9. it
10. was
11. for
12. you
13. he
14. on
15. as
16. are
17. they
18. with
19. be
20. at

Pre-Primer Passage

Overview: The passage (20 words) will help determine how well the student is able to read connected text.

Materials Needed: The pages in the manual containing the passage, a 3" X 5" card, and the Record Booklet.

PROCEDURE

1. Duplicate the appropriate section of the Record Booklet.

2. Place the short passage (20 words) before the student, and cover everything but the title and illustration. Activate the student's background by saying, **"Look at the picture, and read the title to yourself. Then tell me what you think this story will be about."** Informally judge the student's background knowledge and record an X along the continuum on the record sheet.

3. Then say, **"Read the story to me. I'll ask you to answer some questions when you are finished."** As the student reads, note any miscues using procedures explained in Section Two of this manual. Record the number of miscues in the box on the record sheet.

4. When the student has finished reading, ask the comprehension questions or invite a retelling using procedures explained in Section Two of this manual. If the questions were used, record the number of questions missed in the box on the record sheet.

SCORING AND INTERPRETATION

Use the scoring guides on the record sheet to evaluate word recognition and comprehension. There are also some specifics of word recognition and comprehension that you can evaluate on a scale of 1 to 5. Then make an overall qualitative judgment of the student's word recognition and comprehension by marking Xs on the continuums on the summary page of the Record Booklet. Refer to this manual for general guidelines and examples of students' responses.

For teaching strategies, consult Sections 3.12 and 3.14 in Johns, Lenski, and Elish-Piper (1999).

The Cat

Pat has a cat.

The cat is big.

Pat likes to feed

the cat every day.

The cat likes Pat.

COPY

Record Booklet
(Teacher Copy)

 Note: This Record Booklet is on the CD-ROM that accompanies the Basic Reading Inventory.

RECORD BOOKLET FOR EARLY LITERACY ASSESSMENTS

Jerry L. Johns, Ph.D.

Student _____   Grade _____   Sex M F   Date of Test _____

School _____   Examiner _____   Date of Birth _____

Address _____   Current Book/Level _____   Age _____

Profile of Emergent Reader

	Low or Not Evident		Some		High or Very Evident

Alphabet Knowledge

_____/26 upper case

_____/28 lower case

Writing

Literacy Knowledge

_____/20

Wordless Picture Reading

sense of story

connects pictures

language use

reading dictation

Caption Reading

words recognized

fluency

ability to repeat text

Auditory Discrimination

_____/12

Phoneme Awareness

_____/12

Phoneme Segmentation

_____/22

Basic Word Knowledge

_____/20

Pre-Primer Passage

word recognition

comprehension/retelling

QUALITATIVE ANALYSIS OF EARLY LITERACY ASSESSMENT INSIGHTS

General Directions: Note the degree to which the student shows behavior or evidence in the following areas. Space is provided for additional items.

	Not Evident Low Seldom Weak Poor				Very Evident High Always Strong Excellent
1. Alphabet knowledge	├——————+——————+——————+——————┤
2. Writing	├——————+——————+——————+——————┤
3. Literacy knowledge	├——————+——————+——————+——————┤
4. Directionality of print	├——————+——————+——————+——————┤
5. Sense of story	├——————+——————+——————+——————┤
6. Tells story with pictures	├——————+——————+——————+——————┤
7. Language use	├——————+——————+——————+——————┤
8. Word knowledge	├——————+——————+——————+——————┤
9. Fluency	├——————+——————+——————+——————┤
10. Ability to repeat text	├——————+——————+——————+——————┤
11. Phonemic awareness	├——————+——————+——————+——————┤
12. Awareness of sounds	├——————+——————+——————+——————┤
13. Spelling	├——————+——————+——————+——————┤
14. Word recognition	├——————+——————+——————+——————┤
15. Comprehension/retelling	├——————+——————+——————+——————┤
16. Following directions	├——————+——————+——————+——————┤
17. General engagement	├——————+——————+——————+——————┤
18. _____	├——————+——————+——————+——————┤
19. _____	├——————+——————+——————+——————┤
20. _____	├——————+——————+——————+——————┤

423

Alphabet Knowledge

(Student copy is on page 391.)

Brief Directions: Present an alphabet sheet from one form. Use 3" X 5" cards to block off everything but the lines being read. If necessary, point to each letter with a finger. Then say, **"Here are some letters. I want to see how many you know."** Place a + above correctly identified letters. Record the student's responses for incorrect letters. Total correct responses, and record the score in the box.

Form A

O	H	S	E	G	P
X	V	I	M	J	D	K
B	T	R	Z	F	N
Y	Q	W	C	U	A	L

☐ **Correct**

b	x	e	c	j	m	g
l	u	r	t	q	h	y
s	d	o	a	k	w	a
i	p	v	f	n	z	g

☐ **Correct**

Observations, Comments, Notes, and Insights

Writing

(No student copy; supply paper and writing instruments.)

Brief Directions: Give the student paper and pencil. Ask the student to do some writing. Record qualitative judgments, observations, and insights below.

	Not Evident Low Seldom Weak Poor				Very Evident High Always Strong Excellent

Directionality

Left to right

Top to bottom

Writing

Scribbles or "cursivelike" scribbles

Letterlike formations

Repeated letters, numbers, words

Variety of letters, numbers, words

Knowledge of first (F) and last
    (L) name

Letter-Sound Relationships

Represents sounds heard at word
    beginnings

Represents sounds heard at word
    endings

Represents sounds heard in
    middles of words

Writing Conventions

Use of word boundaries

Use of punctuation

Overall Message Intent (check one)

_____ Student indicated no message intent.

_____ Student talked about but did not read or pretend to read what was written.

_____ Student was able to read what was written.

Teacher could make sense of writing independently. _____ yes _____ no

Observations, Comments, Notes, and Insights

Literacy Knowledge

(Student copy of *New Shoes*)

Brief Directions: Show the book, *New Shoes,* to the student. Say, **"I'd like you to show me some of the things you know about reading. You won't have to read."** Ask the following questions as *you* read the book to the student. Circle correct (+) or incorrect (–) responses. Total correct responses.

Page

	+	–	1. Hand the book to the child and say, **"Show me the front of this book."**
1	+	–	2. Say, **"Point to where I should start reading."** *Read page 1.*
2	+	–	3. Ask, **"Which way should I go?"** Check for knowledge of left to right. *Read first line of page 2.*
2/3	+	–	4. Ask, **"Where should I go after that?"** Check for knowledge of a return sweep to the left. *Read rest of page 2 and page 3.*
3	+	–	5. On page 3, point to the comma and ask, **"What's this or what's this for?"**
4	+	–	6. *Read text on page 4.* Point to a period and ask, **"What's this or what's this for?"**
5	+	–	7. *Read text on page 5.* Point to the exclamation mark and ask, **"What's this or what's this for?"**
6	+	–	8. *Read text on page 6.* Point to the question mark and ask, **"What's this or what's this for?"**
6	+	–	9. Point to a lower-case letter (m, y, s) and say, **"Find a capital letter like this, find an upper-case letter like this, or find the big one like this."** Repeat for each letter.
7	+	–	10. *Read text on page 7.* Say, **"Show me one letter."** (Two 3" X 5" cards may be useful for items 10–19.)
	+	–	11. Say, **"Now show me two letters."**
	+	–	12. Say, **"Show me only one word."**
	+	–	13. Say, **"Now show me two words."**
	+	–	14. Say, **"Show me the first letter of a word."**
	+	–	15. Say, **"Show me the last letter of a word."**
	+	–	16. Say, **"Show me a long word."**

+ – 17. Say, **"Show me a short word."**

+ – 18. Say, **"Show me a sentence."**

8–9 + – 19. ***Read text on pages 8 and 9.*** Point to a capital letter (I, O, M) and say, **"Find a small letter like this or find a lower-case letter like this."** Repeat for each letter.

10 + – 20. ***Read text on page 10.*** Close the book, and hand it to the child with back cover showing and say, **"Show me the title or show me the name of the book."**

☐ **Total Correct**

Qualitative Judgments of Literacy Knowledge

	Not Evident **Low** **Seldom** **Weak** **Poor**				**Very Evident** **High** **Always** **Strong** **Excellent**

Overall engagement

Understanding of print
directionality

Knowledge of punctuation

Correspondence of upper-case
with lower-case letters

Knowledge of *letter* and *letters*

Knowledge of *word* and *words*

Ability to frame a sentence

Observations, Comments, Notes, and Insights

Wordless Picture Reading

(Student Copy is on page 410.)

Student's Dictation

Wordless Picture Reading

(Student Copy is on page 411.)

Student's Dictation

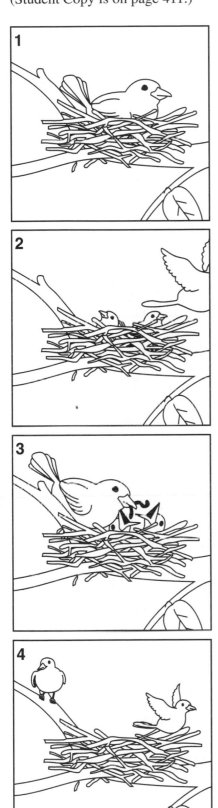

Caption Reading

(Student copy is on page 413.)

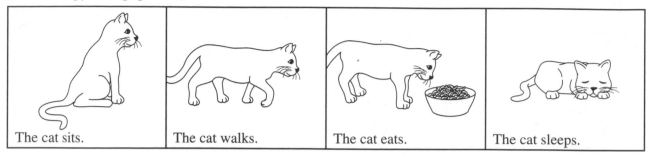

| The cat sits. | The cat walks. | The cat eats. | The cat sleeps. |

Qualitative Judgments of Caption Reading

If the student read the story, check the most characteristic statement:

___ The student's reading is an exact match to the text.

___ The student's reading closely matches the text.

___ The student's reading is somewhat related to the text but is based on the illustrations.

___ The student's reading is related mostly to the illustrations.

If you read the story first, check the statement most characteristic of the student's reading:

___ The student used memory to read the text with high accuracy.

___ The student used memory and illustrations to read the text with fair accuracy.

___ The student seemed to use a combination of memory and mostly illustrations to read the text.

___ The student did not seem to remember your reading and relied almost entirely on the illustrations to read the text.

	Not Evident Low Seldom Weak			Very Evident High Always Strong
Other Reading Behaviors	Poor			Excellent
Reads left to right	├————┼————┼————┼————┤
Reads top to bottom	├————┼————┼————┼————┤
Points to word and says it correctly	├————┼————┼————┼————┤
Demonstrates letter-sound relationships	├————┼————┼————┼————┤
Uses monitoring (rereads; corrects)	├————┼————┼————┼————┤
Points to correct words (if requested by you)	├————┼————┼————┼————┤
Engagement	├————┼————┼————┼————┤
Confidence as a reader	├————┼————┼————┼————┤

Auditory Discrimination

(No student copy is needed.)

		Correct	Incorrect
1.	bad — dad	_____	_____
2.	buff — bus	_____	_____
3.	watch — watch	_____	_____
4.	ball — bowl	_____	_____
5.	fall — fall	_____	_____
6.	sink — think	_____	_____
7.	lag — lad	_____	_____
8.	tot — top	_____	_____
9.	set — sit	_____	_____
10.	foam — phone	_____	_____
11.	rode — rode	_____	_____
12.	lab — lad	_____	_____

Total Correct ☐

Phoneme Awareness (Spelling)

(Teacher and student copy)

_____

_____

1. _____

2. _____

3. _____

4. _____

5. _____

6. _____

7. _____

8. _____

9. _____

10. _____

11. _____

12. _____

Correct   _____ Beginnings (B)   _____ Middles (M)   _____ Ends (E)

Observations, Comments, Notes, and Insights

Phoneme Segmentation*

(No student copy needed.)

Directions: Today we're going to play a word game. I'm going to say a word and I want you to break the word apart. You are going to tell me each sound in the word in order. For example, if I say "old," you should say "/o/-/l/-/d/." *(Administrator: Be sure to say the sounds, not the letters, in the word.)* Let's try a few together.

Practice items: *(Assist the child in segmenting these items as necessary.)* ride, go, man

Test items: *(Circle those items that the student correctly segments; incorrect responses may be recorded on the blank line following the item.)* The correct number of phonemes is indicated in parentheses.

1.	dog (3) _____	12.	lay (2) _____
2.	keep (3) _____	13.	race (3) _____
3.	fine (3) _____	14.	zoo (2) _____
4.	no (2) _____	15.	three (3) _____
5.	she (2) _____	16.	job (3) _____
6.	wave (3) _____	17.	in (2) _____
7.	grew (3) _____	18.	ice (2) _____
8.	that (3) _____	19.	at (2) _____
9.	red (3) _____	20.	top (3) _____
10.	me (2) _____	21.	by (2) _____
11.	sat (3) _____	22.	do (2) _____

Total Correct ☐

* The author, Hallie Kay Yopp, California State University, Fullerton, grants permission for this test to be reproduced. The author acknowledges the contribution of the late Harry Singer to the development of this test. Adapted from Hallie Kay Yopp, "A Test for Assessing Phonemic Awareness in Young Children," *The Reading Teacher*, 49 (September 1995), 20–29.

Basic Word Knowledge

(Student copy is on page 418.)

Brief Directions: Present one form of words. Ask the student to identify words. Say, **"I want to see if you know some words. Let's begin with this one."** Use a plus (+) for correct responses. Record the student's responses for incorrect words. Total correct responses and put the score in the box.

1.	the _____	11.	for _____
2.	of _____	12.	you _____
3.	and _____	13.	he _____
4.	to _____	14.	on _____
5.	a _____	15.	as _____
6.	in _____	16.	are _____
7.	is _____	17.	they _____
8.	that _____	18.	with _____
9.	it _____	19.	be _____
10.	was _____	20.	at _____

☐ Total Correct

Observations, Comments, Notes, and Insights

Student Copy is on page 420.

EE-1 (Pre-Primer) Activating Background: Look at the picture and read the title to yourself. Then tell me what you think this story will be about.

Background: Low ├──────┼──────┤ High

The Cat

	MISCUES						
	Substitution	Insertion	Omission	Reversal	Repetition	Self-Correction of Unacceptable Miscue	Meaning Change (Significant Miscue)
Pat has a cat.							
The cat is big.							
Pat likes to feed							
the cat every day.							
The cat likes Pat.							
TOTAL							

Word Recognition Scoring Guide		
Total Miscues	Level	Significant Miscues
0	Independent	0
1	Ind./Inst.	—
2	Instructional	1
3	Inst./Frust.	2
4	Frustration	3

Total Miscues ☐   Significant Miscues ☐

WPM

)1200

EE-1 (Pre-Primer)
Comprehension Questions

T 1. _____ What is this story mostly about?
(a cat)

F 2. _____ Who feeds the cat?
(Pat)

F 3. _____ How often is the cat fed?
(every day)

E 4. _____ What might the cat be fed?
(any logical response; cat food;
scraps)

I 5. _____ Why do you think the cat likes
Pat?
(any logical response; Pat feeds it)

Retelling Notes

☐ Questions
Missed

Comprehension Scoring Guide	
Questions Missed	Level
0	Independent
1	Ind./Inst.
1½	Instructional
2	Inst./Frust.
2½ +	Frustration

Retelling
Excellent
Satisfactory
Unsatisfactory

Qualitative Analysis of Word Identification and Comprehension				
(1 = not evident; 5 = very evident)				
Word Identification		Comprehension	
Uses graphophonic information	1 2 3 4 5	Makes predictions	1 2 3 4 5
Uses semantic information	1 2 3 4 5	Seeks to construct meaning	1 2 3 4 5
Uses syntactic information	1 2 3 4 5	Understands topic and major ideas	1 2 3 4 5
Knows basic sight words automatically	1 2 3 4 5	Remembers facts or details	1 2 3 4 5
Possesses sight vocabulary	1 2 3 4 5	Evaluates ideas from passages	1 2 3 4 5
Possesses numerous strategies	1 2 3 4 5	Makes and supports appropriate inferences	1 2 3 4 5
Uses strategies flexibly	1 2 3 4 5	Engagement with passage	1 2 3 4 5

Important Note: If the scoring guides are used, teacher judgment is especially important because of the length of the passage and the limited number of questions. Retelling may be particularly useful at this level.

Appendix B

Procedures for Eliciting and Evaluating Passage Retellings

Retelling Procedure 1*

NARRATIVE PASSAGES

1. Ask the student to retell the passage by saying: "Tell me about (name of passage) as if you were telling it to someone who has never heard it before."

2. Use the following prompts only when necessary:

   "What comes next?"

   "Then what happened?"

   If the student stops retelling and does not continue with the above prompts, ask a question about the passage that is based on that point in the passage at which the student has paused. For example, "What did the boys do after raking the leaves?"

3. When a student is unable to retell the story, or if the retelling lacks sequence and detail, prompt the retelling step by step. The following questions may be helpful:

   "Who was the passage about?"

   "When did the story happen?"

   "Where did the story happen?"

   "What was the main character's problem?"

   "How did he (or she) try to solve the problem? What was done first/next?"

   "How was the problem solved?"

   "How did the story end?"

* Adapted from: Lesley Mandel Morrow, "Retelling Stories: A Strategy for Improving Young Children's Comprehension, Concept of Story Structure, and Oral Language Complexity," *The Elementary School Journal,* 85 (May 1985), 647–61.

Retelling Procedure 2*

COMPREHENSION

Directions: Indicate with a checkmark the extent to which the reader's retelling includes or provides evidence of the following information.

	None	Low Degree	Moderate Degree	High Degree

RETELLING

1. Includes information directly stated in text.

2. Includes information inferred directly or indirectly from text.

3. Includes what is important to remember from the text.

4. Provides relevant content and concepts.

5. Indicates reader's attempt to connect background knowledge to text information.

6. Indicates reader's attempt to make summary statements or generalizations based on text that can be applied to the real world.

7. Indicates highly individualistic and creative impressions of or reactions to the text.

8. Indicates the reader's affective involvement with the text.

9. Demonstrates appropriate use of language (vocabulary, sentence structure, language conventions).

10. Indicates reader's ability to organize or compose the retelling.

11. Demonstrates the reader's sense of audience or purpose.

12. Indicates the reader's control of the mechanics of speaking or writing.

Interpretation: Items 1–4 indicate the reader's comprehension of textual information; items 5–8 indicate metacognitive awareness, strategy use, and involvement with text; items 9–12 indicate facility with language and language development.

*Adapted from: Pi A. Irwin and Judy N. Mitchell and cited in *Reexamining Reading Diagnosis: New Trends and Procedures,* edited by Susan Mandel Glazer, Lyndon W. Searfoss, and Lance M. Gentile. Newark, Delaware: International Reading Association, 1988, pp. 128–49.

Retelling Procedure 3*

STORY STRUCTURE

General Directions: To evaluate passages for story structure, place a check next to the element if the student includes it. Include the number of points scored for each element based on retelling.

1. *Characters* (5 points)

   Introduction of characters (2 points main characters, 1 point for each additional,   _____
   total of 5 points)

2. *Setting* (5 points)

   A time or place where the story happens (5 points)   _____

   OR

   A general setting statement (5 points)

3. *Theme* (10 points) = gist   _____

   Initiating events that set the goal for the story

   OR

   A goal becomes evident for the main character to achieve or a problem is evident to solve

4. *Plot Episodes* (10 points)   _____

   Events leading toward accomplishing the goal or solving the problem (adjust maximum
   raw score to equal 10 based on number of events)

5. *Resolution* (10 points)   _____

   The problem is solved or goal is reached (8 points)
   The story is ended (2 points)

6. *Sequence* (10 points)   _____

   Story is told with elements in the structural order listed above (10 points all in order; 6.6
   points 3 in order; 3.3 points 2 in order; 1 point 1 in order; 0 none in order; omitted elements
   are not scored)

Total Points   _____

×2

Retelling Score   ▢

*Adapted from: Jodi Grant, "Deciding What's Important for Readers to Remember," Paper Presented at the Annual Conference of the International Reading Association, Atlanta, 1984.

Retelling Procedure 4*

EXPOSITORY PASSAGES

Independent Level

Retelling will generally reflect:

1. the text structure
2. organization of how the material was presented
3. main ideas and details contained in the material

Instructional Level

Retelling will generally reflect:

1. less content than at an independent level
2. some minor misinterpretations and inaccuracies
3. organization that differs, in some respects, to the way it was presented in the material

Frustration Level

Retelling will generally be:

1. haphazard
2. incomplete
3. characterized by bits of information not related in any logical or sequential order

---

*Adapted from: Marjorie Seddon Johnson, Roy A. Kress, and John J. Pilulski, *Informal Reading Inventories* (2nd ed.) Newark, Delaware: International Reading Association, 1987.

Retelling Procedure 5*

NARRATIVE AND EXPOSITORY—HOLISTIC APPROACH

General Directions: This holistic approach for evaluating retellings can be used with both narrative and expository text.

► The criteria for each of the five levels of retellings (5 = highest level) are described in Table 1.

► To categorize the principal qualities of each level of richness in comparison with all other levels, use Table 2.

Table 1   Judging Richness of Retellings

Level	Criteria for Establishing Level
5	Student generalizes beyond text; includes thesis (summarizing statement), all major points, and appropriate supporting details; includes relevant supplementations; shows high degree of coherence, completeness, comprehensibility.
4	Student includes thesis (summarizing statement), all major points, and appropriate supporting details; includes relevant supplementations; shows high degree of coherence, completeness, comprehensibility.
3	Student relates major ideas; includes appropriate supporting details and relevant supplementations; shows adequate coherence, completeness, comprehensibility.
2	Student relates a few major ideas and some supporting details; includes irrelevant supplementations; shows some degree of coherence; some completeness; the whole is somewhat comprehensible.
1	Student relates details only, irrelevant supplementations or none; low degree of coherence; incomplete; incomprehensible.

Table 2   Checklist for Judging Richness of Retellings

	5	4	3	2	1
Generalizes beyond text	X				
Thesis (summarizing) statement	X	X			
Major points	X	X	X	?	?
Supporting details	X	X	X	X	?
Supplementations	Relevant	Relevant	Relevant	Irrelevant	Irrelevant
Coherence	High	Good	Adequate	Some	Poor
Completeness	High	Good	Adequate	Some	Poor
Comprehensibility	High	Good	Adequate	Some	Poor

---

*Adapted from Pi A. Irwin and Judy Nichols Mitchell, "A Procedure for Assessing the Richness of Retellings," *Journal of Reading,* 26 (February 1983), 391–96.

Appendix

C

Form E: Extra Passages

Form E contains an extra passage at third grade and an extra passage at fifth grade. Because there is a transition from the graded word lists to the graded passages, some teachers find these extra "practice" passages helpful.

These passages may also be used for oral and silent reading to help verify, supplement, or expand knowledge and insights about the student's reading.

PASSAGES

Tom's Day

Today was Tom's birthday. This was supposed to be a special day. Instead, it was a very bad day. He was going to have a birthday party, but his mom was out of town. Jeff, his best friend, had forgotten his birthday. Besides, it was raining. "What a gloomy day," Tom said as he jammed his cold hands into his pockets. He shuffled slowly down the street kicking a stone.

He unlocked the back door and opened it. Wham! He was knocked over by Rusty. Rusty barked and greeted him with a wet lick. As Tom got to his feet, everyone shouted, "Surprise!"

Student Copy is on page 444.

E 3183 (Grade 3) Activating Background: Read the title to yourself; then tell me what you think will happen.

Background: Low ├────┼────┤ High

Tom's Day

Tom's Day	MISCUES					Self-Correction of Unacceptable Miscue	Meaning Change (Significant Miscue)
	Substitution	Insertion	Omission	Reversal	Repetition		
Today was Tom's birthday. This							
was supposed to be a special day.							
Instead, it was a very bad day. He							
was going to have a birthday party,							
but his mom was out of town. Jeff,							
his best friend, had forgotten his							
birthday. Besides, it was raining.							
"What a gloomy day," Tom said as							
he jammed his cold hands into his							
pockets. He shuffled slowly down							
the street kicking a stone.							
He unlocked the back door and							
opened it. Wham! He was knocked							
over by Rusty. Rusty barked and							
greeted him with a wet lick. As							
Tom got to his feet, everyone							
shouted, "Surprise!"							
TOTAL							

Word Recognition Scoring Guide		
Total Miscues	Level	Significant Miscues
0–1	Independent	0–1
2–4	Ind./Inst.	2
5	Instructional	3
6–9	Inst./Frust.	4
10 +	Frustration	5 +

Total Miscues □   Significant Miscues □

_____ WPM
)6000

E 3183 (Grade 3)
Comprehension Questions

T   1. _____ What is this story about?
            (Tom's birthday; a bad day; a
            surprise)

F   2. _____ How was the weather?
            (raining; gloomy)

F   3. _____ Where was Tom's mom?
            (out of town)

F   4. _____ Who is Tom's best friend?
            (Jeff)

F   5. _____ What was Tom doing as he
            walked down the street?
            (kicking a stone)

F   6. _____ Who knocked Tom down?
            (his dog, Rusty)

F   7. _____ How did Rusty greet Tom?
            (barked; licked him)

I   8. _____ Which season could it be? Why?
            (any logical response because of
            cold hands, the rain, or kicking a
            stone)

E   9. _____ What would probably happen at a
            surprise party?
            (any logical response)

V   10. _____ What does "jammed" mean?
            (push; shove; put his hands in
            hard; real far; fast; quick)

Retelling Notes

☐ Questions Missed

Comprehension Scoring Guide	
Questions Missed	Level
0–1	Independent
1½–2	Ind./Inst.
2½	Instructional
3–4½	Inst./Frust.
5 +	Frustration

Retelling
Excellent
Satisfactory
Unsatisfactory

The Astonished Students

There was once a student in Germany named Kristof who thought he could do anything he wanted to do. He was very courageous. One Friday, he coaxed his friend Petra to go in the dark forest. They would build a bonfire. She took the invitation, but was scared. She had heard the legend of the "Furious Scientist." He appeared with the mist of the night. Petra and Kristof went into the forest. The horizon was getting dark. They hiked for ten minutes. Suddenly, both of them left. They were frantically holding their heads talking about a horrifying mist they saw.

E 8595

Student Copy is on page 447.

E 8595 (Grade 5) Activating Background: Read the title to yourself; then tell me what you think will happen.

Background: Low ├──────┼──────┤ High

The Astonished Students

	MISCUES						
	Substitution	Insertion	Omission	Reversal	Repetition	Self-Correction of Unacceptable Miscue	Meaning Change (Significant Miscue)
There was once a student in Germany							
named Kristof who thought he could do							
anything he wanted to do. He was very							
courageous. One Friday, he coaxed his friend							
Petra to go in the dark forest. They would							
build a bonfire. She took the invitation, but							
was scared. She had heard the legend of the							
"Furious Scientist." He appeared with the							
mist of the night. Petra and Kristof went into							
the forest. The horizon was getting dark.							
They hiked for ten minutes. Suddenly, both of							
them left. They were frantically holding their							
heads talking about a horrifying mist they							
saw.							
TOTAL							

Word Recognition Scoring Guide		
Total Miscues	Level	Significant Miscues
0–1	Independent	0–1
2–4	Ind./Inst.	2
5	Instructional	3
6–9	Inst./Frust.	4
10 +	Frustration	5 +

Total Miscues ☐   Significant Miscues ☐

$\overline{)6000}$ WPM

E 8595 (Grade 5)
Comprehension Questions

T 1. _____ What is the story about?
(Kristof and Petra's walk in the woods)

F 2. _____ Where did Kristof live?
(in Germany)

F 3. _____ How did Kristof get Petra to come with him?
(he coaxed her)

F 4. _____ What did they plan to do in the forest?
(build a bonfire)

F 5. _____ Who or what did the legend speak of?
("Furious Scientist")

F 6. _____ When did they go into the forest?
(on Friday night)

F 7. _____ What were Petra and Kristof doing as they left the forest?
(holding their heads; talking about a horrifying mist they saw)

I 8. _____ How do you think Kristof and Petra felt as they left the forest? Why?
(any logical response)

E 9. _____ Do you believe that Kristof and Petra really saw something during the night? Why?
(any logical response)

V 10. _____ What is "mist"?
(like a fog; haze)

	Retelling Notes

☐ Questions Missed

Comprehension Scoring Guide	
Questions Missed	Level
0–1	Independent
1½–2	Ind./Inst.
2½	Instructional
3–4½	Inst./Frust.
5 +	Frustration

Retelling
Excellent
Satisfactory
Unsatisfactory

449

Appendix

D

Summary Sheets

 Note: These summary sheets are on the CD-ROM that accompanies the Basic Reading Inventory.

Summary of Student's Oral Reading Performance on the Basic Reading Inventory

Jerry L. Johns, Ph.D.

SUMMARY OF STUDENT'S MISCUES IN ORAL READING			
Substitutions			
Different Beginnings	Different Middles	Different Endings	Different in Several Parts

Insertions	Omissions	Repetitions	Miscellaneous

Basic Reading Inventory
Miscue Tally and Reading Behavior
Summary Charts

Jerry L. Johns, Ph.D.

Directions: Record the number of miscues from all passages at the student's independent, instructional, and instructional/frustration levels. Total each category. Follow the same procedure for the other reading behaviors. Then make qualitative judgments about the student's reading and check the appropriate columns at the bottom of the cover page of the performance booklet.

Passages Read	Type of Miscue			
	Substitution	Insertion	Omission	Reversal
PP				
P				
1				
2				
3				
4				
5				
6				
7				
8				
TOTALS				

Passages Read	Other Reading Behaviors		
	Repetition	Self-Correction of Unacceptable Miscue	Meaning Change
PP			
P			
1			
2			
3			
4			
5			
6			
7			
8			
TOTALS			

Qualitative Summary of Miscues on the Basic Reading Inventory

Jerry L. Johns, Ph.D.

MISCUE	TEXT	GRAPHIC SIMILARITY			CONTEXT		Self-Correction of Unacceptable Miscues
		Beginning	Middle	End	Acceptable	Unacceptable	
	Column Total						
	Number of Miscues Analyzed						
	Percentage						

PREDICTION STRATEGY

Graphic Similarity — B M E

100%		
90		
80		
70		
60		
50		
40		
30		
20		
10		

___% ___% ___%

Miscues Acceptable in Context

100%
90
80
70
60
50
40
30
20
10

___%

CORRECTION STRATEGY

Unacceptable Miscues Self-Corrected

100%
90
80
70
60
50
40
30
20
10

___%

Summary of Student's Comprehension Performance on the Basic Reading Inventory

Jerry L. Johns, Ph.D.

ANALYSIS BY TYPE OF QUESTION										
Grade	Fact Oral	Fact Silent	Topic Oral	Topic Silent	Evaluation Oral	Evaluation Silent	Inference Oral	Inference Silent	Vocabulary Oral	Vocabulary Silent
P	__/6	__/6	__/1	__/1	__/1	__/1	__/1	__/1	__/1	__/1
1	__/6	__/6	__/1	__/1	__/1	__/1	__/1	__/1	__/1	__/1
2	__/6	__/6	__/1	__/1	__/1	__/1	__/1	__/1	__/1	__/1
3	__/6	__/6	__/1	__/1	__/1	__/1	__/1	__/1	__/1	__/1
4	__/6	__/6	__/1	__/1	__/1	__/1	__/1	__/1	__/1	__/1
5	__/6	__/6	__/1	__/1	__/1	__/1	__/1	__/1	__/1	__/1
6	__/6	__/6	__/1	__/1	__/1	__/1	__/1	__/1	__/1	__/1
7	__/6	__/6	__/1	__/1	__/1	__/1	__/1	__/1	__/1	__/1
8	__/6	__/6	__/1	__/1	__/1	__/1	__/1	__/1	__/1	__/1
9	__/6	__/6	__/1	__/1	__/1	__/1	__/1	__/1	__/1	__/1
10	__/6	__/6	__/1	__/1	__/1	__/1	__/1	__/1	__/1	__/1
11	__/6	__/6	__/1	__/1	__/1	__/1	__/1	__/1	__/1	__/1
12	__/6	__/6	__/1	__/1	__/1	__/1	__/1	__/1	__/1	__/1
Ratio Missed	__/___	__/___	__/___	__/___	__/___	__/___	__/___	__/___	__/___	__/___
Percent Missed	__%	__%	__%	__%	__%	__%	__%	__%	__%	__%
Total Ratio Missed	__/___		__/___		__/___		__/___		__/___	
Total Percent Missed	__%		__%		__%		__%		__%	

ANALYSIS BY LEVEL OF COMPREHENSION			
	Lower-Level Comprehension (Fact Questions Only) Oral	Lower-Level Comprehension (Fact Questions Only) Silent	Higher-Level Comprehension (All Other Questions) Oral	Higher-Level Comprehension (All Other Questions) Silent
Ratio Missed	__/___	__/___	__/___	__/___
Total Ratio Missed	__/___		__/___	
Total Percent Missed	__%		__%	

Informal Assessment of Comprehension Engagement on the Basic Reading Inventory

Jerry L. Johns, Ph.D.

	PP	P	1	2	3	4	5	6	7	8	9	10	11	12
Correct responses especially full, fresh, or elaborated (numerals circled)*														
Incongruent incorrect responses **unrelated** to the passage in some meaningful, logical way (numerals with Xs)*														

*Refers to numerals circled beside the comprehension questions in the performance booklet.

INFORMAL GUIDELINES FOR EVALUATING ENGAGEMENT

1. More than one elaboration of a correct response per passage "can be taken as evidence of an alert mind that is engaged and being driven by meaning. It is too soon to say if any significant meanings can be attached to the absence of elaborations, or how much of this can be expected with different types of questions and formats" (Manzo and Manzo, 1993, p. 467).
2. More than three incongruent responses to comprehension questions are "an indication that engagement was weak and nonproductive" (Manzo and Manzo, 1993, p. 467).

Basic Reading Inventory
Class Summary Chart

Jerry L. Johns, Ph.D.

Student	Date	Levels				Comprehension					Word Recognition						
		Ind.	Inst.	Frust.	Lis.	Fact	Topic	Inference	Evaluation	Vocabulary	Substitutions	Corrections	Repetitions	Omissions	Punctuation	Phonics	Context

Consistent Strengths (+) and/or Weaknesses (−)

References

Ackland, Robert T. "Let's Look at Reading: Interactive Professional Development Using Informal Reading Inventories." Doctoral dissertation, University of Illinois at Chicago, 1994 (*Dissertation Abstracts International,* 1994, vol. 55/11, p. 3477).

Adams, Marilyn Jager. *Beginning to Read: Thinking and Learning About Print* (A Summary prepared by Steven A. Stahl, Jean Osborn, and Fran Lehr). Champaign: University of Illinois, 1990.

Allington, Richard L., and Anne McGill-Franzen. "Word Identification Errors in Isolation and in Context: Apples vs. Oranges." *The Reading Teacher,* 33 (April 1980), 795–800.

Alvermann, Donna E. Interfacing Microcomputers with Video-Cassettes: A Program for Teaching the IRI. Paper presented at the meeting of the College Reading Association, Pittsburgh, 1985.

Anderson, Betty, and Rosie Webb Joels. "Informal Reading Inventories." *Reading Improvement,* 23 (Winter 1986), 299–302.

Bader, Lois A. *Bader Reading and Language Inventory* (3rd ed.). Upper Saddle River, NJ: Prentice-Hall, Inc., 1998.

Barr, Rebecca, Camille L.Z. Blachowicz, and Marilyn Wogman-Sadow. *Reading Diagnosis for Teachers: An Instructional Approach* (3rd ed.). New York: Longman, 1995.

Beldin, H. O. "Informal Reading Testing: Historical Review and Review of the Research." In William K. Durr (Ed.), *Reading Difficulties: Diagnosis, Correction, and Remediation.* Newark, DE: International Reading Association, 1970, pp. 67–84.

Betts, Emmett A. "Adjusting Instruction to Individual Needs." In Nelson B. Henry (Ed.), *Reading in the Elementary School.* (The Forty-eighth Yearbook of the National Society for the Study of Education, Part II). Chicago: The University of Chicago Press, 1949, pp. 266–80.

Betts, Emmett A., Mabel Everett, and Frances Rodewald. "Remedial Reading." *Journal of Exceptional Children,* 2 (February 1936), 88–91.

Betts, Emmett A. "Reading Problems at the Intermediate Grade Level." *The Elementary School Journal,* 40 (June 1941), 737–46.

Betts, Emmett Albert. *Foundations of Reading Instruction.* New York: American Book Company, 1946.

Betts, Emmett Albert. *The Prevention and Correction of Reading Difficulties.* Evanston, IL: Row, Peterson and Company, 1936.

Blanchard, Jay S. *Computer-Based Reading Assessment Instrument.* Dubuque, IA: Kendall/Hunt Publishing Company, 1985.

Bolenius, Emma Miller. *Teacher's Manual of Silent and Oral Reading.* Boston: Houghton Mifflin Company, 1919.

Botel, Morton. *Botel Reading Inventory.* Chicago: Follett Educational Corporation, 1966.

Bristow, Page Simpson, John J. Pikulski, and Peter L. Pelosi. "A Comparison of Five Estimates of Reading Instructional Level." *The Reading Teacher,* 37 (December 1983), 273–79.

Brittain, Mary M. "Informal Reading Procedures: Some Motivational Considerations." *The Reading Teacher,* 24 (December 1970), 216–19.

Brown, Joel, Kenneth S. Goodman, and Ann M. Marek. (Comps. and Eds.). *Studies in Miscue Analysis: An Annotated Bibliography.* Newark, DE: International Reading Association, 1996.

Brown, Sandra R. "A Comparison of Five Widely Used Standardized Reading Tests and an Informal Reading Inventory for a Selected Group of Elementary School Children." Doctoral dissertation, University of Georgia, Athens, 1963 (*Dissertation Abstracts,* 1964, vol. 25, p. 996).

Burke, Carolyn L., and Kenneth S. Goodman. "When a Child Reads: A Psycholinguistic Analysis." *Elementary English,* 47 (January 1970), 121–29.

Burns, Paul C., and Betty D. Roe. *Burns/Roe Informal Reading Inventory* (3rd ed.). Boston: Houghton Mifflin Company, 1989.

Burns, Paul C., and Betty D. Roe. *Burns/Roe Informal Reading Inventory* (4th ed.). Boston: Houghton Mifflin Company, 1993.

Burns, Paul C., and Betty D. Roe. *Burns/Roe Informal Reading Inventory* (5th ed.). Boston: Houghton Mifflin Company, 1999.

Burns, Paul C., Betty D. Roe, and Elinor P. Ross. *Teaching Reading in Today's Elementary Schools.* Boston: Houghton Mifflin Company, 1996.

Buros, Oscar Krisen. *The Seventh Mental Measurements Yearbook.* Highland Park, NJ: The Gryphon Press, 1972.

Caldwell, JoAnne. "A New Look at the Old Informal Reading Inventory." *The Reading Teacher,* 39 (November 1985), 168–73.

Carroll, John B., Peter Davies, and Barry Richman. *Word Frequency Book.* Boston: Houghton Mifflin Company, 1971.

Carver, Ronald P. "Silent Reading Rates in Grade Equivalents." *Journal of Reading Behavior,* 21 (1989), 155–66.

Christie, James F. "The Qualitative Analysis System: Updating the IRI." *Reading World,* 18 (May 1979), 393–99.

Cohn, Marvin, and Cynthia D'Alessandro. "When Is a Decoding Error Not a Decoding Error?" *The Reading Teacher,* 32 (December 1978), 341–44.

Collins, Martha D., and Earl H. Cheek, Jr. *Diagnostic-Prescriptive Reading Instruction* (4th ed.). Dubuque, IA: Wm. C. Brown Communications, Inc., 1993.

Conrad, Lori L., and Nancy L. Shanklin. "Using Miscues to Understand Students' Reading." *Colorado Reading Council Journal,* 10 (Spring 1999), 21–32.

Cooper, J. Louis. "The Effect of Adjustment of Basal Reading Materials on Reading Achievement." Doctoral dissertation, Boston University, Boston, 1952.

Crawley, Sharon J., and King Merritt. *Remediating Reading Difficulties* (2nd ed.). Dubuque, IA: Brown and Benchmark Publishers, 1996.

Cunningham, Patricia M., Dorothy P. Hall, and Margaret Defee. "Non-ability Grouped, Multilevel Instruction: A Year in a First-grade Classroom," *The Reading Teacher,* 44 (April, 1991), 566–71.

Dale, Edgar, and Joseph O'Rourke. *The Living Word Vocabulary: The Words We Know.* Elgin, IL: Dome, Inc., 1976.

D'Angelo, Karen, and Robert M. Wilson. "How Helpful Is Insertion and Omission Miscue Analysis?" *The Reading Teacher,* 32 (February 1979), 519–20.

Davis, Beth G., and Bonnie Lass. *Elementary Reading: Strategies That Work.* Needham Heights, MA: Allyn and Bacon, 1996.

Dunkeld, Colin G. "The Validity of the Informal Reading Inventory for the Designation of Instructional Reading Levels: A Study of the Relationships Between Children's Gains in Reading Achievement and the Difficulty of Instructional Materials." Doctoral dissertation, University of Illinois, Urbana, 1970 (*Dissertation Abstracts,* 1971, vol. 31, p. 6274).

Durrell, Donald. "Individual Differences and Their Implications with Respect to Instruction in Reading." In Guy Montrose Whipple (Ed.), *The Teaching of Reading* (The Thirty-sixth Yearbook of the National Society for the Study of Education, Part I). Bloomington, IL: Public School Publishing Company, 1937, pp. 325–56.

Ekwall, Eldon E. "Informal Reading Inventories: The Instructional Level." *The Reading Teacher,* 29 (April 1976), 662–65.

Ekwall, Eldon E. "Should Repetitions Be Counted as Errors?" *The Reading Teacher,* 27 (January 1974), 365–67.

Ekwall, Eldon E. *Ekwall Reading Inventory* (2nd ed.). Boston: Allyn and Bacon, 1986.

Ekwall, Eldon E. "Informal Reading Inventories: The Instructional Level." *The Reading Teacher,* 29 (April 1976), 662–65.

Ekwall, Eldon E., and James L. Shanker. *Ekwall/Shanker Reading Inventory* (3rd ed.). Boston: Allyn and Bacon, 1993.

Emans, Robert. "Teacher Evaluation of Reading Skills and Individualized Reading." *Elementary English,* 42 (March 1965), 258–60.

Estes, Thomas H., and Joseph L. Vaughan, Jr. "Reading Interest and Comprehension: Implications." *The Reading Teacher,* 27 (November 1973), 149–53.

Evory, Ann (Ed.). *Contemporary Authors* (first revision, vol. 33–36). Detroit: Gale Research Company, 1978, pp. 101–2.

Farr, Roger. "Putting It All Together: Solving the Reading Assessment Puzzle." *The Reading Teacher,* 46 (September 1992), 26–37.

Felknor, Catherine. "Use of Individual Reading Inventories with Fourth-Grade Students on Individual Literacy Plans." *Colorado Reading Council Journal,* 11 (Spring 2000), 15–17.

Felknor, Catherine, Victoria Winterscheidt, and Laura Benson. "Thoughtful Use of Individual Reading Inventories." *Colorado Reading Council Journal,* 10 (Spring 1999), 10–20.

Flynt, E. Sutton, and Robert B. Cooter, Jr. *Reading Inventory for the Classroom.* Scottsdale, AZ: Gorsuch Scarisbrick, Publishers, 1993.

Flynt, E. Sutton, and Robert B. Cooter, Jr. *English-Español Reading Inventory for the Classroom.* Upper Saddle River, NJ: Prentice-Hall, Inc., 1999.

Flynt, E. Sutton, and Robert B. Cooter, Jr. *Reading Inventory for the Classroom* (2nd ed.). Scottsdale, AZ: Gorsuch Scarisbrick, Publishers, 1995.

Flynt, E. Sutton, and Robert B. Cooter, Jr. *Reading Inventory for the Classroom* (3rd ed.). Upper Saddle River, NJ: Prentice-Hall, Inc., 1998.

Flynt, E. Sutton, and Robert B. Cooter, Jr. *Reading Inventory for the Classroom* (4th ed.). Upper Saddle River, NJ: Prentice-Hall, Inc., 2001.

Forman, Joan, and Mary Ellen Sanders. *Project Leap First Grade Norming Study: 1993–1998.* Unpublished Manuscript, 1998.

Froese, Victor. "Functional Reading Levels: From Graded Word Lists?" 1974, Microfiche ED 102 520.

Gates, Arthur I. *The Improvement of Reading* (Rev. ed.). New York: The Macmillan Company, 1935.

Gillet, Jean Wallace, and Charles Temple. *Understanding Reading Problems: Assessment and Instruction* (4th ed.). Glenview, IL: Scott, Foresman/Little Brown Higher Education, 1994.

Gillet, Jean Wallace, and Charles Temple. *Understanding Reading Problems: Assessment and Instruction* (5th ed.). New York: Addison Wesley Longman, Inc., 2000.

Gillis, M. K., and Mary W. Olson. *Elementary IRIs: Do They Reflect What We Know About Text Type/ Structure and Comprehension?* Unpublished manuscript, 1985.

Glazer, Susan Mandel, and Carol Smullen Brown. *Portfolios and Beyond: Collaborative Assessment in Reading and Writing.* Norwood, ME: Christopher-Gordon Publishers, Inc., 1993.

Goodman, Kenneth S. "A Linguistic Study of Cues and Miscues in Reading." *Elementary English,* 42 (October 1965), 639–43.

Goodman, Kenneth S. "Analysis of Oral Reading Miscues: Applied Psycholinguistics." In Frank Smith (Ed.), *Psycholinguistics and Reading.* New York: Holt, Rinehart and Winston, Inc., 1973, pp. 158–76.

Goodman, Kenneth S. "The Search Called Reading." In Helen M. Robinson (Ed.), *Coordinating Reading Instruction.* Glenview, IL: Scott, Foresman and Company, 1971, pp. 10–14.

Goodman, Yetta M. "Reading Diagnosis—Qualitative or Quantitative?" *The Reading Teacher,* 26 (October 1972), 32–37.

Goodman, Yetta M., and Ann M. Marek. *Retrospective Miscue Analysis.* Katonah, NY: Richard C. Owen Publishers, Inc., 1996.

Goodman, Yetta M., and Carolyn L. Burke. *Reading Miscue Inventory Manual: Procedure for Diagnosis and Evaluation.* New York: The Macmillan Company, 1972.

Goodman, Yetta M., Dorothy J. Watson, and Carolyn L. Burke. *Reading Miscue Inventory: Alternative Procedures.* New York: Richard C. Owen Publishers, 1987.

Gray, William S. "Methods of Testing Reading II." *The Elementary School Journal,* 16 (February 1916), 281–98.

Gunning, Thomas G. *Assessing and Correcting Reading and Writing Difficulties.* Boston: Allyn and Bacon, 1998.

Gunning, Thomas G. *Best Books for Beginning Reading.* Boston: Allyn and Bacon, 1998.

Gunning, Thomas G. *Creating Reading Instruction for All Children* (3rd ed.). Boston: Allyn and Bacon, 2000.

Hardy, Norman D., and Max E. Jerman. *Readability Estimator.* Seattle: Berta-Max, Inc., 1985.

Harris, Albert J., and Edward R. Sipay. *How to Increase Reading Ability* (9th ed.). New York: Longman, 1990.

Harris, Theodore L., and Richard E. Hodges (Coeds.). *A Dictionary of Reading and Related Terms.* Newark, DE: International Reading Association, 1981.

Harris, Theodore L., and Richard E. Hodges (Eds.). *The Literacy Dictionary: The Vocabulary of Reading and Writing.* Newark, DE: International Reading Association, 1995.

Hasbrouck, Jan E., and Gerald Tindal. "Curriculum-Based Oral Reading Fluency Norms for Students in Grades 2 Through 5." *Teaching Exceptional Children,* 24 (Spring 1992), 41–44.

Hays, Warren S. "Criteria for the Instructional Level of Reading." 1975, Microfiche ED 117 665.

Helgren-Lempesis, Valerie A., and Charles T. Mangrum II. "An Analysis of Alternate-Form Reliability of Three Commercially Prepared Informal Reading Inventories," *Reading Research Quarterly,* 21 (Spring 1986), 209–15.

Homan, Susan P., and Janell P. Klesius. "A Re-examination of the IRI: Word Recognition Criteria." *Reading Horizons,* 26 (Fall 1985), 54–61.

Hood, Joyce. "Is Miscue Analysis Practical for Teachers?" *The Reading Teacher,* 32 (December 1978), 260–66.

Hunt, Lyman C., Jr. "The Effect of Self-Selection, Interest, and Motivation Upon Independent, Instructional, and Frustrational Levels." *The Reading Teacher,* 24 (November 1970), 146–51, 158.

International Reading Association. *Making a Difference Means Making it Different.* (A Position Statement). Newark, DE: International Reading Association, 2000.

IOX, *Basic Skills Word List: Grades 1–12.* Los Angeles: IOX, 1980.

Johns, Jerry L. *Advanced Reading Inventory.* Dubuque, IA: Wm. C. Brown Company Publishers, 1981.

Johns, Jerry L. *Basic Reading Inventory.* Dubuque, IA: Kendall/Hunt Publishing Company, 1978.

Johns, Jerry L. *Basic Reading Inventory* (3rd ed.). Dubuque, IA: Kendall/Hunt Publishing Company, 1985.

Johns, Jerry L. *Basic Reading Inventory* (4th ed.). Dubuque, IA: Kendall/Hunt Publishing Company, 1988.

Johns, Jerry L. *Basic Reading Inventory* (6th ed.). Dubuque, IA: Kendall/Hunt Publishing Company, 1994.

Johns, Jerry L. *Basic Reading Inventory* (7th ed.). Dubuque, IA: Kendall/Hunt Publishing Company, 1997.

Johns, Jerry L. *Basic Reading Inventory: Pre-Primer Through Grade Twelve and Early Literacy Assessments* (8th ed.). Dubuque, IA: Kendall/Hunt Publishing Company, 2001.

Johns, Jerry L. *Computer-Based Advanced Reading Inventory* (Grade 7–College). DeKalb, IL: Northern Illinois University, 1986.

Johns, Jerry L. "Emmett A. Betts on Informal Reading Inventories" (Open to Suggestion Column). *Journal of Reading,* 34 (March 1991), 492–93.

Johns, Jerry L. (Comp.). *Informal Reading Inventories: An Annotated Reference Guide.* DeKalb, IL: Northern Illinois University, 1993.

Johns, Jerry L. "Informal Reading Inventories: A Holistic Consideration of the Instructional Level." In Nancy D. Padak, Timothy V. Rasinski, and John Logan (Eds.). Twelfth Yearbook of the College Reading Association, 1990a, pp. 135–40.

Johns, Jerry L. "Informal Reading Inventories: A Survey Among Professionals." *Illinois School Research and Development,* 13 (Fall 1976), 35–39.

Johns, Jerry L. *Secondary & College Reading Inventory* (2nd ed.). Dubuque, IA: Kendall/Hunt Publishing Company, 1990b.

Johns, Jerry L. *Spanish Reading Inventory* (2nd ed.). Dubuque, IA: Kendall/Hunt Publishing Company, 2001.

Johns, Jerry L. "Using Informal Reading Inventories in Classroom and Clinic." In Lillian R. Putnam (Ed.). *How to Become a Better Reading Teacher: Strategies for Assessment and Intervention.* Columbus, OH: Merrill, 1996, pp. 113–22.

Johns, Jerry L., and Anne Marie Magliari. "Informal Reading Inventories: Are the Betts Criteria the Best Criteria?" *Reading Improvement,* 26 (Summer 1989), 124–32.

Johns, Jerry L., and Peggy VanLeirsburg. "How Professionals View Portfolio Assessment." *Reading Research and Instruction,* 32 (Fall 1992), 1–10.

Johns, Jerry L., and Peggy VanLeirsburg. Portfolio Assessment: A Survey Among Professionals. Literacy Research Report No. 1. DeKalb, IL: Northern Illinois University Reading Clinic, 1990.

Johns, Jerry L., and Susan Davis Lenski. *Improving Reading: A Handbook of Strategies* (2nd ed.). Dubuque, IA: Kendall/Hunt Publishing Company, 1997.

Johns, Jerry L., and Susan Davis Lenski. *Improving Reading: Strategies and Resources* (3rd ed.). Dubuque, IA: Kendall/Hunt Publishing Company, 2001.

Johns, Jerry L., Sharon Garton, Paula Schoenfelder, and Patricia Skriba. *Assessing Reading Behavior: Informal Reading Inventories* (An Annotated Bibliography). Newark, DE: International Reading Association, 1977.

Johns, Jerry L., Susan Davis Lenski, and Laurie Elish-Piper. *Early Literacy Assessments & Teaching Strategies.* Dubuque, IA: Kendall/Hunt Publishing Company, 1999.

Johnson, Marjorie Seddon, and Roy A. Kress. *Informal Reading Inventories.* Newark, DE: International Reading Association, 1965.

Johnson, Marjorie Seddon, Roy A. Kress, and John J. Pikulski. *Informal Reading Inventories* (2nd ed.). Newark, DE: International Reading Association, 1987.

Johnston, Peter. Prior Knowledge and Reading Comprehension Test Bias. (Technical Report No. 289). Champaign, IL: Center for the Study of Reading, 1983.

Johnston, Peter, and Richard Allington. "Remediation." In Rebecca Barr, Michael L. Kamil, Peter B. Mosenthal, and P. David Pearson (Eds.). *Handbook of Reading Research, Volume II.* New York: Longman, 1991, pp. 984–1012.

Jorgenson, Gerald W. "Relationship of Classroom Behavior to the Accuracy of the Match Between Material Difficulty and Student Ability." *Journal of Educational Psychology,* 69 (February 1977), 24–32.

Kalmbach, James R. "Evaluating Informal Methods for the Assessment of Retellings." *Journal of Reading,* 30 (November 1986), 119–27.

Kender, Joseph P. "Analysis of Factors Associated with Informal Reading Tests at the Eighth Grade Level." Doctoral dissertation, University of Pennsylvania, Philadelphia, 1966.

Kender, Joseph P. "Informal Reading Inventories." *The Reading Teacher,* 24 (November 1970), 165–67.

Kibby, Michael W. *Practical Steps for Informing Literacy Instruction: A Diagnostic Decision-Making Model.* Newark, DE: International Reading Association, 1995.

Killgallon, Patsy Aloysius. "A Study of Relationships Among Certain Pupil Adjustments in Language Situations." Doctoral dissertation, Pennsylvania State College, State College, 1942 (*Doctoral Dissertations,* 1943, vol. 10, p. 75).

Klesius, Janell P., and Susan P. Homan. "A Validity and Reliability Update on the Informal Reading Inventory with Suggestions for Improvement." *Journal of Learning Disabilities,* 18 (February 1985), 71–76.

Kragler, Sherry. "Vygotsky and At-Risk Readers: Assessment and Instructional Implications." In Lisbeth Dixon-Kraus (Ed.). *Vygotsky in the Classroom: Mediated Literacy Instruction and Assessment.* White Plains, NY: Longman Publishers, 1996, pp. 149–60.

Ladd, Eleanor. "A Comparison of Two Types of Training with Reference to Developing Skill in Diagnostic Oral Reading Testing." Doctoral dissertation, Florida State University, Tallahassee, 1961 (*Dissertation Abstracts,* 1962, vol. 22, p. 2707).

Lenski, Susan Davis. *Schools that Succeed on the IGAP Reading Test.* Bloomington, IL: Illinois Reading Council, 1998.

Lenski, Susan Davis, and Jerry L. Johns. *Improving Writing: Resources, Strategies, and Assessments.* Dubuque, IA: Kendall/Hunt Publishing Company, 2000.

Lenski, Susan Davis, Mary Ann Wham, and Jerry L. Johns. *Reading & Learning Strategies for Middle & High School Students.* Dubuque, IA: Kendall/Hunt Publishing Company, 1999.

Leslie, Lauren, and JoAnne Caldwell. *Qualitative Reading Inventory.* Glenview, IL: Scott, Foresman/Little Brown Higher Education, 1990.

Leslie, Lauren, and JoAnne Caldwell. *Qualitative Reading Inventory—II.* New York: HarperCollins College Publishers, 1995.

Leslie, Lauren, and JoAnne Caldwell. *Qualitative Reading Inventory—III.* New York: Longman, 2001.

Leu, Donald J., Jr., and Charles K. Kinzer. *Effective Literacy Instruction, K–8* (4th ed.). Upper Saddle River, NJ: Prentice-Hall, Inc., 1999.

Leu, Donald J., Jr., and Charles K. Kinzer. *Effective Reading Instruction in the Elementary Grades.* Columbus, OH: Merrill Publishing Company, 1987.

Lipson, Marjorie Y., and Karen K. Wixson. *Assessment and Instruction of Reading Disability.* New York: HarperCollins Publishers, 1991.

Lipton, Aaron. "Miscalling While Reading Aloud: A Point of View." *The Reading Teacher,* 25 (May 1972), 759–62.

Lowell, Robert E. "Problems in Identifying Reading Levels with Informal Reading Inventories." In William K. Durr (Ed.), *Reading Difficulties: Diagnosis, Correction, and Remediation.* Newark, DE: International Reading Association, 1970, pp. 120–26.

Maginnis, George H. "Emmett Albert Betts." In John F. Ohles (Ed.), *Biographical Dictionary of American Educators* (vol. 1). Westport, CT: Greenwood Press, 1978, pp. 125–26.

Manning, John C. "Ariston Metron." *The Reading Teacher,* 48 (May 1995), 650–59.

Manzo, Anthony V., and Ula C. Manzo. *Literacy Disorders.* Fort Worth, TX: Harcourt Brace Jovanovich, Inc., 1993.

Manzo, Anthony V., and Ula C. Manzo. *Teaching Children To Be Literate.* Fort Worth, TX: Harcourt Brace College Publishers, 1995.

Manzo, Anthony V., Ula C. Manzo, and Michael C. McKenna. *Informal Reading-Thinking Inventory.* Fort Worth, TX: Harcourt Brace College Publishers, 1995.

Marzano, Robert J., Jean Larson, Geri Tish, and Sue Vodehnal. "The Graded Word List Is Not a Shortcut to an IRI." *The Reading Teacher,* 31 (March 1978), 647–51.

McCormick, Sandra. *Instructing Students Who Have Literacy Problems.* Englewood Cliffs, NJ: Prentice-Hall, Inc., 1995.

McCormick, Sandra. *Instructing Students Who Have Literacy Problems* (3rd ed.). Upper Saddle River, NJ, Prentice-Hall, Inc., 1999.

McCormick, Sandra. *Remedial and Clinical Reading Instruction.* Columbus: Merrill Publishing Company, 1987.

McCracken, Robert A. "The Development and Validation of the IRI for the Individual Appraisal of Reading Performance in Grades One Through Six." Doctoral dissertation, Syracuse University, Syracuse, New York, 1963 (*Dissertation Abstracts,* 1963, vol. 24, p. 5200).

McCracken, Robert A. *Standard Reading Inventory.* Bellingham, WA: Pioneer Printing Company, 1966.

McNaughton, Stuart. "The Influence of Immediate Teacher Correction on Self-Corrections and Proficient Oral Reading." *Journal of Reading Behavior,* 13 (Winter 1981), 367–71.

McTague, Becky. "Lessons From Reading Recovery for Classroom Teachers." *Illinois Reading Council Journal,* 25 (Winter 1997), 42–49.

Micro Power & Light. *Readability Calculations.* Dallas, TX: Micro Power & Light Co., 1995.

Millsap, Lucille N. "A Study of Teachers' Awareness of Frustration Reading Levels Among Their Pupils in Basal Readers." Doctoral dissertation, University of Oregon, Eugene, 1962 (*Dissertation Abstracts,* 1962, vol. 23, p. 2809).

Morris, Judith A. "An Investigation of Informal Reading Inventory Scoring Criteria with Average Second- and Fourth-Grade Students." Unpublished doctoral dissertation, Northern Illinois University, 1990.

Morrow, Lesley Mandel. "Retelling Stories: A Strategy for Improving Young Children's Comprehension, Concept of Story Structure, and Oral Language Complexity." *The Elementary School Journal,* 85 (May 1985), 647–61.

Morrow, Lesley Mandel. "Retelling Stories as a Diagnostic Tool." In Susan Mandel Glazer, Lyndon W. Searfoss, and Lance M. Gentile (Eds.). *Reexamining Reading Diagnosis and Instruction.* Newark, DE: International Reading Association, 1988, pp. 128–49.

National Reading Panel. *Teaching Children To Read: An Evidenced-Based Assessment of the Scientific Research Literature on Reading and Its Implications for Reading Instruction.* Washington, DC: U.S. Department of Health and Human Services, 2000.

Newman, Harold. "Oral Reading Miscue Analysis Is Good but Not Complete." *The Reading Teacher,* 31 (May 1978), 883–86.

Norton, Donna E. *The Impact of Literature-Based Reading.* New York: Macmillan Publishing Company, 1992.

Olson, Mary W., and M. K. Gillis. Text Type and Text Structure: An Analysis of Three Secondary Informal Reading Inventories. Unpublished manuscript, 1985.

Opitz, Michael F. *Rhymes & Reasons: Literature and Language Play for Phonological Awareness.* Portsmouth, NH: Heinemann, 2000.

Patty, Delbert L. "A Comparison of Standardized Oral Reading Test Scores and Informal Reading Inventory Scores." Doctoral dissertation, Ball State University, Muncie, IN, 1965 (*Dissertation Abstracts,* 1966, vol. 26, p. 5302).

Pehrsson, Robert S. "Challenging Frustration Level." *Reading & Writing Quarterly: Overcoming Learning Difficulties,* 10 (July–September 1994), 201–08.

Pikulski, John. "A Critical Review: Informal Reading Inventories." *The Reading Teacher,* 28 (November 1974), 141–51.

Pikulski, John J., and Timothy Shanahan. "Informal Reading Inventories: A Critical Analysis." In John J. Pikulski and Timothy Shanahan (Eds.), *Approaches to the Informal Evaluation of Reading.* Newark, DE: International Reading Association, 1982, pp. 94–116.

Powell, William R. "Reappraising the Criteria for Interpreting Informal Inventories." In Dorothy L. DeBoer (Eds.), *Reading Diagnosis and Evaluation.* Newark, DE: International Reading Association, 1970, pp. 100–09.

Powell, William R. "The Validity of the Instructional Reading Level." In Robert E. Leibert (Ed.), *Diagnostic Viewpoints in Reading.* Newark, DE: International Reading Association, 1971, pp. 121–33.

Raphael, Taffy E. "Teaching Question Answer Relationships, Revisited." *The Reading Teacher,* 39 (February 1986), 516–22.

Recht, Donna R. "The Self-Correction Process in Reading." *The Reading Teacher,* 29 (April 1976), 632–36.

Reutzel, D. Ray, and Robert B. Cooter, Jr. *Teaching Children to Read* (3rd ed.). Upper Saddle River, NJ: Prentice-Hall, Inc., 2000.

Richek, Margaret Ann, JoAnne Schudt Caldwell, Joyce Holt Jennings, and Janet W. Lerner. *Reading Problems: Assessment and Teaching Strategies* (3rd ed.). Boston: Allyn and Bacon, 1996.

Rinsky, Lee Ann, and Esta de Fossard. *The Contemporary Classroom Reading Inventory.* Dubuque, IA: Gorsuch Scarisbrick, Publishers, 1980.

Rinsland, Henry D. *A Basic Vocabulary of Elementary School Children.* New York: The Macmillan Company, 1945.

Sakiey, Elizabeth, and Edward Fry. *3,000 Instant Words.* Highland Park, NJ: Drier Educational Systems, 1979.

Schell, Leo M. "The Validity of the Potential Level via Listening Comprehension: A Cautionary Note." *Reading Psychology,* 3 (July–September 1982), 271–76.

Schell, Leo M., and Gerald S. Hanna. "Can Informal Reading Inventories Reveal Strengths and Weaknesses in Comprehension Subskills?" *The Reading Teacher,* 35 (December 1981), 263–68.

Schlieper, Anne. "Oral Reading Errors in Relation to Grade and Level of Skill." *The Reading Teacher,* 31 (December 1977), 283–87.

Silvaroli, Nicholas J. *Classroom Reading Inventory.* Dubuque, IA: Wm. C. Brown Company Publishers, 1969.

Silvaroli, Nicholas J. *Classroom Reading Inventory* (7th ed.). Dubuque, IA: Wm. C. Brown Communications, Inc., 1994.

Silvaroli, Nicholas J. *Classroom Reading Inventory* (8th ed.). Dubuque, IA: Brown & Benchmark Publishers, 1997.

Smith, Laura, and Constance Weaver. "A Psycholinguistic Look at the Informal Reading Inventory Part I: Looking at the Quality of Reader's Miscues: A Rationale and an Easy Method." *Reading Horizons,* 19 (Fall 1978), 12–22.

Spache, George D. *Diagnosing and Correcting Reading Disabilities.* Boston: Allyn and Bacon, Inc., 1976.

Spiegel, Dixie Lee. "A Comparison of Traditional Remedial Programs and Reading Recovery: Guidelines for Success for All Programs." *The Reading Teacher,* 49 (October 1995), 86–96.

Stieglitz, Ezra L. *The Stieglitz Informal Reading Inventory.* Boston: Allyn and Bacon, 1992.

Stieglitz, Ezra L. *The Stieglitz Informal Reading Inventory* (2nd ed.). Boston: Allyn and Bacon, 1997.

Sucher, Floyd, and Ruel A. Allred. *Sucher-Allred Reading Placement Inventory.* Oklahoma City: The Economy Company, 1973.

Tatham, Susan Masland. "Comprehension Taxonomies: Their Uses and Abuses." *The Reading Teacher,* 32 (November 1978), 190–94.

Taylor, Stanford E., Helen Frackenpohl, Catherine E. White, Betty Willmon Nieroroda, Carole Livingston Browning, and E. Patricia Birsner. *EDL Core Vocabularies in Reading, Mathematics, Science, and Social Studies.* New York: EDL/McGraw-Hill, 1979.

Thorndike, Edward L. "Improving the Ability to Read." *Teachers College Record,* 36 (November 1934), 123–44.

Thorndike, Edward L., and Irving Lorge. *The Teacher's Word Book of 30,000 Words.* New York: Teachers College, 1944.

Tierney, Robert J. "Literacy Assessment Reform: Shifting Beliefs, Principled Possibilities, and Emerging Practices." *The Reading Teacher,* 51 (February 1998), 374–90.

Vacca, Jo Anne L., Richard T. Vacca, and Mary K. Gove. *Reading and Learning to Read.* Boston: Little, Brown and Company, 1987.

Vacca, Jo Anne L., Richard T. Vacca, and Mary K. Gove. *Reading and Learning to Read* (3rd ed.). New York: HarperCollins College Publishers, 1995.

Vacca, Jo Anne, Richard T. Vacca, and Mary K. Gove. *Reading and Learning to Read* (4th ed.). New York: Addison Wesley Longman, Inc., 2000.

Valencia, Sheila. "A Portfolio Approach to Classroom Reading Assessment: The Whys, Whats, and Hows." *The Reading Teacher,* 34 (January 1990), 338–40.

VanLeirsburg, Peggy, and Jerry L. Johns. "Portfolios: Teachers' Perceptions and Practices." *Michigan Reading Journal,* 29 (Fall 1995), 14–23.

Vygotsky, L. S. *Mind in Society* (Edited by Michael Cole, Vera John-Steiner, Sylvia Scribner, and Ellen Souberman). Cambridge, MA: Harvard University Press, 1978.

Waldo, Karl Douglas. "Tests in Reading in Sycamore Schools." *The Elementary School Journal,* 15 (January 1915), 251–68.

Walker, Barbara J. *Diagnostic Teaching of Reading: Techniques for Instruction and Assessment* (3rd ed.). Columbus: Merrill, an imprint of Prentice-Hall, Inc., 1996.

Walker, Barbara J. *Diagnostic Teaching of Reading* (4th ed.). Upper Saddle River, NJ: Prentice-Hall, Inc., 2000.

Walter, Richard B. "History and Development of the Informal Reading Inventory." 1974, Microfiche ED 098 539.

Wheat, Harry Grove. *The Teaching of Reading*. Boston: Ginn and Company, 1923.

Whipple, Guy Montrose, Ed. *Report of the National Committee on Reading*. (The Twenty-fourth Yearbook of the National Society for the Study of Education, Part I). Bloomington, IL: Public School Publishing Company, 1925.

Wilde, Sandra. *Miscue Analysis Made Easy*. Portsmouth, NH: Heinemann, 2000.

Williamson, Leon E., and Freda Young. "The IRI and RMI Diagnostic Concepts Should be Synthesized." *Journal of Reading Behavior,* 5 (July 1974), 183–94.

Windell, Idajean. "Development and Evaluation of a Module to Train Special Education Teacher Trainees to Determine a Pupil's Instructional Reading Level." 1975, Microfiche ED 111 142.

Woods, Mary Lynn, and Alden J. Moe. *Analytical Reading Inventory* (3rd ed.). Columbus: Charles E. Merrill Publishing Company, 1985.

Woods, Mary Lynn, and Alden J. Moe. *Analytical Reading Inventory* (4th ed.). Columbus: Merrill Publishing Company, 1989.

Woods, Mary Lynn, and Alden J. Moe. *Analytical Reading Inventory* (5th ed.). Columbus: Merrill, 1995.

Woods, Mary Lynn, and Alden J. Moe. *Analytical Reading Inventory* (6th ed.). Upper Saddle River, NJ: Prentice-Hall, Inc., 1999.

Yopp, Hallie Kay. "A Test for Assessing Phonemic Awareness in Young Children." *The Reading Teacher,* 49 (September 1995), 20–29.

Yopp, Hallie Kay, and Ruth Ellen Yopp. "Supporting Phonemic Awareness Development in the Classroom." *The Reading Teacher,* 54 (October 2000), 130–43.

Zeno, Susan M., Stephen H. Ivens, Robert T. Millard, and Raj Duvvuri. *The Educator's Word Frequency Guide*. Brewster, NY: Touchstone Applied Science Associates, Inc., 1995.

Index

How to Use the "Basic Reading Inventory" CD-ROM

INSTALLATION PROCEDURES

The installation procedures described below allow you to install Adobe Acrobat Reader™ 4.0.5 and QuickTime™ 4.1.2 on your hard drive. If your computer already has Adobe Acrobat Reader™ 4.0.5 or QuickTime™ 4.1.2, you do not need to go through any installation procedure! Just pop the CD into your CD-ROM or DVD drive and you're ready to access all of the information on the CD. If you have an earlier version of Reader™ or QuickTime™, you will need to install the latest versions of these programs for the CD to run efficiently. If you don't know whether or not your computer has Adobe Acrobat Reader™ or QuickTime™, test it. PC users can open the CD-ROM or DVD drive and attempt to access the program by double-clicking on "BRI." Macintosh™ users should double-click on the BRI icon.

WINDOWS™ INSTALLATION

Read the preceding paragraph to make sure you need the installation.

Place the *Basic Reading Inventory* CD-ROM in the CD-ROM or DVD drive of the computer.

Double-click on "My Computer."

Double-click on the CD-ROM or DVD drive. It should be labeled "BRI."

To install Adobe Acrobat Reader™, double-click on "Install Reader" folder.

Double-click on the Reader icon and follow the directions on the screen.

To install QuickTime™, double-click on Explorer or Netscape, depending on which one your computer uses to access the Internet.

Double-click on the QuickTime™ icon and follow the directions on the screen.

Restart your computer.

Remember to keep the CD in the drive because only the Reader and QuickTime™ have been installed on the hard drive. To access the *Basic Reading Inventory* Booklets and Videos:

Double-click on "My Computer" to access your CD-ROM or DVD drive.

Double-click on the drive which should be labeled "BRI" to arrive at the opening screen.

From the opening screen, you can find information on the CD by clicking on "Menu," which has forms and videos organized by page numbers referenced in the textbook. Click on the title of any of the forms or videos to go directly to that title.

MACINTOSH™ INSTALLATION

Read the preceding installation procedures to make sure you need the installation.

Place the BRI CD-ROM in the CD-ROM or DVD drive.

Double-click on the BRI icon.

To install Adobe Acrobat Reader™, double-click on "Reader."

Double-click on "Reader Installer" and follow the directions on the screen.

To install QuickTime™, double-click on Explorer or Netscape, depending on which one your computer uses to access the Internet.

Double-click on the QuickTime™ icon and follow the directions on the screen.

Restart your computer.

Remember to keep the CD in the drive because only the Reader and QuickTime™ have been installed on the hard drive. To access the *Basic Reading Inventory* Booklets and Videos:

Double-click on the BRI icon to arrive at the opening screen.

Double-click on "Menu" to go to the main menu listing all of the contents.

From the opening screen, you can find information on the CD by clicking on "Menu," which has forms and videos organized by page numbers referenced in the textbook. Click on the title of any of the forms or videos to go directly to that title.

NAVIGATING THE CD-ROM

From the Menu page, you can access any of the topics listed simply by clicking on a particular title. Once you have reached a specific booklet, you can navigate through the booklet by clicking on the left or right facing arrows in the toolbar at the top of the page to move forward or backward through the booklet. Clicking on the left arrow with a vertical bar to the left of it will take you to the first page of the booklet. Clicking on the right arrow with the vertical bar to the right of it, will take you to the last page of the booklet. To return to the Menu, simply click on the "Return to Menu" button found on the first page of each booklet.

You can also access any of the videos from the Menu page. Click on the title of any video. Once the video has loaded, click anywhere on the screen to start the video. When finished, click on "Menu" to return to the Menu page.

PRINTING FROM THE DATABASE

Each booklet of *Basic Reading Inventory* is a Portable Document File, or PDF. Each PDF begins with page 1. When you print, you will need to tell the computer the PDF page numbers you want, rather than the original page numbers. The page number in the toolbar at the lower left of your screen is the PDF page number that tells you where you are in the PDF file.

Located in the top left hand corner of the first page of each booklet (PDF file) in a red box are the page numbers you will need to print each complete booklet. To print individual pages, look for the page number listed in the top right hand corner of each individual page.

To print, go to *File* and select *Print*. WARNING: The default in the print menu is set to print an entire PDF file. Unless you want to print an entire booklet, you need to specify the *page number*. (*Page number* refers to the PDF page numbers, **NOT** the original page numbers.)

Basic Reading Inventory Administration and Scoring Procedures

To determine a student's independent, instructional, and frustration levels, administer the graded word lists and graded passages included in the Basic Reading Inventory as follows:

WORD RECOGNITION IN ISOLATION: Select a graded word list at a reading level that will be easy for the student. Ask the student to pronounce the words rapidly. Record the student's responses in the sight column beside the corresponding word list in the performance booklet.

Return to mispronounced or unknown words for an attempt at analysis and note the student's responses in the analysis column. Administer successive word lists until the student is no longer able to achieve a **total** score of at least 14 correct words or until the student becomes frustrated.

Scoring: Total the correct responses in the sight and analysis columns. Consult the criteria on the scoring guide at the bottom of the word lists to determine a rough estimate of the reading level achieved on each graded word list. Record the number-correct scores and the reading levels on the summary sheet of the performance booklet.

WORD RECOGNITION IN CONTEXT: Ask the student to read aloud the passage graded one level *below* the highest independent level achieved on the graded word lists. As the student reads the passage, record all miscues such as omissions, repetitions, substitutions, and the like on the corresponding copy of the passage found in the performance booklet.

Scoring: Count the number of *total* miscues or *significant* miscues (those that affect meaning) in each graded passage.

To determine reading levels from the word recognition in context scores, consult the criteria on the scoring guide at the bottom of the passage. Record the score and the reading levels on the summary sheet of the performance booklet.

COMPREHENSION: Ask the comprehension questions that accompany the passage in the performance booklet and record the student's responses. Continue administering graded passages until the student has many word recognition miscues or is unable to answer half the comprehension questions. Also, watch for behavior associated with frustration: lack of expression, word-by-word reading, excessive anxiety, and so on.

Scoring: Count the number of comprehension questions missed.

To convert these scores into reading levels, consult the criteria on the scoring guide at the bottom of the questions. (Teacher judgment must be exercised at the pre-primer level because the limited number of questions may not permit precise measurement of achievement.) Record the scores and the reading levels on the summary sheet of the performance booklet.